Contents

Preface

How many times have you heard friends and family tell you to visit a place before it's discovered and everybody starts going there? Get off the beaten track, they say. Follow the path less travelled, they advise you. *See it before it's too late*, they may even warn you.

This book is about those fundamental ideas in tourism. What do we mean by too late? How do we recognise too late when we see it, and what do we do about it when we get there? Even better, how do we avoid ever getting to the point of too late?

These are the fundamental questions of sustainable tourism. First, we want to avoid "too lateness" – a form of intergenerational inequity, as what we are actually saying is "you should have seen it 10, 20, 50 years ago! It was so much better then". Second we also want to promote intragenerational equity, that we all have access to development opportunities to improve the economic (including financial), environmental and social conditions that we live in.

Sustainability and its origins will be defined in Chapter 1 of this book. For now, suffice it to say that sustainability in general has been very challenging to put into mainstream practice. When it comes to tourism, a number of challenges specific to this sector add to the difficulty of implementing sustainability.

First, tourism is not a clear-cut set sector when it comes to defining it. We may be fairly confident that the travel agent who booked your trip, the airline and hotel that you use are part of the tourism sector. But what about the taxi that got you from the airport to the hotel, or the train that took you from your home to the airport for that matter? What about the restaurants you will eat in, the supermarkets you'll use to buy the toothpaste you forgot to bring? The banks where you'll withdraw cash, and the police who will keep you safe in a destination? And each of these services has its own supply chain to think about – leading to a series of Russian Dolls, each one hiding another inside.

This interlinking of supply chains and diverse sectors and regions begs the question: does the whole complex system need to be sustainable – from tourism generating region to host destination, and all the carbon emitting transportation along the way – for tourism itself to be sustainable? The purists would argue "yes". The pragmatists might convince us otherwise, pointing out the value of trade-offs, and the need to start somewhere.

Second, tourism inevitably has impacts: the act of observation always changes the observed. The trick is to minimise the negative impacts and maximise the positive impacts. Sustainability is a process, like it or not, and it is incremental and adaptive. Tourism in particular, not only influences its environment, but is highly influenced by its environment (think rainy days, a pilot strike, a spike in the value of local currency, a nearby earthquake, or a terrorist attack). Cause and effect is not always immediately apparent and linear relationships do not always exist, making managing this diffuse sector even more challenging. Finally, sustainable tourism means different things to different people.

Unpacking sustainable tourism therefore requires a good understanding of what it means, why it's proving difficult to implement and what its positive and negative impacts actually are. We need to understand the policy framework that binds sustainable tourism practices, as well as the diversity of individual choices that practitioners make within that framework, how they operationalise those choices and work with partners to implement sustainability. We'll review some cases where these have been most effectively carried out and how we know that they are being effective. Finally we'll then look at the future of sustainable tourism; how innovations are influencing sustainable practices and what the future trends are that need to be addressed.

The learning sequence will be as follows:

Section 1: Introduction

1: Definitions and origins of sustainable tourism

This chapter sets out the need for sustainability and the global framework for sustainability and how it relates to tourism. It looks at the various agreements and goals that exist as a framework for considering sustainability goals within tourism, and reviews the triple bottom line approach to sustainability

2: Challenges to implementing sustainability in tourism

This chapter examines the idea of a business case for sustainability, and asks why, if the business case is so clear, is it still so poorly developed in tourism? It also raises the question of tourism's carbon footprint, system-based incentives and disincentives for applying sustainability in practice.

3: Impacts of tourism

This chapter reviews the types of impacts, positive and negative associated with tourism, and introduces the types of case studies that will bring the material to life throughout the remaining book chapters.

Section 2: Managing for sustainability

4: Sustainable tourism policy frameworks

This chapter reviews the policy frameworks in which operators function, and how these affect consumer behaviour in tourism. It explains the importance of different policy structures to achieve the types of positive impacts outlined in Chapter 3 and contrasts progressive and less progressive approaches

5: Governance and partnerships

Based on Chapter 4, this chapter explores how partnerships can best be leveraged to integrate sustainability. This includes community groups, NGOs, certification agencies, etc.

6: Ethics and values

This chapter builds on Chapters 1-5 and explores how ethics and values bring to bear on integrating sustainability into business practice. It explores why the discussion of sustainability itself is problematic, and why any operationalisation of the principles must start with an understanding of how values play into the operationalisation of sustainability

7: Measures and tools

This chapter explores the different types of tools available to practitioners to measure, track and develop their pathway towards sustainability.

8: Operationalising sustainable tourism

This chapter presents business practices that have adopted a sustainability value and ethic, and looks at how sustainability is operationalised into business practice. It uses actual cases, and draws out lessons from those cases around the influence of policy, supply chains, and trade-offs to maximise benefits and minimise negative impacts

Section 3: Future of sustainable tourism

9: The future of sustainable tourism: change and innovation

This chapter looks at some of the big issues that tourism will be facing in the next 20-50 years and asks how well we are prepared for these changes. Existing research suggests that tourism does not engage very well with the larger issues of geopolitical stability, a transition away from the carbon economy, etc. This chapter also reviews the types of innovation that are assisting the transition to sustainability as well as well as providing a framework for understanding innovation and its role in tourism as part of the service industry.

10: Concluding remarks

This chapter integrates the material presented in previous chapters and asks readers to think about how the systems-based, supply chain approach can be applied to respond to the bigger future challenges to sustainability in tourism

The textbook and its exercises along with supplementary material are designed to help you as a student or a practitioner appreciate the complexity of implementing sustainable tourism, but at the same time to help you focus on what you want to achieve in terms of sustainability.

It provides you with a range of resources and knowledge that you'll need to implement sustainability, including examples environmental impact assessments and indicators, an awareness of policy and regulations, and techniques to successfully engage with community. And it will hopefully inspire you by looking at a number of actual businesses who practice sustainability, and who give an honest account of challenges and rewards of doing so.

Downloading and using the AR app

Introduction to Sustainable Tourism uses augmented reality (AR) to provide readers with additional resources to better understand the material presented in the textbook. The hyperlinks in the text are accompanied by QR codes so that readers can easily access these additional resources on their smartphones and tablets while reading the print version of the book. But there's more.

Readers are invited to download the free *Introduction to Sustainable Tourism AR App* from the Android Play Store or the Apple App Store. The app's Scan function will access the podcasts, videos documents and webpages behind the hyperlinks, (look for the standard QR codes) and also sets of multiple choice questions (identified by the '**Test yourself**' boxes). The app also contains a useful glossary of key terms in the field of sustainability and tourism.

To get the app, simply the follow instructions below:

1   Go to the app store (Android Play Store or the Apple App Store) on your smartphone or tablet.

2   Search for *Introduction to Sustainable Tourism AR App* which has this logo.

3   Download the app – it's free so you won't have any charges.

The app's landing page has three buttons:

AR Scan starts the scanner function

Glossary opens a glossary of key terms in the field of sustainability and tourism

About tells you more about this app

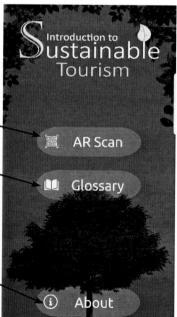

4 Press the AR Scan button and you are ready to use the AR scanner in the app with the textbook. Simply find the location of the AR icons in the text.

☐ The standard QR icons lead you to additional resources in the form of URL links, podcasts and videos.

☐ The codes in **Test yourself** boxes will give you access to the multiple choice questions that test your understanding of what you have read in each chapter. These cannot be accessed by a standard QR reader.

5 Scan the icon in the textbook with the AR scanner, and it will trigger the AR content. You will have access to the additional content as long as you hover the scanner over the AR icon in the textbook.

6 To go access new content from another icon, simply pull the device away from the AR code, and this will reset the camera. Allow a couple of seconds to reset the AR Tracker if codes become stuck, and scan new codes.

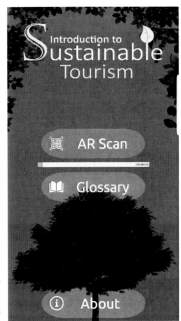

Return ———

7 The 'Return' button will take you back to the app's landing page.

8 To look up an item in the glossary, click the Glossary button and scroll through the list.

Section 1: Introduction

 Introduction

Sustainability is often represented as resting on the three founding pillars of social, environmental and economic sustainability (people, planet and profit) – a firm, immovable foundation, upon which all else rests. Build these correctly at the start and the rest will follow, freeing you up to focus on the day to day running of operations.

For this book, however, I invite you to think of sustainability as three juggling balls – representing people, planet and profit. Your job is to keep those three balls moving through the air, always dynamic, never resting. Take your eye off one of the balls, and it is sure to fall to the ground, in all likelihood taking at least one other ball with it.

To keep all three balls moving gracefully through the air, you are going to need several things – not least hand to eye coordination! You will need focus – "what am I trying to achieve?"

You will need skill – "what resources, knowledge and experience do I have at my disposal?"

And you will need to practice.

Because, ultimately, sustainability comes down to a set of decisions – decisions that you will have to make repeatedly for as long as you are involved in sustainable tourism.

The first aim of this book is to help you focus, decide what you want to achieve in terms of sustainability. And maybe to start with, you will only be able to keep two of those balls in the air, perhaps even only one. The second aim of this book is to highlight the types of resources and knowledge that you'll need to keep those balls in the air. This may include environmental impact assessments and indicators, an awareness of policy and regulations, or techniques to successfully engage with community. Finally, the third aim of this book is demonstrate how you practice these things. We'll do this by looking at actual businesses and how they manage to keep two or three balls in the air at any one time.

The structure of this book is geared towards understanding how an individual makes decisions that move towards or away from sustainability practices within a given set of influencers. These will be the focus of Sections 2: Managing for Sustainability and 3: The Future of Sustainable Tourism.

First, however, we must understand what sustainability means in a tourism context, why it has proven so difficult to implement, and what both positive and negative outcomes of sustainable tourism might look like. Combined with the chapter on ethics, this will give you a lens through which to view the implementation of sustainability.

Key words and concepts

- Sustainability
- Three pillars of people, place and profit
- Sustainable tourism
- Brundtland report
- Sequence of tourism platforms

- UNEP and UNWTO
- Sustainable Development Goals
- One Planet Programme
- Tourism master plans
- Ecotourism

1.1 The concept of sustainability

To begin, let's consider how we should think about the broader concept of sustainability.

Sustainability, when stripped right back to its bare bones, is about relationships. Relationships to people (social sustainability), planet (environmental sustainability) and profit (economic sustainability).

But what does that mean? It's your relationships with your employees, your customers, your dependents and family. It's your suppliers, local producers, the community who share the same space and resources as you. It's the people who set the rules for what you can and can't do. It's also the people who look to you for leadership, as a role model to set the best example of what might be. It's how you treat those close to you, as well as those who may seem different for their gender, age, education, religion, race, and ability.

It's also the environment in which you live. The landscape, both biotic (living) and abiotic (non-living). It's how you change the habitat around you, by using rocks and wood as construction material, clearing the landscape to build tourism infrastructure, using water for cleaning and production, lighting up spaces that were previously dark. It's how you dispose of your waste material, on land, in water and in the air. It's the other creatures that share your space – those that may need the same resources as you. It's both direct and indirect, through your suppliers, as well as the practices that you encourage or discourage at your site.

Finally, it's your wallet, your banker, your shareholders, your dependents, your supply chain, your employees. It's also your financial security, your level of comfort, your ability to take care of the unexpected, to cope with a rainy day. It's your dreams... of what might be and how to get there.

Ultimately these are all facets of the same thing: your ability to function well, both now and in the future. And in the next section, we will get to the official definitions of sustainability and how they align with this fuzzier concept of sustainability. Intermingled with this, it's your sense of your place within a complex web of other beings, some of whom will have competing needs, as well as rules and policies that govern you, hampering or facilitating your sustainability goals. It's your sense of responsibility and your sense of agency – of having an effect (positive or negative) on the world around you.

Question

In your current role, name and describe three relationships which have a sustainability-related link. How do you think about these in the long-term? What do you do to maintain these relationships?

Now think back to your juggle act. See the size of the task ahead? Make no mistake, it's no simple ask to bring about greater sustainability in tourism. Along the way, we'll meet some people who will share their journeys of learning how to juggle all three balls at once – they will tell us how it is at once exhausting and rewarding. And always challenging.

1.2   Sustainable development

Our engagement with the concept of sustainability in the West, arose more or less straight out of one woman's relationship with the environment around her. Her name was Rachel Carson and she was an environmental scientist, public servant and avid writer born in 1907 in rural USA. Her best known book *Silent Spring* published in 1962 is often said to have spearheaded the Western environmental movement that we recognise today.

The book's primary concern was the impact of pesticides on human health, while observing the direct impacts it was having on rural ecosystems. The title *Silent Spring* warned of a day when we would no longer hear birdsong come springtime. Her book caused much controversy, but highlights valuing our relationship with ourselves (the health concerns that she raised) as well as with the natural environment. In this vein she is noted to have said: "The human race is challenged more than ever before to demonstrate our mastery – not over nature but of ourselves."

A suite of environmental regulations, governmental agencies, environmental defence organisations, environmental studies and popular science books followed the publication of *Silent Spring*. But it was two decades later that sustainability was formally linked to the concept of development and defined in the 1987 Brundtland report, *Our Common Future: Report of the World Commission of Environment and Development*, commission by the United Nations and which laid out the fundamental principles of sustainability and sustainable development.

Download the Brundtland report:

http://www.un-documents.net/our-common-future.pdf

This report produced perhaps the most widely recognised definition of sustainable development as:

> *"development that meets the needs of the present without compromising the ability of future generations to meet their own needs".*

Five basic principles of sustainability are identified in the report:

1 The idea of holistic planning and strategy making

2 The importance of preserving essential ecological processes

3 The need to protect both human heritage and biodiversity

4 The need to develop in a way that sustains productivity over the long-term for later generations

5 The need to achieve a better balance of fairness and opportunity between nations.

Sustainable development is therefore deliberate – planned with forethought, adaptive but not necessarily reactive to opportunities. It is inclusive – it considers everybody, regardless of power status, and even non-human beings. It values more than just economic outcomes – it places importance on cultural heritage, social wellbeing and biodiversity. And it is holistic, it recognises that humans, as a species, live in closed system (Planet Earth) with finite resources (e.g. fossil fuels) as well as renewable resources; it argues that any activity in one part of that system will affect other parts – as we'll discuss using chocolate (and beer and coffee) as an example in Section 1.7.

Despite setting out some broad principles linking sustainability to development, the Brundtland report arguably did little to clarify how these principles would translate into business practice and governmental policy. A starting point for a number of countries has been to produce environmental accounts – statistics that track natural capital against a range of measures, e.g. metallic and non-metallic minerals, fossil fuels, accessible timber, and land available for use. The idea behind this, although rarely the practice, is the so-called 'constant natural capital rule', where future generations are left with natural capital assets that are valued (economically, culturally, spiritually, aesthetically and so forth) as the stock that we currently possess, as per the environmental accounts.

Three issues that should become immediately apparent are as follows:

Test yourself

1 How do we balance these different values, e.g. how do we weigh up economic values vs spiritual values?

2 How do we measure and articulate some of the less tangible (non-market driven) values in a way that they can be agreed and entered into the debate?

3 Is it acceptable to maintain a constant stock, but allow specific assets to be interchanged, e.g. replacing natural products with engineered ones?

Question

Consider this scenario: a recreational area is popular with nature lovers who use it as a place of tranquillity and escape. More recently, a tourism operator has started to use the same space for jet ski tours, impacting on the noise levels, as well as opening it up to new users and creating an economic return from the place and new jobs in the area. How would you balance these two uses and their associated values?

These questions underpin one of the central impediments to the implementation of sustainable development: it is an inherently contested term. What has value to me, may hold a completely different value for you – and where one is objective and measurable, and the other intangible and subjective, how can these be compared? It's an apple and an orange situation, in a world which enjoys the occasional glass of cider! In Hall's words (1998, p.22) "political reality rather than ecological reality has been the order of the day", showing where our decision-makers' values tend to lie.

To make matters even more complicated, the very principle of growth encapsulated in the 'development' aspect of sustainable development appears to cause a lack of consensus amongst the proponents of sustainability, and has generated ongoing discussions of how sustainable development, including sustainable tourism, might be operationalised. It is not surprising therefore that the world has been relatively slow to put sustainability into practice at the scale required by reports such as the Brundlandt report.

Few sectors are able to claim sustainability, and even fewer embrace the type of inter-sectoral sustainability recommended by policy reports. The latter is particularly important for tourism as this sector crosses over between transport, accommodation, food and beverage, natural and build heritage (national parks, historic buildings), man-made purpose-build attractions (theme parks, casinos), tourism intermediaries (agents), as well as all the indirect suppliers of tourism products and services. Sustainability in tourism is arguably even trickier than in many other sectors.

1.3 Sustainable tourism

Test yourself

We now understand the origin of the concept of sustainability and how it was linked to industries such as tourism through the idea of sustainable development.

So what exactly is sustainable tourism?

The official definitions of sustainable tourism, according to the UN World Tourism Organisation – the peak body for tourism as a sector – is:

"Tourism that takes full account of its current and future economic, social and environmental impacts, addressing the needs of visitors, the industry, the environment and host communities"

All three juggling balls are clearly present in that definition, as well as the central idea of a relationship with others (in this case the visitor, the industry, environment and host communities). The UNWTO expands on this definition by stating that sustainable tourism must:

"maintain ecological processes and conserve natural heritage and biodiversity; respect the authenticity, traditional values and cultural heritage of host communities and contribute to cross-cultural understanding; and, ensure viable businesses, and distribute economic benefits to all stakeholders equitably"
(UNEP & UNWTO, 2005).

Sustainable tourism is a relative newcomer to the sustainable development agenda, despite its substantial economic size in terms of revenue and employment and almost continual growth since the end of WWII. Because of the relative newness of the concept, we have relatively little understanding of what sustainable tourism should look like or how we should get there – although some may argue that there has been a lot of talk about and very little practice of sustainability in tourism.

The year 2017 was officially nominated the Year of Sustainable Tourism – with much fanfare about the positive impacts of tourism as represented in the UNWTO's *Travel.Enjoy.Respect* video.

Watch the video: https://www.youtube.com/watch?v=49c2DdJN4Uc

The IY2017 promotion is very appealing, but the story of sustainable tourism is more complicated than that.

Test yourself

Mass tourism, as represented by coastal resort destinations of Europe (think Costa Brava, Malaga, Ibiza and so forth) is typically the business model against which sustainable tourism is held up and compared. We can all recognise issues of unsustainable tourism when it is presented to us in the form of sprawling hotel developments, polluted beaches, excessive drinking and drug use. In these cases, it is a question of convincing destination managers to place holds on further tourism development; undertake some lengthy and often costly regeneration activities within the destination; and radically change marketing strategies.

Australia's hub of tourism, the City of Gold Coast, is the perfect example of this approach in the period of 2016-2018. The city receives around 5 million visitors per year, with a resident population of just over half a million people. Compare that to the nearby city of Brisbane, the state's capital, where the ratio of tourists to residents is a much lower 3.5 visitors per resident (compared to 10 for the Gold Coast). By any measure, the Gold Coast can therefore be considered a mass tourism destination, with a well-established range of man-made (bars, shops and theme parks) and natural attractions (beaches, sunshine and national parks). Its popularity, however, has also created a sense of over-development and an image of the 'glitter strip' that can be unappealing to some.

In an effort to overcome the destination's state of stagnation, local government proposed several strategies: hosting a mega-event (the 2018 Commonwealth Games), developing a cruise ship terminal and putting out a bid for a second casino. In August 2017, the state's Premier withdrew support for a major development on one of the region's more popular recreational areas, the Spit, based on community opinion that the area should be preserved as a low development site. In her announcement, the Premier reported that:

> "what we know about the Spit, is very clearly, it is iconic to Queensland, it is iconic to the Gold Coast, and I want to see that area transformed into beautiful parklands with storey limits, within the city plan."

(Palaszczuk, cited in the Brisbane Times, 4 August 2017).

BRISBANETIMES.COM.AU
Palaszczuk shrugs off criticism over Southport Spit casino decision
Premier Annastacia Palaszczuk says feedback on the government's decision to dump the $3 billion casino and resort development on the Gold Coast's Spit has been...

Figure 1. 1: Palasszczuk's decision to maintain low development at a popular Australian recreation spot, earmarked for $3 billon redevelopment. https://www.brisbanetimes.com.au/national/queensland/palaszczuk-shrugs-off-criticism-over-southport-spit-casino-decision-20170804-gxpdpq.html

While some have argued that the Premier's decision was foolhardy, creating an impression that the state of Queensland is too fickle for secure development investments, it is this type of decision that represents a commitment to keeping all three balls in the air at once: environmental risk assessments were taken into consideration, and local resident sentiment about losing access to recreational amenities were acknowledged.

This type of action is rare when it comes to mass tourism, for a range of political reasons. The so-called alternative forms of tourism – those that do strive for the principles put forward by the UNWTO – face a different type of problem: some academics argue that these forms of tourism have not been around long enough, with enough systematic research and monitoring, across a wide enough spectrum of geographic, economic and cultural conditions, for a good understanding of the thresholds that demarcate the transition from sustainable to unsustainable tourism. In three decades of research, we have not yet developed a blueprint for sustainable tourism that can inform management decisions.

Others argue sustainable tourism has reached a level of stagnation. There is a lot of reinventing the wheel going on, along with a lot of political decisions about how to apply (nor not) those principles.

At the most basic level is the understanding that we must be able to:

1 Identify the immediate and extended effects of tourism;

2 Minimise its negative economic, social and environmental impacts;

3 Maximise its positive economic, social and environmental impacts;

4 Select and record the most appropriate indicators to track how tourism is performing with regards to those impacts; and

5 Manage those impacts to within an acceptable range.

If you know that much, you are ahead of the game. The remainder of this book will build your understand of how to best achieve these basic principles.

At a higher, more conceptual level, Weaver (2006) raises some interesting questions around the role of sustainable tourism – should we aim to protect the status quo or be remedial? Does the term 'sustainability' evoke the idea of sustaining the existing situation, i.e. maintaining the status quo? This may be appropriate in situations where no negative impacts are occurring and no further growth is being encouraged. However, few tourism businesses or attractions fall into that category, either in terms of their impacts or in their attitude towards future growth.

On the contrary, many tourism businesses, attractions and destinations are already witnessing some form of negative impacts, with one or two of the three juggling balls falling out of the air, most often as managers focus their attention on another of those balls. And here it must be emphasised that it is not always the focus on financial sustainability that causes the other two (environmental and social) to fall to the ground. Tourism is a business, and without long-term financial viability, it is doomed to fail on all three measures.

A balanced approach is required and how we get there can be likened to a pendulum swinging from strong growth and development to protecting the status quo to somewhere in the middle – these ways of thinking about tourism are described by Jafari's and later McBeth's sequence of tourism platforms, discussed next.

1.4   A sequence for thinking about sustainable tourism

Four ways of thinking about tourism development and management can be identified in any discourse on the topic. Listen to any town mayor, property developer, environmental group, or tourism researchers and consultants discuss a proposed new tourism development and you'll be able to place it in one of the four categories below.

The four categories are known as the Platforms of Tourism (Jafari, 2001). By learning to recognise them in practice, you'll have a better understanding of a tourism proponent's (or opponent's) starting position, their assumptions and most importantly, their blind spots. You can make a more informed decision about how to engage with their discourse.

The Advocacy platform

The first 'platform' is known as the *Advocacy* platform, and as the name suggests, it is the starting point for those who believe that tourism's benefits outweigh any possible negative impacts. Tourism was the 'smokeless industry' in stark contrast to the smoke-belching factories of the time. The Advocacy platform has largely been driving the more recent development of mass tourism as a part of a liberal, modernist expression of freedom after the geopolitical conflicts of the 1980s (e.g. the end of the Cold War, the processes of decolonisation) and with rise of affluent middle classes who want to travel for business and leisure.

The thinking behind the Advocacy platform was perhaps most common back in the 1950s to 60s, where tourism was considered an ideal economic (and sometimes social) development tool with few or no negative impacts, and therefore to be promoted with little to no government interference or management. Not only does tourism investment generate direct revenue and jobs, but servicing it creates new markets for other local economic sectors such agriculture, fisheries, carpenters, mechanics, craftsmen, etc.

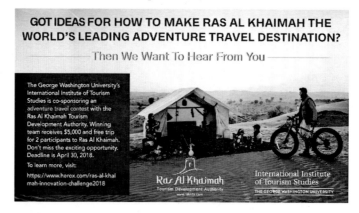

Figure 1.2: One example of tourism's use a tool for development in regional areas.

Another argument in favour of tourism development is that it creates low skilled jobs that are accessible to groups who may be facing poor employment prospects otherwise. The economic benefits generated by tourism also provides an incentive to protect the natural and built heritage that attracts tourists to the destination, thereby creating yet more reasons to advocate for the development of tourism.

This platform can still be identified in many places, which see tourism as a low impact solution for sustainable development.

The Cautionary platform

If the Advocacy platform represents a pendulum swinging to the right, then what goes up must come down, and across. As the pendulum swings across to the left, we find the so-called '*Cautionary*' platform. At this stage, in the 1970s, the negative impacts of tourism started to be noted, with a consequent call for greater regulation and planning by the public sector.

Where the growth of the destination has been promoted through advocacy, the increasing number of visitors in a destination or at an attraction will eventually exceed a capacity threshold, where social and natural resources of the destination are no longer sufficient to accommodate the number of tourists present. This commonly referred to as the destination's carrying capacity, which marks a tipping point from sustainable to unsustainable tourism. Indeed, each of us can think of destinations that were once pristine, uncrowded, inexpensive and 'authentic', that now feel crowded, polluted, overpriced and inauthentic as the destination has become more popular, and more and more tourism development has been allowed within the destination.

For those who adopt a Cautionary approach, each and every argument presented by the Advocacy group can be countered with an opposing argument; yes, jobs are created but these are low paid, seasonal and often casual, offering little job security and career advancement prospects. Large tourism developments often source their products outside the local community, creating a 'leakage' effect, few economic indirect benefits stay within the destination. Cultural attractions become 'commodified' to suit the tastes and needs of foreigners, rather than maintaining their original meaning. Natural attractions become degraded through trampling, souvenir collection, etc.

T+L • TRIP IDEAS

Go Here, Not There: Undiscovered Places to Visit Now

**These destinations offer fewer crowds and similar attributes
to their more popular counterparts, making them fine
alternatives to hot spots that are at their max.**

KRISTA SIMMONS AUGUST 24, 2015

This second position can be largely summed up by the belief that mass tourism contains the seed of its own destruction.

The tourism area life-cycle

One of the best known models in tourism traces this effect through the tourism area life-cycle (Butler, 1980). In the Life-cycle model, Butler traces the evolution of destinations over time, in a broadly S-curve approach, from little tourism activity, through a stage of investment in tourism, to a breach of the tourism area's carrying capacity.

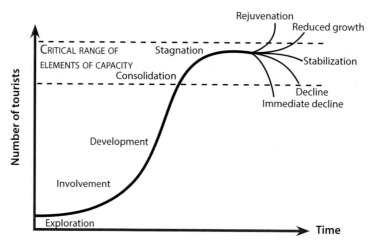

Figure 1.3: Butler's tourism area life cycle

The model starts with an *exploration* stage with low visitor numbers and low levels of tourism development. During this stage, there is little to no tourism development per se (i.e. if you have seen a destination advertised as being "off the beaten track", then that destination has already passed the exploration stage), with the steady and low number of tourists making use of local amenities and infrastructure. Locals do not work in tourism as such, but are prepared to accommodate visitor needs and learn to welcome the outsider's interest and injection of cash into the community.

This brings about the following stage, where locals actively seek tourism opportunities for their development potential. This becomes the *involvement* stage, quickly followed by an *development* stage (often indicating an advocacy approach) of high visitor numbers and high development. This is point where negative impacts such as overcrowding, price inflation, traffic congestion, pollution and so forth become apparent to the majority of stakeholders (visitors, locals, managers and business owners), and the tourism area's carrying capacity is said to have been breached.

At this point, the tourism area may either go into decline as potential visitors avoid the area that is now perceived to be overcrowded, overpriced and too 'touristy', investment dries up, and residents lose interest in tourism, or the tourism area may stagnate, with steady numbers of visitors still arriving, but remaining above the carrying capacity, and so continuing to put undue pressure on the tourism area. Alternatively, the tourism area be managed into a state of rejuvenation, by either reducing the number of visitors, e.g. through a demarketing strategy, or by increasing the area's carrying capacity, sometimes done through site 'hardening' (more on these in Chapter 7).

While the tourism area life-cycle model has never been empirically supported by research, it is nevertheless appealing as it encapsulates the sustainable vs unsustainable states of tourism. The former fall beneath the carrying capacity threshold, whilst the latter are above it.

Note that sustainable tourism can occur at two points along the Time (x) axis. The first is before the threshold has been crossed, but visitor numbers are still growing. Weaver calls this "circumstantial sustainable tourism", in that there is no deliberate effort to keep tourism to a sustainable level, it just so happens that visitors numbers are low enough, albeit growing, to not inflict significant negative impacts on the area. The second is in the stabilization stage, where decision-makers have pro-actively engaged in strategies to bring visitor numbers below the threshold. Weaver refers to this as "deliberate sustainable tourism".

The Adaptancy platform

The latter reflects the next two stages of Jafari's platforms, where the pendulum swings back to a middling position. These are known as the *Adaptancy* platform of the 1980s and the *Knowledge-based* platform of the 1990s. The former, the Adaptancy platform called for the move away from mass tourism towards alternative forms of tourism, such as ecotourism, community-based or volunteer tourism, which emphasised small-scale development, i.e. staying well below that carrying capacity threshold, while seeking maximum benefits for the environment and local communities. It was at this point that we saw the start of the sustainable tourism discourse.

The Knowledge-based platform

The Adaptancy platform was followed by a recognition that small-scale, locally-led tourism did not always yield the greatest social, environmental and economic benefits within tourism destinations. Rather than adopting an ideologically-based approach to tourism development (e.g. "the bigger the better" vs "small is beautiful"), private and public sectors should adopt a Knowledge-based platform, which promotes planning for specific tourism activities best suited to minimise impacts, maximise benefits and build capacity within tourism destinations.

As a result, the concept of sustainable tourism, as we understand it, i.e. underpinned by research, consultation, and planning and management, entered the mainstream in the 1990s. This marked the beginning of deliberate attempts to identify that carrying capacity line for each tourism area – through the use of indicators (more on these in Chapter 7), and cooperative private/public efforts to keep visitor numbers below that carrying capacity threshold, while maximising economic, social and environmental benefits.

Figure 1. 4: "They knew" – controversy over the optimistic forecasting of economic benefits from Australia's largest event of the decade, vs the report on a review of research into impacts of mega-events released by the local university in the year leading up to the event.

Tourism areas where this has been achieved remain few and far between, however, due to a number of challenges to be covered in Chapter 2, and leading to the stagnation in our understanding and implementation of sustainable tourism that we just mentioned before.

The Sustainability and Ethics-based platforms

To overcome this stagnation, two further platforms have been added to the sequence of tourism platforms described above (Advocacy, Cautionary, Adaptancy and Knowledge-based). These additional platforms reflect two important contributions that explain this stagnation and seek to overcome it – contributions that explain, in the first instance, why sustainable tourism is not achieving its desired outcomes, and second, why true sustainability has indeed proven difficult to build into the practice of sustainable tourism and its operations.

These contributions are best presented by reading the original paper by MacBeth (2005), but are summarised here. First is the *Sustainability* platform itself. In creating this fifth platform, McBeth sought to label and acknowledge a transitional phase between the knowledge-based platform and the ethics-based platform. While the former is objective and "frontier-thinking", the latter represents a more thoughtful, reflexive approach to tourism development.

Thus, the sixth platform proposed by MacBeth is an *Ethics-based* platform, which moves away from a growth imperative, and instead understands business and its impacts from a value-based, ethical perspective. Macbeth argues that this perspective should serve as a starting point for all operations-level decision-making in order to achieve the goals of triple bottom line sustainability. This issue of an ethics-based approach to sustainable tourism will be explored in greater detail in Chapter 6.

1.5   The institutional framework for sustainable tourism

While Chapter 4 will review the policy-based and legislative framework that shapes the implementation of sustainable tourism, it is worth briefly covering some of the institutional context that drives the sustainability agenda within tourism. These can include:

- ☐ International agreements,
- ☐ National policies,
- ☐ Peak bodies,
- ☐ Lobbyists – specific to tourism as well as social and environmental groups,
- ☐ Supporting resources such as guide books, websites and travel agents.

At an international level, the United Nations covers sustainable tourism in a number of key documents particularly through the UN Environment Program (UNEP), which convened the Earth Summit, the UN's 1992 Conference on Environment and Development in Rio de Janeiro, Brazil, and the UN World Tourism Organisation, the United Nations agency responsible for the promotion of responsible, sustainable and universally accessible tourism

First, let's review UNEP's influence on sustainable tourism development. Over 170 national governments attended the Earth Summit, marking it as the largest conference on sustainability at the time, and this saw the creation of *Agenda 21*, a blueprint for sustainable development. Part of Agenda 21 was to encourage sustainable development to be operationalised at an international level, but more importantly at a national, regional or local level. We'll review Agenda 21 under national policies rather than at the international level. Over time the outcomes of the conference became more formalised and in 2002 the UNEP created its Sustainable Tourism Programme, which aimed to facilitate the implementation of *Agenda 21*.

Find our more at UNEP's web site:

https://www.unenvironment.org/

UN ﴾☉﴿
environment

Another decade on, in 2014, the Sustainable Tourism Programme launched its 10-Year *Framework of Programmes on Sustainable Consumption and Production Patterns* (recently rebranded as *One Planet – Sustainable Tourism Programme*). This tied in neatly with the UN Development Programme's new Sustainable Development Goals (SDGs), replacing the previous Millennium Goals. Goal 12 (of 17 SDGs) is to promote the Responsible Consumption and Production, forming the umbrella for *One Planet – Sustainable Tourism Programme* for greater sustainability in tourism through "efficiency, innovation and adaptability".

The Programme lists four objectives:

1. Integrating sustainable consumption and production (SCP) patterns in tourism related policies and frameworks

2. Collaboration among stakeholders for the improvement of the tourism sector's SCP performance

3 Fostering the application of guidelines, instruments and technical solutions to prevent and mitigate tourism impacts and to mainstream SCP patterns among tourism stakeholders

4 Enhancing sustainable tourism investment and financing.

Read more at One Planet: http://sdt.unwto.org/about-10yfp-stp

It is primarily managed through the UN World Tourism Organisation (UNWTO), as well as several national government ministries of tourism and/or environment, and a 22-member Multi-Stakeholder Advisory Committee (MAC), consisting of governmental agencies, non-governmental organisations, private sector businesses, intergovernmental organisations, national cleaner production centres as well as academia and UN agencies.

The UNWTO offers leadership in delivering technical reports and statistics on the tourism market; developing sustainable tourism policies and instruments, education and training; and providing technical assistance for tourism sustainable development projects around the world. Its membership includes 156 countries, with associate and affiliate members representing the private sector, educational institutions, tourism associations and local tourism authorities.

The UNWTO's vision of the *One Planet - Sustainable Tourism Programme* is for a tourism sector that has "globally adopted SCP [sustainable consumption practices] resulting in enhanced environmental and social outcomes and improved economic performance" (UNWTO, 2018). The UNWTO is more expansive than UNEP in linking the *One Planet* programme to SDGs, seeing the potential for sustainable tourism to also contribute to SDG8 focusing on decent work and economic growth, SDG13 addressing climate change or SDGs14 (sustainably use and conserve marine resources) and SDG15 (sustainably use and conserve terrestrial resources).

SUSTAINABLE DEVELOPMENT GOALS

Figure 1.5: The 17 Sustainable Development Goals, part of UNWTO's One Planet programme

The UNWTO also works specifically on a number of 'hot' topics within tourism, related to economic, social and environmental sustainability. These are climate change, both its impacts on tourism and tourism's contribution to greenhouse gas emissions, ecotourism and protected areas; small island developing states (which can have a particularly high reliance on tourism as well as limited resources and fragile socio-cultural and natural environments); and wetlands, again a particularly vulnerable ecosystem with a vital role to play for freshwater resources, fisheries and so forth.

Finally, the UNWTO also promotes the 1999 *Global Code of Ethics for Tourism* (GCET), a set of 10 principles directed at governments, the travel industry, communities and tourists alike, to promote social, economic and environmental sustainability in tourism. On the basis of the 10 principles set out in the code of ethics, the UNWTO offers a programme of work on tourism resilience, encouraging members to assess and mitigate social, economic and environmental risks related to tourism, plan for and respond effectively to crises (e.g. disease pandemics, natural disasters, acts of terrorism). The Code itself will be covered in Chapter 6. Finally, the UNWTO works on facilitating tourist travel, primarily visa procedures, to ensure destinations maximise their opportunities to benefit from tourism development opportunities.

A number of additional international institutions and frameworks also influence sustainable tourism development, albeit in a more tangential way (e.g. RAMSAR's protection of wetlands, or CITES ban on the trade of endangered species exports), but we'll leave these to be covered in greater detail in Chapter 4.

At a national level, many national and state governments who attended UNEP's Rio Summit have legislated or advised that local authorities devise strategies to implement Agenda 21 locally, as well as formulated policy at the national level to support sustainable tourism development. These are most effective when they involved:

1 A long-term comprehensive, integrated and inclusive strategy.

2 Extensive collaboration and participation of all relevant actors.

3 A move towards cross-sectoral harmonisation of policy and decision-making processes for improved integration (Bennett, 1997).

These can be implemented at a national level, using a top-down approach such as Bhutan's national tourism plan, or at a regional level, using a community-led, bottom-up approach. Teoh (2015) discusses how Bhutan's commitment to Gross National Happiness (GNH), as an alternative to Gross Domestic Product (GDP), has informed the development of tourism in that small country situated between India and China. GHN represents an alternative development paradigm that values its people's happiness over material wealth. It is founded on four pillars, namely:

1 The conservation and preservation of the natural environment

2 Cultivation and promotion of culture

3 Good governance

4 Sustainable and equitable socio-economic development (Ura & Galay, 2004).

Figure 1.6: Bhutan's tourism marketing campaign is based on its unique GNH index.

The GNH approach was applied in tourism through a tourism development strategy based on a *high value, low volume* approach. The strategy was formally used to limit the number of tourists arriving in the country, while encouraging high yield tourists, as well as controlling the distribution of visitors around the country and ensuring that the benefits of tourism, through the Royalty fee, support the rest of Bhutan's GNH plan.

It was typically considered to be an example of Weaver's "deliberate alternative tourism", that is small scale tourism based on strong regulatory frameworks. These regulations focus on:

☐ A high tariff system (c.US$200/night/person) to deter budget travellers;

☐ A Royalty fee (US$65/night/person);

☐ Physically limited access to Bhutan, either overland or through limited flight capacities;

☐ Itineraries follow restricted routes, with approved drivers and guides, accommodation and food choices.

However, there were still some concerns about Bhutan's ability to balance managing its tourism impacts with delivering the type of high value, exclusive experience that justified tourists' expenses. A review of Bhutan's tourism strategy by an American consultancy firm, McKinsey and Company, suggested a move to *high value, low impact* – i.e. focussing on managing visitor impacts rather than visitor numbers. This move was perceived by some stakeholders to compromise the GNH philosophy in favour of delivering higher economic benefits (through increased tourist numbers), and it was felt that the American consultants had not truly understood the nature of Bhutan's GNH plan, and the country's emphasis on balancing economic sustainability with social and environmental sustainability.

Another example, this time at a regional level is Tofino is presented by Sheppard, Dodds and Williams (2015). Tofino is a nature-based tourism destination off the coast of British Columbia, best known for its rugged coastline, beautiful beaches, and outdoor recreation opportunities. Tofino's popularity as a destination is increasing, putting greater pressure on social and environmental resources, and prompting the local community to devise a local tourism master plan. The Master Plan addresses issues such as a lack of adequate community facilities, seasonality issues, and lack of adequate infrastructure (e.g. sewage treatment plants, limited water availability), and a high dependence on imported commodities to provide for its residents and visitors, as well as upholding local residents' sense of place.

The first step of this community plan was the recognition that sustainability itself has different meanings for different people, e.g. business as usual for some, or a conservation and limits to growth approach for others. The move towards greater sustainability from a governance approach has therefore focused on breaking down barriers between these two viewpoints through inclusiveness, transparency, participation and performance in public policy and decision-making.

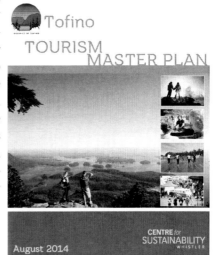

Figure 1.7: Tofino's Tourism Master Plan, an example of placing community values and the environment alongside economic opportunities. https://www.youtube.com/watch?v=KGnoGpi7Dmo

Watch this video on Tonfino community values. https://www.youtube. com/watch?v=WZ0TP3uieO4

From a practical perspective, local researchers Shepphard et al. (2015) suggested a framework that maps out the areas of concern for tourism stakeholders, and recommends indicators set out against each of these that include both values-based criteria, as well as technical measures of sustainability to ensure a more holistic approach to sustainable tourism development.

They also proposed a five step practical approach to develop their sustainable tourism master plan, including:

1 The establishment of a baseline sustainability footprint.

2 The identification of specific measurable actions for sustainability that match the current master plans.

3 The communication of all results and goals to both residents and visitors.

4 The use of RMI (development-incentive based funds) to upgrade core infrastructure.

5 The provision of incentives to tourism-related businesses to undertake sustainability practices, and report and publicise their efforts to guests.

The results was the creation of a long-term visioning process that involved all stakeholders, and clarified some of the different perceptions of sustainability within the local community. This represents a concerted, community-led, bottom-up approach which is relatively rare in the tourism sector.

While community-led approaches like the one above are rare in tourism, a number of peak bodies or trade associations also provide technical reports, blueprints to planning, and training workshops/capacity building in sustainable tourism to assist national and regional governments develop their sustainable tourism plans. A good example is the World Travel & Tourism Council (WTTC), a membership-based organisation that represents all sectors of the tourism and travel industry, with the view to providing "empirical evidence to promote awareness of Travel & Tourism's economic contribution; to expand markets in harmony with the environment; and to reduce barriers to growth" (WTTC, 2018).

With regards to sustainable tourism development, WTTC produced a guide to sustainability reporting to help tourism companies understand the key concepts behind reporting, provide an overview of regulations and trends that drive sustainability, and to help businesses identify the implications and opportunities offered by becoming more sustainable. In conjunction with this guide, WTTC promotes its annual Tourism for Tomorrow awards to recognise "best practice in sustainable tourism within the industry globally, based upon the principles of environmentally friendly operations; support for the protection of cultural and natural heritage; and direct benefits to the social and economic well-being of local people in travel destinations around the world" (WTTC, 2018).

Figure 1.8: Tourism for Tomorrow 2019. Watch the video. <u>https://www.wttc.org/tourism-for-tomorrow-awards/about-the-awards</u>

Examples of other peak bodies involved in sustainable tourism include the Global Sustainable Tourism Council (GSTC) and the Pacific Asia Travel Association (PATA). GSTC manages a number of global tourism sustainability standards at the destination and business levels to promote minimum requirements for tourism to protect and sustain the world's natural and cultural resources, while ensuring tourism meets its potential as a tool for conservation and poverty alleviation. PATA offers a number of funds to promote sustainable tourism in general, as well as to protect cultural heritage, the natural environment, and deliver education programs to support sustainability.

There are also a number of non-governmental organisations that are not trade associations or peak bodies who also lobby for greater sustainability in tourism. Examples of these include the Centre for Responsible Travel (CREST), in the USA, or Tourism Concern in the UK. They are not-for-profit groups who advocate for sustainable travel by offering best practice guidelines, consulting, sharing expertise on impact measurement and management, and may also promote particular travel services that they deem to have a strong track record in sustainable tourism practices.

Finally, a number of guidebooks and booking platforms exist to enable travellers (and in some cases tourism providers looking to develop more sustainable supply chains) identity and buy sustainable tourism experiences. Tourism Concern offers its own ethical travel guidebook, while major travel guidebook companies such as the Rough Guide or Lonely Planet also offer their own sustainability-oriented guidebooks, e.g. the *Rough Guide to a Better World*, an "essential guide to how the world can be a better place for everyone", or the *Lonely Planet's Guide to Responsible Travel*, a mini-guidebook featuring Lonely Planet's best tips and ideas for having a positive impact on the world while traveling.

1.6   Ecotourism: the poster child of sustainable tourism

Any talk of sustainable tourism will eventually turn to a discussion of ecotourism. More than any other sub-sector of tourism, ecotourism represents the balance of environmental, social and economic sustainability. It is often what comes to mind when sustainable tourism is discussed in the public arena, by non-experts in tourism, to the point where it sometimes used interchangeably with sustainable tourism. Weaver (2006) refers to it as the "conscience of sustainable tourism", while others such as Butcher warn of 'ego-tourism', a word play that suggests that there might be more to ecotourism than meets the eye.

Ecotourism rose to prominence in the 1990s. The concept is often attributed to Brazilian conservationist Ceballos-Lascurain, who defined ecotourism as travel "to relatively undisturbed or uncontaminated natural areas with the specific objective of studying, admiring, and enjoying the scenery and its wild plants and animals as well as any cultural aspects (both past and present) found in these area" (1987, p.13). Since then the International Ecotourism Society (TIES) and the United Nations Environment Program have taken the lead on establishing a set of ecotourism principles. As well as its defining characteristic of being nature-based, the three main principles are that ecotourism should:

1 Minimise damage to the environment, or better still leave the environment in a better state than before;

2 Provide economic benefits to the local community, both directly and indirectly through ecotourism's supply chain;

3 Encourage and develop a greater awareness of the natural and socio-cultural environment in which the ecotourism activities take place, through a deliberate and strategic interpretive program.

As with sustainable tourism itself, these characteristics can be interpreted to varying degrees to produce a range of ecotourism products, from largely nature-based offerings with some interpretive signage, to more extensive programs that directly support wildlife conservation and natural protection. A number of studies have developed spectra of ecotourism, hard to soft, deep green to light green, to reflect the range of services that can be offered under the banner of ecotourism.

The general principle, however, is that the stricter interpretations of the ecotourism ethos will encourage small group sizes, with independent travellers who are able to fit in with local customs and meet local people. The learning aspect of the experience is high, and often accompanied by a relatively high level of physical challenge, be it in the living conditions, or the modes of transport used to view nature. In these cases, a strong emphasis is placed on maximising positive social and environmental outcomes as well as economic benefits. For example, a native guide might be hired along with an interpreter to provide local employment and develop a sense of pride and custodianship over the natural asset, rather than employ an external guide who might speak more languages but has fewer local ties and knowledge, and is less likely to spend or invest her or his salary in the local community.

At the other end of the spectrum are the weaker interpretations of ecotourism; where the focus remains on nature, but less attention is spent on the learning aspect, or in maximising benefits to local people and the local natural environment. This form of ecotourism will be made more accessible to visitors with less specialised knowledge or interest in the natural features, who might be less tolerant for physical hardships (have mobility or other health issues, etc.), and need a greater supportive, more familiar framework as part of their tourism experience. An example might be a guided game drive in the Kruger National Park, a 3 hour tour with a National Park's appointed tour guide, in an open bus which seats approximately 25 people, provides limited interpretation and may disturb wildlife in its efforts to secure good wildlife sightings for its more mainstream customers.

The difference between these two extreme forms of ecotourism leads us to some of the issues that we will discuss in subsequent chapters. For example, the need to balance managing negative and positive impacts with the tourism experience itself, the role of ethics in tourism, issues of greenwashing, labelling and monitoring those labels, and finally, the role of the tourist (demand-side) versus the provider (supply-side) in managing impacts. Is being an ecotourist context-specific (on one day of my holiday, I may be an ecotourist and on the next a shopping tourist) and if so, who bears the responsibility for delivering the ecotourism experience?

1.7   Complex relationships in practice

Finally, I promised you a discussion of chocolate (and beer and coffee), arguably staples of any hedonic day of tourism. Chocolates feature on the menu of aeroplanes, cafes and restaurants, as little welcome gifts in hotel rooms, at vending machines and kiosks in every bus station and train station. All festivals and events, be they music, sporting or art, will feature some chocolate in their catering (not to mention coffee and/or beer).

Some countries, e.g. Ghana, have built an entire tourism campaign around chocolate, with each arriving tourist welcomed to the country with chocolate. Chocolate factories have become tourist attractions in their own right, with Cadbury's Birmingham factory attracting half a million visitors each year. Chocolate even has its own niche sub-sector within food and wine tourism; the chocolate tourism website features the best destinations to visit for your chocolate fix and a list of chocolate festivals and events to add to your calendar, e.g. Honk Kong's annual Chocolate Trail, a celebration of all things chocolate at the Harbour City Shopping Mall.

Figure 1.9: Ghana celebrates chocolate

The ubiquitous popularity of chocolate has led to concerns of a worldwide chocolate shortage. Demand outstripped supply back in 2012, as the Chinese and Indian markets grew, as well as the popularity of dark chocolate with its higher cocoa content. By 2020 we may face a shortfall of 1 million metric tons of chocolate. Chocolate prices have been rising as this shortfall grows, while research into increasing chocolate production has become a priority for some of the major players such as Mars, Inc., albeit with concerns of a watered down chocolatey taste.

But chocolate woes don't end there. In 2015, *The Guardian* newspaper ran a story titled "No more beer, chocolate or coffee: how climate change could ruin your weekend" (Guardian, 2015). Its second line read thus:

"Not taking global warming seriously enough? Our failure to act, and bad weather, will mean many of the pleasures we take for granted will disappear."

The central argument of the article is that changes to climate are creating rising temperatures and a lack of water in hop growing regions, threatening hop production. Temperatures in the cocoa producing regions of Ghana and the Ivory (which produce 70% of the world's cocoa) are set to rise by 2°, making those regions too hot and dry for cocoa trees. Meanwhile, crippling poverty is driving Africa cocoa farmers to look for other sources of income, such as the more stable production of corn.

The growing demand for chocolate and the increasingly difficult growing conditions for the cocoa bean are likely to compound the sustainability issues already facing chocolate. Most notably, chocolate production has long been associated with human rights concerns around the use of child labour, particularly where children are working in hazardous conditions (e.g. use of pesticides without proper protective gear, or use of potentially dangerous tools such as machetes), or even international child trafficking for forced labour in cocoa farms.

In 2001, US senator Thomas Harkin, and US Congressman, Eliot Engel, introduced the Harkin-Engel Protocol that addresses the "growing and processing of cocoa beans and their derivative products in a manner that complies with ILO Convention 182 concerning the prohibition and immediate action for the elimination of the worst forms of child labor". It is a voluntary public-private agreement between governments, the global cocoa industry, cocoa producers, cocoa laborers, non-governmental organizations. Progress towards the targets set out in the agreement is monitored by the US-based Tulane University whose last report in 2015 found that 2.03 million children were still found in hazardous work in cocoa production in Ghana and the Ivory Coast.

Meanwhile, finding new areas to produce cocoa have led to the deforestation of parts of the Peruvian and Brazilian Amazon. This has obvious habitat impacts for wildlife living in the cleared area, but also raises concern around greenhouse gas emissions linked to land-use change such as deforestation. Cadbury's lifecycle analysis estimates that 1 Dairy Milk chocolate bar (49g) releases 169g of CO2-equalivent emissions, based on the production of raw ingredients such as cocoa, cocoa butter, milk and sugar, and from packaging and distribution, but not including emissions from land-use change.

The point of this example is the following:

In order to be truly sustainable, even something as a small chocolate treat welcoming you at check-in is becoming a luxury in terms of what the Earth can produce under a changing climate, and would need careful scrutiny for its social sustainability impacts – both in terms of fair pay for farmers, and even more alarmingly for hazardous and forced child labour – as well as environmental sustainability linked to habitat clearing through the expansion of cocoa farms, and greenhouse gas emissions in the production of chocolate's raw ingredients, its packaging and its distribution. Conversely, the carbon emission impacts of travel on climate change and the resulting issues of cocoa production would also need to be taken into consideration.

Repeat this example for every aspect of the tourism supply chain, not only beer and coffee, but all of your food and beverages, your construction materials, your furnishings and interior design, your energy, water, gas and heating supply, your waste disposal (landfill and recycling), your employment practices, and those of your suppliers, and so on and so forth and you can see the scale of the challenge of sustainable tourism.

This example also tries to highlight why we must take a systems thinking approach to sustainable tourism management, where cause and effect do not always have linear relationships, and adopt a holistic perspective of the interlinking elements that form a dynamic system, and recognise that these dynamic systems may be nested within other systems. More on this in the next chapter!

Review

In summary, it is important to understand sustainability as a dynamic process, one which requires ongoing engagement, practice, skill and focus. A good rule of thumb is to view sustainability as a form of relationship-building, with a diversity of stakeholders, both human and non-human; anything that contributes to resilient, positive and trusting relationships is likely to be moving in the direction of sustainability, any actions that don't are likely to be moving in the opposite direction.

Of course, this is a rule of thumb only – the official definition of sustainable development was provided in Section 1.2. as "development that meets the needs of the present without compromising the ability of future generations to meet their own needs". This raises immediate questions around the value of my needs versus your needs, versus the needs of those people who are not even born yet.

Moreover, some argue that there is an inherent tension between the idea of development, and the growth associated with it, and the idea of sustainability, which lends itself to a more status quo orientation. One simple way of thinking about this tension has been put forward as the 'constant natural capital rule' where each generation should preserve the natural stock for the next, whilst living off the 'interest' only of that stock.

This would also apply to sustainable tourism, which follows a similar definition: "tourism that takes full account of its current and future economic, social and environmental impacts, addressing the needs of visitors, the industry, the environment and host communities". This definition applies equally to forms of mass tourism and to alternative tourism, e.g. ecotourism, and begs the question of whether tourism should be remedial in cases where sustainability thresholds have already been crossed, or encourage a status quo.

The answer to this question depends to some extent on your position in Jafari's tourism platforms: advocacy, cautionary, adaptancy or knowledge-based and McBeth's more recent additions of the sustainability and the ethics-based platforms. It will also depend on the specific tourism area's level of development according to Butler's Tourism Area Lifecycle Model, with Weaver's reminder not to confuse circumstantial sustainable tourism with deliberate sustainable tourism.

To assist tourism areas achieve the deliberate sustainable tourism, a number of international agreements, national and regional policies and lobbying or advisory organisations exist to provide best practice guidelines. At the international level, these are primarily driven by UNEP and UNWTO's *One Planet-Sustainable Tourism Programme*, which aligns with UNDP's Sustainable Development Goals. At the national and regional level, we find examples of both a top-down, government-led approach to implementing sustainable tourism and a bottom-up, community-led approach.

Finally, to illustrate the issue of sustainability in the tourism sector, we used the example of chocolate as a value-added pleasure to the tourism experience, and demonstrated how even something as small as a 50g bar of chocolate can have implications for social, environmental and economic sustainability, raising serious considerations around human rights, land clearing and climate change. Extrapolating from a small candy bar to the entire tourism supply chain illustrates the scale of the challenge, even for a 'green' tourism sector such as ecotourism!

Questions and exercises

1 Why is thinking about sustainability in the form of relationships a good rule of thumb? Can you find any examples of where this rule of thumb wouldn't work?

2 Think about a destination that you know well, what platform does it operate from: advocacy, cautionary, adaptancy, knowledge-based or ethics-based? Where would you place it on Butler's tourism area lifecycle?

3 Who are the key players in promoting sustainable tourism and what roles do they play?

4 Which of the 17 SDGs is sustainable tourism most closely aligned with?

5 Are ecotourism and sustainable tourism the same thing? Justify your answer.

6 How is a juggling metaphor useful in describing sustainable tourism development? How would you apply it to the example of chocolate in tourism in Section 1.7.

Multiple choice questions

1 Which of the following is one of the basic principles of holistic planning in the Brundtland report:

a) The need to protect both human heritage and biodiversity

b) The need to protect destination authenticity

c) The need to ensure financial viability

2 Sustainability values economic outcomes more than outcomes on the natural or social environments: True or false

3 Which of the following is not an accepted part of the constant natural capital rule?

a) We should audit all of current natural assets including accessible timber, land available for use, etc.

b) We should live of the "interest" of those assets, and leave the stock intact for future generations

c) We should interchange natural products with engineered products to allow us to use natural stock as necessary.

4 There are three components to sustainable tourism, which are looking at current impacts, looking at future impacts, and addressing the needs of four different stakeholder groups: True or false

5 Which is the correct sequence of platforms?

a) Advocacy → adaptancy → cautionary → knowledge → ethical → sustainable

b) Knowledge → advocacy → cautionary → adaptancy → sustainable → ethical

c) Advocacy → cautionary → adaptancy → knowledge → sustainable → ethical

Further reading

Bramwell, B. & Lane, B. (1993) Sustainable tourism: An evolving global approach. *Journal of Sustainable Tourism,* **1**(1), 1-5.

Bramwell, B., Higham, J., Lane, B. & Miller, G. (2017) Twenty five years of sustainable tourism and the Journal of Sustainable Tourism: looking back and moving forward. *Journal of Sustainable Tourism,* **25**(1), 1-9.

Boluk, K., Cavaliere, C.T. & Higgins-Desbiolles, F. (2017). Critical thinking to realize sustainability in tourism systems: reflecting on the 2030 sustainable development goals. *Journal of Sustainable Tourism,* **25**(9), 1201-1204.

Buckley, R. (2012). Sustainable tourism: research and reality. *Annals of Tourism Research,* **39**(2), 528-546.

Font, X. & McCabe, S. (2017) Sustainability and marketing in tourism: its contexts, paradoxes, approaches, challenges and potential. *Journal of Sustainable Tourism,* **25**(7), 869-883.

Garrod, B., & Fyall, A. (1998). Beyond the rhetoric of sustainable tourism?. *Tourism Management,* **19**(3), 199-212.

Miller, G., Rathouse, K. Scarles, C., Holmes, K. & Tribe, J. (2010). Public understanding of sustainable tourism. *Annals of Tourism Research,* **37**(3), 627-645.

Sharpley, R. (2000) Tourism and sustainable development: Exploring the theoretical divide. *Journal of Sustainable Tourism,* **8**(1), 1-19.

References

Bennett, G., (1997). Niederlande, the Dutch National Environmental Policy Plan. In *Nationale Umweltpläne in ausgewählten Industrieländern,* edited by M. Jänicke, A. Carius and H. Jörgens. Berlin: Springer. pp.73-85.

Brundtland, G. H. (1987). What is sustainable development? *Our Common Future,* 8-9.

Butler, R. W. (1980). The concept of a tourist area cycle of evolution: implications for management of resources. *Canadian Geographer/Le Géographe canadien,* **24**(1), 5-12.

Ceballos-Lascurain, H. (1987) The future of ecotourism, *Mexico Journal January,* 13-14.

Guardian (2015) No more beer, chocolate or coffee: how climate change could ruin your weekend, https://www.theguardian.com/environment/2015/jun/09/no-beer-chocolate-coffee-how-climate-change-ruin-your-weekend

Hall, C.M. (1998). Historical antecedents of sustainable development and ecotourism: New labels on old bottles? In C.M. Hall & A. Lew (eds.), *Sustainable Tourism Development: Geographical perspectives* (pp. 13-24). London: Addison-Wesley Longman.

Jafari, J. (2001). The scientification of tourism. In V. Smith and M. Brent (eds.) *Hosts and Guests Revisited: Tourism issues of the 21 century* (pp. 28-41). New York: Cognizant.

MacBeth, J. (2005). Towards an ethics platform for tourism. *Annals of Tourism Research*, **32**(4), 962-984

Sheppard, V. Dodds, R. and Williams, P. (2015). Good governance: managing growth and long-term resort destination sustainability and resilience. In Hughes, M., Weaver, D. & Pforr, C., *The Practice of Sustainable Tourism: Resolving the paradox*, Routledge, Oxford.

Teoh, S., (2015). The governmentality approach to sustainable tourism: Bhutan's tourism governance, policy and planning. In Hughes, M., Weaver, D. & Pforr, C., *The Practice of Sustainable Tourism: Resolving the paradox*, Routledge, Oxford, pp-113-132.

UNEP & UNWTO (2005). *Making Tourism More Sustainable - A Guide for Policy Makers*, p.p.11-12

UNWTO (2018) http://sdt.unwto.org/content/highlights-oneplanet-sustainabletourism (accessed July 2018).

Ura, K., & Galey, K. (Eds.) (2004). *Gross National Happiness and Development*. Thimpu: Centre for Bhutan Studies.

Weaver, D. (2006). *Sustainable Tourism: Theory and Practice*. Oxford: Butterworth: Heinemann.

WTTC (2018) https://www.wttc.org/summits/the-global-summit-2018/ (accessed July 2018).

2 Challenges to Implementing Sustainability Practices in Tourism

Introduction

So has sustainability in tourism actually reached a point of stagnation?

The answer on the surface may well be 'yes'. At first glance, it would appear that tourism has moved little beyond flight carbon offset schemes, high efficiency lightbulbs, and towel re-use schemes. The cynics would also point to 'greenwashing' within tourism, talking up environmental benefits to give the appearance of greater sustainability than is actually occurring. Why would this be?

The inclusion of sustainability-related behaviours within a business (green-washing or otherwise) tends to happen for one or several of three reasons.

1. To ward off the imposition of tighter government regulation on tourism activities

2. To tap into this apparently growing market of green consumers, who seek out environmentally and socially sustainable products and services

3. To enhance the social licence of businesses operating in sensitive areas (cruise ships travelling to the highly sensitive Antarctic environment, for example).

Test yourself

Another commonly-cited reason for adding a sustainability strategy to a business' priorities is the so-called business case for sustainability. Briefly, this is the argument that businesses who perform better on social and environmental indicators also perform better financially – a direct link can be made between investing in sustainability and economic returns. Unfortunately this sentiment is often translated into "investing in sustainability leads to greater profits", which the evidence does not always support. Instead, the argument is much more nuanced, involving risk minimisation, a 'slow' (longer-term) approach to business growth and success, and investing in relationships, as discussed in Chapter 1.

This chapter examines this notion of a business case for sustainability, and asks why, if the business case is so clear, are sustainability practices still so poorly developed in tourism? It reviews challenges that are specific to the travel and tourism sector that make implementation of sustainable tourism even more complex. These include:

☐ The private/public sector nature of tourism, and the need for what Weaver (2015) refers to as 'enlightened self-interest'.

☐ The scale-related issues of tourism and integrating practices across tourists to single businesses to destinations, and destinations to host regions and generating regions.

☐ The issue of inseperability in tourism where production and consumption are linked in ways that do not occur in most sectors.

☐ The infrequent nature of tourism purchases.

☐ The 'footloose' nature of much of the sector.

☐ The influence of business size on sustainability practices.

☐ The need for local, context-based, yet multi-disciplinary knowledge.

The chapter also raises the tricky question of tourism's relationship with climate change. Tourism and climate change have a two-way relationship, as tourism has a significant carbon footprint and is therefore a major contributor to climate change, and is also highly vulnerable to changes in the climate. While the former, tourism's carbon footprint, will be covered in Chapter 3, this chapter will consider how tourism is vulnerable, directly and indirectly, to a changing climate.

Key words and concepts

- Business case for sustainability
- Corporate Social Responsibility
- Slack resources/good management approach
- Tragedy of the commons
- Inseparability of tourism experiences

- Global-local nexus
- Carbon calculators
- Theory of Planned Behaviour
- Intergovernmental Panel on Climate Change
- Systems thinking

2.1 The business case for sustainability

'Green is gold' is the key phrase when discussing the business case for sustainability; proving how enterprises do well (Corporate Financial Performance or CFP) by doing good (Corporate Social Responsibility or CSR) has become a form of holy grail in the business literature (Garay & Font, 2012, p.335).

But it turns out that it is not that simple. The research into this area is divided equally between those studies that say CSR activities do have a positive effect on CFP, and those studies that say there is either no effect at best, or at worst, a negative effect. Several explanations are provided for these contradictory findings. First, the relationship is far more complex and nuanced than simple cause and effect; second it depends on what is being measured; and third, it depends on the measures being used.

At the very least, one aspect of the relationship that researchers do appear to agree on is that it is bi-directional; a good CSR performance is as much likely to influence as be influenced by good CFP. This complex, bi-direction relationship between CSR and CFP is often explained by two alternative approaches: the 'slack resources' approach and the 'good management' approach.

The slack resources approach recognises that a company with strong CFP will generate extra resources that can be invested in CSR. In this case 'doing well' actually paves the way for 'doing good' by providing the slack or additional resources needed to invest in CSR initiatives (Singal, 2014).

The good management approach is that CSR forms part of a suite of best practice activities designed to actively engage internal and external stakeholders, provide clear channels of communication, transparency and accountability, and so forth. CFP may improve through CSR implementation by developing capabilities such as closer internal and communication and interaction, a clearer articulation of the owner's vision, greater management flexibility and improved external relationships (Garay & Font, 2012).

It could be argued therefore that CSR and CFP are actually part of a 'virtuous cycle' (Singal, 2014). A study of the Nanshan Cultural Tourism Zone in Hainan, China, found that their improved environmental performance, and the social recognition and positive press that came with it, caught the attention of the local government, who then 'adopted' it as a flagship attraction, and provided the attraction with further assistance and support, effectively expanding the virtuous cycle.

So if the business case for implementing sustainability is not straightforward, what motivates businesses to invest in social and environmental sustainability? Much of the literature has focused on engaging in CSR for three reasons:

1 Increasing operational efficiency, to reduce energy and water consumption and therefore costs (eco-efficiency)

2 Forestalling risk by preventing brand damage and ensuring an ongoing social licence to operate (legitimisation)

3 Selling to the environmental niche, by tapping into new markets, increasing sales and enhancing the company image in this space a (competitive advantage).

Question

2

We saw in Chapter 1, how ecotourism and sustainability are being conflated. The following article discusses why eco-resorts have become so successful. Read the article and determine which reasons are being presented as part of the good business case for sustainability in hotels.

Why eco-resorts are the new black

https://www.couriermail.com.au/travel/australia/green-is-gold-for-australian-hotels-and-resorts-as-ecotourism-becomes-a-billiondollar-industry/news-story/1deabe06b638c330c72d116fa696fc6a

The first of these reasons, eco-efficiency, represents a direct relationship between cost management and environmental performance, and is perhaps the area where the 'green is gold' argument has received the strongest empirical support. The latter two arguments represent indirect links, and require a bit more unpacking.

In the economics literature the legitimisation argument can be related to a 'transaction cost economics' approach, whereby CRS effectively avoids higher costs from more formalised contractual compliance mechanisms and aligning more closely with social norms (Garay & Font, 2012). The competitive advantage argument have often been linked to a resource-based view that holds that the skills and resources (such as relationships with stakeholders, an engagement with higher order learning and embracing innovation) lead to a product that cannot be easily imitated by other firms (Garay & Font, 2012).

There is also a growing body of literature that suggests that reducing the environmental impact of the private sector is likely to have significant social returns, even if they do not yield significant private returns. Which for some, is a good enough reason to engage in CSR activities, and aligns more closely with an altruism approach, accepting society and nature as the business' greatest stakeholders. Businesses that adopt this approach often seek to protect the environment for its own intrinsic value, have made a low footprint lifestyle choice and have a strong social commitment (Garay & Font, 2012).

In fact, the notion of a business' 'Purpose Imperative' is replacing the whole idea of sustainability in some circles. The CEO of one of the World's largest investment management corporations wrote an open letter in 2018 to all the CEO's of his clients that makes exactly this point:

"Society is demanding that companies, both public and private, serve a social purpose. To prosper over time, every company must not only deliver financial performance, but also show how it makes a positive contribution to society. Companies must benefit all of their stakeholders, including shareholders, employees, customers, and the communities in which they operate. Without a sense of purpose, no company, either public or private, can achieve its full potential. It will ultimately lose the license to operate from key stakeholders".

Read the full letter here: https://www.blackrock.com/corporate/investor-relations/2018-larry-fink-ceo-letter

In studies that have actually tested the 'green is gold' relationship, it would appear that there is a positive correlation between *environmental performance* and economic performance (e.g. the eco-efficiency argument) but not necessarily between *environmental management* and economic performance (Rodriguez and Cruz, 2007). In their study, Garay and Font (2012) found that eco-saving practices correlate positively (albeit only slightly) with the financial situation of the business, as did environmental impact assessment and fair wages, but activities such a local development support, heritage protection and promoting the consumption of local products did not.

Henderson (2015) suggests that businesses focus on CSR as a form of strategic hedging of long-term bets. She argues that three key variables in the 'green is gold' argument are actually very uncertain:

☐ Will mainstream consumers come to value sustainable products and services enough to pay a premium for them?

☐ How and/or when will increasingly severe environmental pressures generate political pressure for the introduction of new regulatory measures?

☐ How and/or when will scientific and technological advances make responding to environmental problems significantly cheaper?

She posits that the two forms of planning – short-to medium term operational thinking, and longer-term strategic planning – rely on two very different forms of leadership, different organisational structures, incentive structures, time frames and formal metrics of performance and success. The latter being much more comfortable with uncertainty, flexibility and indeed failure if the hypothesised future state does not actually come about.

In studying radical innovation adoption in small to medium accommodation businesses, Coles et al., (2014) found that it was the desire for first mover advantage to make the business stand out that often prompted greater environmental management measures. At the other extreme, Singal (2014) reminds us that non-operational CSR initiatives are the first areas to be cut in tourism firms under financial stress.

She also suggests that this type of management responds much more effectively to scenario analysis and specific types of framing. She uses the following example to illustrate her point: rather than ask a business "is global warming real?' the question could be much better presented as a "is there a real possibility that an increased perception that global warming is real may lead to increased regulation of global warming gasses?" (Henderson, 2015, p.21).

A word of caution is also required here. In an interesting framing experiment of energy saving behaviours, researchers Steinhorst et al., (2015) found that asking a sample of German businesses to save energy (i) to reduce their costs, or (ii) to reduce their carbon emissions, they found that both had similar effects on energy saving behaviours. However, only the latter led to spill-over effects into other pro-environmental behaviours – because the environment was front and centre of the second framing argument, i.e. was made salient, and because the respondents in that group realised that changes in their actions could make a positive difference, they were more likely to try out other pro-environmental behaviours. The researchers then ask the question; is the reverse also true? Does the cost reduction argument lead to a search for other ways to cut costs, some of which may actually be detrimental to sustainability?

They caution us to be mindful of the law of unintended consequences when using the 'green is gold' argument.

2.2   Challenges specific to the tourism sector

Tourism's apparent stagnation in the implementation of sustainability principles can, at least in part, be accounted for by a number of features that are specific to the sector itself. The extent of public private partnerships, geographical scale-related issues, the inseparability of the tourism experience, the infrequent nature of tourism purchases, the footloose nature of much of the sector, the prevalence of small to medium sized enterprises and the balance between local context-based knowledge and multi-disciplinary, technical expertise are some of the main challenges facing tourism and the implementation of sustainability.

In addition to all of these, is the idea that we cannot manage tourism as a series of separate pieces with linear relationships between them. Instead, it must be viewed as a complex, interrelated and dynamic whole system (as I tried to show in Chapter 1's example of chocolate in tourism). As you read through the following sections, look for where this idea of a tourism system is impacting on its management in terms of sustainability.

Test yourself

The dominance of the private sector

First, let's discuss private-public partnerships. Tourism is a fragmented sector, involving a range of different stakeholders and sectors, visitors and host communities, government immigration departments, destination marketing organisations, travel agents, tour agents, transport providers, accommodation providers and so forth, who all make up a complex and interrelated dynamic system (Table 2.1).

Table 2.1: The UNWTO's (2008) list of consumption products grouped by purpose, according to their categorization as internationally comparable tourism characteristic products

Category	Examples	No. of sub-categories
Package travel, holidays and tours	Tour operator, reservation services, inland water transport of passengers on cruises	5
Accommodation	Room of unit accommodation, campsites, timeshares, rental property management, rooms or units in students' residences	16
Food and beverage	Meal serving with full restaurant services, or limited services, other food and/or beverage services	4
Local and international transportation	Railway transport, taxis, car rental, inland water transport, sightseeing tours, baggage handlers, parking lots, highway/bridge/tunnel, vehicle maintenance and repair serviecs, etc.	59
Recreation, cutlure & sporting activities	Leasing of pleasure and leisure equipment, reservation services for events, tour guides, visitor information services, gambling and betting, museums, zoos and botanical gardens, performing artists, etc.	21
Shopping	Goods purchased by visitors within their shopping activity	1
Other	Credit card services, car, property and travel insurance, foreign exchange, cultural education, medical services, etc.	37

Already we see a mix of private and public sectors, then add to the mix that many attractions are held in public trust (e.g. sea, sand and sun of 3S tourism, national parks, historic city precincts, museums, or even the national character of a place), and paid for by local government. Meanwhile, access to those attractions is often controlled by the private sector, who benefit from the public investment into managing those attractions. Just take a look at Figure 2.1 overleaf, that shows some of the World's most popular tourist attractions and consider how many are actually held in the public interest.

Question

In Figure 2.1, how many of the destinations (many of which are attractions, not destinations) are privately owned and managed and how many are cultural and natural heritage that are managed by the public sector?

Figure 2.1: The world's most popular travel destinations.

This may at worst lead to a form of 'tragedy of the commons' or at best contribute to a lack of clear industry leadership, where fuzzy boundaries of responsibility lead to the old story of four people called Everybody, Somebody, Anybody, and Nobody. The story goes like this:

"There was an important job to be done and Everybody was asked to do it. Everybody was sure Somebody would do it. Anybody could have done it, but Nobody did it. Somebody got angry about that, because it was Everybody's job. Everybody thought Anybody could do it but Nobody realized that Everybody wouldn't do it. It ended up that Everybody blamed Somebody when Nobody did what Anybody could have done."

The Everybody, Somebody, Anybody, and Nobody story is particularly salient when it comes to climate change and travel – an issue that will be discussed in Section 2.3, as well as in Chapter 3. Briefly, when it comes to curbing the significant carbon emissions arising from transport and accommodation in tourism, everybody believes that somebody else should take the lead, and the end result, according to prominent researchers such as Gössling, and Hall (e.g. Gössling et al., 2015) is that nobody is really doing much at all.

There's an interesting discussion about the value of airline carbon offsets here: http://www.abc.net.au/radionational/programs/lifematters/burning-question:-are-airline-carbon-offsets-worth-it/9638320

Test
yourself

For example, a study of travel agents' response to tourism's carbon footprint found that frontline staff had very little knowledge of the issue, and did not feel that it was their role to advise clients to behave in a more environmentally-friendly way. Their managers on the other hand, were aware of the issues, but "shifted the responsibility down the value chain by calling on suppliers to produce more carbon efficient products, up the value chain by calling on customers to change their behaviour, or externally, by calling for government to act" (McKercher et al, 2014, p.690).

Indeed one of their respondents argued that:

"it would be easier if customers began to request low carbon products [leading the] industry to respond to such a request to develop more low caborn products instead of the other way around"

(McKercher et al., 2014, p.691).

Meanwhile, a parallel study of UK tourists' attitudes towards air travel found that a major barrier to changing travel patterns was that the responsibility for climate change lies with "governments, businesses and other countries" but not with the individual (Hares et al., 2010). This way of thinking effectively enters us into a Catch 22 – a paradoxical situation from which an individual cannot escape because of contradictory rules.

In addition to the issue of leadership and responsibility, any private/public partnership is further complicated by differences in ideologies, mandates, power imbalances, accountability and openness in responding to changing circumstances. With the exception of weather, cultural and natural heritage attractions, much of the tourism sector is dominated by the private sector. And, unless guided by intrinsic corporate social responsibility (CSR) values, the private sector rely on the business case for sustainability, which as we have seen in Section 2.1. can be misleading. The public sector, on the other hand, with its mandate to represent its citizens and with less imperative to produce short-term economic returns, ought to be in a better position to pursue sustainability, in cases where it can influence the private sector's practices.

Scale-related issues

The scale-related issues of tourism form another key set of challenges. Tourism scholars refer to a global-local nexus – to understand tourism sustainability, we must recognise the influence of large multinational businesses and institutions, national regulations, regional contexts, community-level influences, and finally the disposition and behaviours of individual tourists. Implementing sustainable tourism requires integrating practices across tourists to single businesses to destinations, and destinations to host regions and generating regions

At the global level, we must understand the broader geo-political forces, e.g. China opening its borders to leisured-based travel, as well as the global priorities of large multinational corporations, trade agreements that create business travel links and pave the way for later leisure travel, through increased travel-related infrastructure and diplomatic relations. These are usually managed at the national level, as are tourism campaigns, run by state managed destination marketing organisations. National governments may also take a lead role in managing broad-based product development that will ultimately shape tourism demand and behaviour.

Regions and communities are usually the ones that play host to inbound tourists. It is their attractions, whether natural, cultural, or economic that draw tourists. It is also at this level that models such as the Tourism Area Lifecycle are developed. Concepts such as carrying capacities or sustainability thresholds are usually applied to destinations at the level of communities and regions, and industry representative bodies are also most likely to occur at the regional level.

Finally, behaviour itself, be it sustainable or unsustainable, occurs at the level of the individual. This is true for both the tourist and for the business. How much energy is consumed at a small to medium sized tourism enterprise depends both up the infrastructure provided by the business, e.g. sensor-operated lights or energy efficient appliances, as well as how the tourists use those. Meanwhile the impetus for using alternative, green energy sources will depend on regional availability and national policies, and so forth. Thus, we have to understand how tourism operates at a sequence of nested scales – from global, national, regional, destination-level, business-level and at the level of individual tourists.

In addition, how information is made available for sustainability-related decision-making represents a scale issue. Even information as basic as the number of travellers each year is difficult to capture as self-drive tourists at a regional, domestic or even international level (e.g. Europe's Schengen Area does not have border controls) cannot easily be recorded for statistical purposes. Similarly, the economic value of tourism, its GDP and employment figures, rely on composite measures of satellite accounts, a complex process using data from other national accounts (e.g. hotels/cafes/restaurants or transport or recreation/culture), censuses/directories, survey data, and databases.

The following reports detail some of the decisions made by the UNWTO on how to measure tourism within a sustainability context.
http://cf.cdn.unwto.org/sites/all/files/docpdf/folderfactsheetweb.pdf and
http://cf.cdn.unwto.org/sites/all/files/docpdf/mstoverviewrev1.pdf

Often making decisions regarding sustainable practices require scaling up data from individual businesses, e.g. energy consumption data from a sample of hotels, or scaling down data at a national or international level, e.g. Australia's international visitor survey, a survey of 40,000 departing, short-term international travellers aged 15 years and over, captured in the departure lounges of the eight major international airports. In both cases, the margin of error as data are scaled up or down is likely to be significant. In the latter case, end-users may also find that the data do not take into account local contexts or variability, making them virtually meaningless for strategic decision-making purposes.

To illustrate this issue in a tourism context, let's take the example of carbon emissions. We would want to know three things: first, what is tourism's current carbon footprint; second, is tourism's carbon footprint growing or decreasing; and third, what is the projected carbon footprint of tourism over the next decade.

The first issue requires an accurate representation of the size and structure of the tourism sector – records of tourism-related businesses across all nations, as well as not only their carbon footprint, but also the carbon footprint up and down the supply chain – i.e. a lifecycle assessment of tourism's carbon footprint. Most figures rely on the last time that such a large endeavour was undertaken was in 2007, 2008 at the time of the Davos Declaration (see Section 2.3), with a new study having just been published in May 2018.

Figure 2.2: Tourism's carbon footprint in increasing rapidly. Read more about it here: http://etn.travel/global-tourisms-carbon-footprint-is-expanding-rapidly-57223/

Second, we want to how technological advances, CSR activities, consumer behaviour and consumer preferences are all affecting tourism's carbon footprint. Do more efficient appliances mean less energy consumed, or do users feel that they can increase their consumption in line with efficiency gains? Is consumer preference for more frequent long-haul holidays outweighing any gains in fuel-efficiency made by the aviation industry and so forth?

Test yourself

Third, we require accurate projections of the number of travellers in the future – will immigration policies change dramatically with any possible geo-political instability? Will travel preferences change away from long-haul destinations with the introduction of a possible carbon tax, or as consumer preferences change? Will technologies such as virtual reality provide substitutes for actual travel?

As you can see, the level of information required comes from many sectors, across borders and vary from micro-levels consumer preferences to macro-level, geo-political systems. It is no easy task collecting that data across such varied scales.

Inseparability of tourism experience production and consumption

Another issue which is particular to the tourism industry is its so-called inseparability. Inseparability is one of the four defining characteristics of the services sector that distinguishes it from manufacturing and other forms of production-based sectors (the other three characteristics are variability, perishability and intangibility). Inseparability means that the tourism experience is largely produced and consumed at the same time.

This has important implications for issues like service recovery – it is difficult to hide mistakes when production and consumption occur at the same time (think of the equivalent of an actor in a play forgetting his or her words). But inseparability of consumption and production also means that, unlike organic vegetables or fairtrade coffee, where a label assures us that certain practices have been adhered to in the their production and we, as consumers have no role to play in the issue, in sustainable tourism, consumers have a much more active role to play in sustainable practices and therefore a larger influence on social, environmental and economic outcomes.

First, our actions have a direct impact, e.g. how we behave at a local cultural ceremony (observing a request to not photograph inside a Buddhist temple for example), or whether we choose to climb a mountain that is considered scared (e.g. Uluru/Ayer's Rock) or resisting the temptation to feed semi-tame wildlife at a picnic site or using the recycling bins available to us. Unlike in most production situations, consumers' actions have a significant direct impact on the sustainability of the sector. In the accommodation sector, for instance, it is estimated that over half of energy and water consumption are linked to the behaviour of the guest, not the business.

Chapter 8 looks at some ways of operationalising sustainability in tourism, with a key focus on inviting tourists to be part of the solution. The video linked below, taken from that same case study on My Green Butler's hospitality intervention gives you an indication of why understanding and managing guest behaviour plays a key role in sustainability.

 Watch the My Green Butler video: https://youtu.be/XLk4M0lp9sU

Second, a tourist who is knowledgeable about sustainability practices may be able to call out unsustainable behaviour and demand a higher standard of behaviour, e.g. an airline which prides itself on its recycling programs yet doesn't appear to separate waste during rubbish collection on a flight. Conversely (and perhaps more frequently) a tourist who is unfamiliar with best practice in sustainability will not be able to call out poor practices.

On a personal note, in 2015 I visited Cuba for the first time and after two weeks of homestays, I decided to book my last night in one of Havana's most historic hotels. Walk-in reservations were managed by a well-groomed, well-spoken, very chic lady in a small office in the basement. After a lengthy conversation about the difficulties of making bookings with an outdated computer system and frequent power blackouts, she showed me her payslip. To my disbelief and dismay, her monthly salary was AU$37/month, i.e. AU$1/ day – in a hotel that was charging several hundred times that as its base rate.

Third, for those of us with a strong sustainability ethics in our daily lives, our ability as tourists to behave in a sustainable manner is highly dependent on the provisions and infrastructure available to us within the destination. For example, we may recycle at home and use low carbon forms of transport (cycling, walking, public transport), but these may not be available to us away from home, or if they are available, we may not know how to access them (think of city bike share systems that have no clear instructions on how to rent the bike). Miller et al.'s (2016) study of pro-environmental behaviours away from home showed that the facilities available to tourists was the third most important factor in their behaviours, after attitudes and habits. This raises important questions about leadership and shared responsibility in co-creating sustainable tourism – an issue that will be discussed further in Chapter 8.

Infrequency of tourism purchases

An issue that is somewhat related to this is the infrequency of tourism purchases and its impact on our ability to understand, assess and weigh up sustainability claims. The literature on green purchases reveals the importance of environmental knowledge, awareness, concern and attitude, availability of product information and product availability, as well perceived consumer effectiveness and transparency of fair trade practices. The latter (perceived consumer effectiveness and transparency of fair trade practices) refer to the previous discussion on inseparability and our ability to assess the tourist experience.

The former (knowledge, awareness, attitude availability of product and product information), however, are largely influenced by the frequency with which we purchase a product or service. Purchase frequency and green consumption is a little counter-intuitive in the case of travel. While habit is often seen as a barrier to pro-environmental switching buying behaviours, occasional or one-off purchases fall into a different category of conscious selection (Lavelle, Rau & Fahy, 2015). In theory, therefore, one-off holiday purchases could be green, were tourists to consider sustainability in their purchasing decision. Ecolabelling in tourism is one way of providing accessible sustainability-related information to allow tourists to choose green tourism businesses. Yet a review of ecolabels' impact on tourists' choices found that they have limited market penetration as they are perceived to:

Test
yourself

☐ Have a low level of reliability,

☐ Lack transparency to consumers

☐ Be based on few or no audits

☐ Have few sanctions for non-compliance (Buckley, 2002).

In the case of tourism purchases, three factors work against the systematic inclusion of sustainability-related factors in purchase decision-making.

First, the infrequent nature of the purchase means that we may never get beyond those early deciding factors of price/value, availability and safety. The five most common factors considered by travellers when booking holidays tend to be price, weather, the wishes of family and friends, travel time and activities (e.g. Hares et al., 2010). Second, tourists' purchases (in particular, leisure-related travel) are often associated with the search for newness – again, this means that intrinsically, we will not build up a familiarity with the purchase that allows us to consider other factors.

For example, Juvan and Dolnicar (2014), and Gössling and Buckley (2016), studied tourists' understanding of carbon footprint calculators and found that only a small percentage of respondents were willing to even engage with these calculators. This may be linked to a phenomenon known as "perplexity of environmental information" (Moisander, 2007, p.406). This perplexity comes about as consumers generally lack the expert knowledge to understand carbon calculations, the confusing information around the environmental impacts of tourism, and increased scepticism about claims of environmental sustainability due to 'greenwashing', an issue we'll come to in Chapter 6.

Question

Try using the following carbon calculators to check the results for yourself. Do they all provide similar results? Is one easier to use than the others? Can you find any others?

■ ICAO Carbon Emissions Calculator: https://www.icao.int/environmental-protection/CarbonOffset/Pages/default.aspx

■ Atmosfair: https://www.atmosfair.de/en/offset/flight/

■ Myclimate: https://co2.myclimate.org/en/footprint_calculators/new

Third, the hedonic, escapist nature of the leisure-based tourism experience means that we may focus less on the 'responsible' side, i.e. the sustainability practices, of a tourism provider. In fact, holidays seem to have a special status in our minds, a symbolic meaning that set them apart from everyday rules and concerns (Becken, 2007). We attach a high value to our holidays, which are imbued with cultural capital, i.e. raising our social standing through the cachet of travelling. In Hares et al.'s (2010) study of UK travellers' perceptions of climate change and air travel, participants went so far as to justify their travel behaviours, including their carbon footprint, as contributing to the greater social good, fostering wellbeing, cross-cultural understanding and economic development of poorer nations.

Some examples of answers given in their study:

"I think that travel's important for people to understand each other's culture... so many social reasons why we need to travel and experience different parts of the world" (p. 470).

"There is more in the media and it does make me think. But it probably makes me think I should travel more now because I might not have the opportunity... in twenty years you just won't be able to get to some of the places that are really accessible now" (p. 469)

Indeed, the so-called attitude/behaviour gap tends to be pronounced in tourism, where tourists may express a positive attitude towards sustainability-oriented behaviours, but may not be willing to enact those behaviours. Gössling and Buckley (2016) found that up to 15% of respondents from a sample of tourist signed up to the German Alternative Tourism Forum, would not refer to carbon labelling in their travel behaviour decisions as "such a label would rather scare me off to book my holiday with this tour operator, because I think they try to make me feel guilty about travelling" (p.365).

Similar results are reported across a range of studies of pro-environmental behaviours when on holiday, all concluding that environmentally friendly behaviours drop in frequency when on vacation, even among those who state that they care about the environment (Dolnicar & Grün, 2009; Wearing et al., 2002). Even more surprisingly, one study found that participants who were most likely to save energy and water at home had the highest travel-related carbon footprint of all study participants (Barr et al., 2011). This raises the issue that any carbon emissions savings achieved at home is likely to be wiped out by this group's holiday behaviour.

The footloose nature of many tourism sub-sectors

Another issue that hinders the move towards greater sustainability in the tourism industry is the comparatively high 'footloose' nature of the industry (Weaver, 2006). To best understand it, we must return to the (fragmented and dynamic) structure of the tourism sector.

At its most basic level, tourism consists of tourists and a tourist-generating region, a transit region where the transport sector is the principle player, and a host destination. Eight main sectors facilitate tourism: intermediaries such as travel agencies, merchandise (guidebooks, travel accessories, luggage, as well as souvenirs), tour operators, transportation, accommodation, food services, attractions and entertainment.

As mentioned, transport dominates the transit region, moving from tourist-generating region to tourism destinations, and is also present to a lesser extent in both generation region and destination. Travel agencies and most merchandise are to be found in the generating region. The remainder, accommodation, food services, attractions, and entertainment are all located in the destination region.

The result of this pattern is twofold. First, tourism impacts are predominantly witnessed in the destination, rather than generating region (an issue touched upon in the discussion of tourism's scale). Second, few of the sectors outlined above are entirely dependent upon tourism for revenue and/or fixed to a particular region. Weaver (2006) therefore argues that these sectors have limited vested interest in safeguarding a sustainable tourism destination.

Let's unpack that bold statement a little further. Of those eight sectors, some are largely footloose in the sense that they can move on to a newer, more pristine destination in response to environmental degradation or social unrest in a tourism area that is stagnant or in decline (using Butler's TALC model). Travel agencies can send tourists to new destinations, similarly with merchandise sales. Large multinational tour operators (both inbound and outbound) can also switch to new locations if necessary. Transport is, by its very nature, footloose, and anyone following patterns of commercial airlines will note how hubs are created and flight routes changed to meet consumer demand. Moreover, when it comes to entertainment, food services and attractions, only part of their market is related to tourism, with residents and/or excursionists making up the remainder.

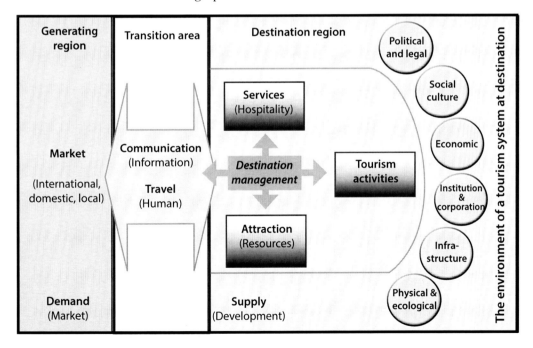

Figure 2.3: A basic model of the tourism system, adapted from Gunn, 1994; Leiper, 1979; Mill & Morrison, 1998; Van Mai & Bosch, Weichard, 1992.

The remaining sector is accommodation, which is believed to contribute up to a quarter of tourism's carbon emissions. With a few exceptions (e.g. cruise ships), accommodation remains fixed within the destination, and has a large and very visible footprint there. The result is that more than most other sectors of tourism, accommodation providers have, or at least should have, a vested interest in keeping the destination sustainable. Much of the literature on sustainability has therefore focussed on the accommodation sector's resource use and waste disposal (e.g. Warren et al., 2018).

With the majority of other tourism sectors not relying on fixed assets (transport will be discussed in Section 2.3. on climate change), there is both less ability to regulate them and they are able to relatively easily move on from a destination that has exceeded its sustainability threshold and is showing evidence of social and environmental degradation. Weaver (2006) adds that the low profit margins of tour operators and the relatively undifferentiated products on offer (think 3Ss) mean that they are looking for cost-cutting options and are highly sensitive to customer complaints over value for money and service quality.

The result is that sustainability considerations become relegated to a value-add, if present at all.

The predominance of small to medium sized enterprises

Alongside the footloose nature of much of the industry, it also has to be pointed out that tourism is characterised by both a small number of multinational companies, with a vast reach and influence, and a very high proportion of small to medium sized tourism enterprises, who dominate the sector in terms of sheer numbers.

For example, within the accommodation sector the five largest hotel groups, Marriot, Hilton, Wyndham, Accor, and Intercontinental control over 30,000 hotels in 127 countries, representing approximately 90 brands. These businesses therefore have significant presence to drive sustainability within destination regions. Their corporate social responsibility programs (available below) represent efforts to minimise resource consumption, reduce waste, hire locally and upskill workers from the local community, address local environmental and social issues, and so forth.

Follow these links to read the CSR strategies of the largest hotel groups.

cr.hilton.com/

www.marriott.com.au/corporate-social-responsibility/corporate-responsibility.mi

www.accorhotels.group/en/commitment/positive-hospitality/acting-here

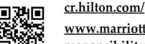
www.wyndhamworldwide.com/category/environment-sustainability

www.ihg.com/intercontinental/content/us/en/support/about-intercontinental#responsiblebusiness

Meanwhile, Airbnb boasts over 4 million listings in 191 countries, and whilst there do not appear to be any sustainability-oriented hosting standards beyond an overriding anti-discrimination policy in line with its "belong anywhere vision", the company itself has a social (but no publically available environmental) sustainability program that includes staff volunteer time, open homes (discounted Airbnb rates for social causes) and disaster relief support, as well as initiatives such as partnering with Make-A-Wish® America and Make-A-Wish® International to grant one wish/day by donating US$1 million in travel credits.

Read about Airbnb's CSR: <u>www.airbnbcitizen.com/social-impact/</u>

There are two points to be made here. The first is that many consider sustainable tourism as synonymous with alternative tourism, and alternative tourism includes the shared economy, such as Airbnb. However, with over 4 million listings and $2.6 billion in revenue, Airbnb cannot be considered part of the alternative tourism sector. Similarly the hotel groups listed above represent approximately $45billion in revenue; tourism sustainability can only occur with these large partners onside, as their influence (as well as that of the largest tour operators, attractions and transport sectors) is vast in terms in communities affected, resources used and tourists as customers. Moreover, these partners have the economies of scale and budgets to make sustainability a reality, using the slack resources approach (c.f. Section 2.1.).

However, whilst these large companies may dominate in terms of market share, footprint, reach and revenue, it is the small to medium-sized enterprises (SMEs) that dominate in terms of sheer numbers of businesses in tourism. An SME is defined in terms of number of employees (usually less than 200) and around 90% of all businesses within a country can be SMEs. They may have less individual impact than a single large hotel chain (Marriott for example employs approximately 177,000 people around the world), but their sheer numbers also make them an important contributor to the implementation of sustainability.

And, as we will see in the examples in Chapter 8, smaller companies may have the knowledge and support to implement sustainability, and may in fact be more agile in greening their own practices as well as their entire supply chains, responding to local social and environmental needs and influencing tourists' behaviours. In a study of CSR in accommodation SMEs, Garay and Font (2012) actually found that the smallest businesses were the ones with strongest CSR-CFP (c.f. Section 2.1.) relationships. Often, however is these SMEs that have the fewest financial and human resources and least technical expertise or even time, to implement sustainability.

The need for technical expertise balanced with local knowledge

Which brings us to the final point of this section; the balance between local context-based knowledge and multi-disciplinary, technical expertise. At the level of the individual, as opposed to systems or regulation, this may be one of the more significant issues in implementing sustainability in tourism.

Listen to Catherine Mohr on the nitty gritty of sustainability
https://www.ted.com/talks/catherine_mohr_builds_green

To explore this further, we turn to one of the core theories of behavioural intention is Ajzen's (1991) Theory of Planned Behaviour, that links one's beliefs to one's actual behaviour.

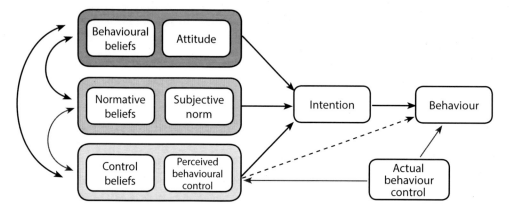

Fig. 2.4: Ajzen's (1991) Theory of Planned Behaviour, linking attitudes, norms and behavioural control to actual behaviour.

Simply put the theory states that one's actual behaviour (in this case, engagement in sustainability-related activities) depends on attitudes towards that behaviour, subjective norms and perceived behavioural control.

☐ **Attitudes** encapsulates both our knowledge of the behaviour and related issue, as well as whether we feel positively or negatively towards that behaviour (do we consider it to be a good thing or bad thing to do?).

☐ **Subjective norm** relates to what significant others in our lives think of the behaviour (is there a social expectation or 'norm' that we do it).

☐ **Perceived behavioural control** describes whether we feel we'll be able to successfully execute the behaviour and/or whether it is likely to be derailed by external forces beyond our control.

The theory of planned behaviour has been widely applied across areas such as healthcare, advertising, pro-environmental behaviours and public relations, albeit with mixed results. As a theory, however, it serves as a good entry point for thinking about sustainability implementation in tourism (similar to Butler Tourism Area Lifecycle Model).

There are several elements at play here. At one level, tourism represents a complex system of interlocking actors, and secondary stakeholders, with multiple material flows (land, energy, water, biodiversity) at varied scales and geographical, social and political contexts, and frequent external shocks such as natural disasters, terrorist attacks, etc. These all relate to the perceived behavioural control – will external factors derail my best efforts and do I really have the ability to execute sustainability-related behaviours?

At the next level, the complex tourism system means that understanding, implementing and evaluating progress in the sustainability of tourism requires complex interdisciplinary, and sometimes even transdisciplinary, methodologies that can reveal cause and effect among its different parts (Budeanu et al., 2016). These relate to knowledge, which in turn relates to attitude (the first dimension of Azjen's theory) – for before I can have a positive or negative attitude towards something, it helps if I have some knowledge about that thing.

Even if we break down the complexity of the tourism system and just focus on one aspect, choosing for example, energy consumption, the level of knowledge required to manage that resource sustainably appears to be lacking.

To demonstrate this, one group of researchers undertook a very revealing study with regards to knowledge and attitudes towards energy consumption in UK-based SMEs in the accommodation sector (Coles et al., 2014). They found that SMTEs (small to medium tourism enterprises) paid little to no attention to information regarding their energy consumption, with little idea how to interpret energy bills and consumption data. Respondents had little knowledge of energy management on their properties – i.e. how to use appliances efficiently, how to benchmark their use against best practice, whether their energy consumption figures were good or bad, and how different sources of energy (gas, wood fuel, coal and renewables) compared against each other. Even more alarmingly, it had apparently not occurred to at least one respondent of the study that switching to a cheaper green tariff did not legitimise a subsequent increase in total consumption and therefore emissions.

Given that energy costs can equate to nearly 1/6 of all business costs, energy efficiency would seem to be a prime candidate for the 'green is gold' approach (c.f. Section 2.1.). Instead, the study found that the SMTE's focus was almost exclusively on revenue management – sales, marking and bookings – as well as servicing guests and maintaining the premises, with cost cuttings coming mostly from staffing arrangements. Coles et al. (2014) found a sustainability literacy gap that is quite staggering, and suggest that:

"before investment in renewable energy solutions or the introduction of dedicated environmental management systems, most SMTEs must innovate in a much simpler way: namely to compile, interpret and act on energy data as part of their routine management processes" (Coles et al., 2014, p.406)

One SMTE owner/manager, Dr Christopher Warren, who has done just this – we'll meet him in Chapter 8 – describes a steep and frustrating learning curve, of grappling with technical reports, confusing providers and often, a lack of site specific knowledge on behalf of suppliers that meant that technologies sold to him under the banner of sustainability often were not suited to the specific climatic (sunshine, cloud cover) or aspect (orientation, size and shape of his cottages) of his particular business.

Not only is the technical and procedural knowledge required to implement sustainability difficult to obtain for a SMTE enterprise, but its implementation at a specific site requires in-depth knowledge of the micro-geographical variations at that site (e.g. is the building north- or south-facing), as well as an understanding of how energy is used within that site, and what, if any, methods can be used to invite a major user of power within a SMTE to collaborate in reducing consumption.

Which brings us to the final point of the Theory of Planned Behaviour: social norms – an issue we have covered previously, and again important here. As you'll see in the interview with Chris Warren, one of the major concerns he had in making his business as sustainable as possible, was requesting that guests be frugal in their energy consumption, effectively working against the social norm that holidays be hedonic and care-free.

Read the interview with Chris at The Conversation here: https://theconversation.com/a-green-and-happy-holiday-you-can-have-it-all-65038

2.3   Climate change

In the middle of all this stands a large, grey, big-eared, long trunked individual – the elephant in this particular room is climate change. And it is there for two reasons. First, tourism is dependent upon a stable climate to function, in terms of seasonal tourism, secure water and food supplies, and transport routes and many of its attractions are vulnerable to changes in climate, weather patterns and weather events. Second, tourism itself adds significantly to greenhouse gas emissions, through transport (primarily aviation) and through the accommodation sector.

The latter will be covered in Chapter 3 on the impacts of tourism, but it is mentioned here for a very specific reason. It is not unforeseeable that there may come a day when travelling for leisure may lose its social legitimacy unless cleaner forms of transport fuel are used and/or may become unaffordable if some form of carbon tax is imposed. Climate change also poses a significant national security threat to regions already under environmental, social and cultural strain from drought, economic recession or ethnic tensions, where additional stressors can, and have, led to violent clashes.

This section will review why tourism is directly and indirectly vulnerable as a result of changing climate. First, however, we need a starting point for the discussion of climate change and tourism and for this we turn to the Intergovernmental Panel on Climate Change (IPCC). The IPCC was jointly established by the World Meteorological Organization (WMO) and the United Nations Environment Programme. (UNEP). Every 6 years a panel of experts produce a series of technical reports and a summary report. The most recent summary, the Fifth Assessment Report, was published in 2014. (**http://www.ipcc.ch/pdf/assessment-report/ar5/syr/AR5_SYR_FINAL_SPM.pdf**)

According to the report, "Climate change will amplify existing risks and create new risks for natural and human systems" (IPCC, 2014, p.13). The extent to which this occurs depends on our actions over the coming decades, and is modelled by the IPCC under four scenarios of future development (Table 2.2.). The best case is a warming of just over 1°C, worst case could be over 6°C.

Table 2.2: IPCC's AR5 predicted temperature increase under four development scenarios.

	More economic focus	**More environmental focus**
Globalisation (homogeneous world)	**A1** rapid economic growth (groups: A1T; A1B; A1Fl) **1.4 - 6.4 °C**	**B1** global environmental sustainability **1.1 - 2.9 °C**
Regionalisation (heterogeneous world)	**A2** regionally oriented economic development **2.0 - 5.4 °C**	**B2** local environmental sustainability **1.4 - 3.8 °C**

The impacts of warmer temperatures are increased hot extremes, heat waves, and changes in precipitation (extended droughts, and increased short, heavy precipitation), increased frequency of cyclones with higher wind speeds and more precipitation, decreases in snow cover, melting of sea ice, glaciers and permafrost, ocean acidification and sea level rise.

As well as the impact on the ecosystem directly affected by the changes, the report has this to say about the impact of climate change on human systems:

In urban areas climate change is projected to increase risks for people, assets, economies and ecosystems, including risks from heat stress, storms and extreme precipitation, inland and coastal flooding, landslides, air pollution, drought, water scarcity, sea level rise and storm surges (very high confidence). [...] Rural areas are expected to experience major impacts on water availability and supply, food security, infrastructure and agricultural incomes, including shifts in the production areas of food and non-food crops around the world (high confidence)." {2.3.2}

[...] From a poverty perspective, climate change impacts are projected to slow down economic growth, make poverty reduction more difficult, further erode food security and prolong existing and create new poverty traps, the latter particularly in urban areas and emerging hotspots of hunger (medium confidence). International dimensions such as trade and relations among states are also important for understanding the risks of climate change at regional scales. {2.3.2}

Climate change is projected to increase displacement of people (medium evidence, high agreement). Populations that lack the resources for planned migration experience higher exposure to extreme weather events, particularly in developing countries with low income. Climate change can indirectly increase risks of violent conflicts by amplifying well-documented drivers of these conflicts such as poverty and economic shocks (medium confidence). {2.3.2}

Tourism will not be immune from these predicted changes, which will affect the whole tourism system. As a result, the UNWTO joined UNEP and WMO to deliver the Davos Declaration in 2007 which asked tourism to "rapidly respond to climate change, within the evolving UN framework and progressively reduce its greenhouse gas emission". The Declaration specifically recognised tourism's role in climate change, and the need to develop strategies to allow tourism to adapt to climate change, as well as ensure that resources are made available to poorer regions and countries who are most vulnerable are able to meet the recommendations (Simpson et al., 2008).

As our understanding of the relationship between climate change and tourism has grown over the last decade, we see that the impacts of climate change will be both direct and indirect.

In terms of direct impacts, specific climates can be major draw cards for tourism – think of snow tourism, and 3S tourism – and changes in the length and quality of snow seasons and summer weather will have direct consequences on the attractiveness of many destinations. Melting snow, increased heat waves, more intense cyclones, more frequent flood events will all have direct impacts on the attractiveness of many tourism destinations, particularly regions such as the Caribbean, Indian Ocean and South Pacific. In some cases, it is predicted that whole islands may disappear with increasing sea levels. The Seychelles and Maldives are countries that are at risk of sea level rise.

Many natural attractions will also be directly affected by climate change: biodiversity loss, reduced landscape aesthetic, and changes in land use are all likely. Severe beach erosion is likely for even mass tourism destinations such as the Gold Coast; the Great Barrier Reef is regularly featured in the media, highlighting concerns for its ongoing survival; while major food and wine destinations are likely to be irrevocably transformed. In some cases, attempts to adapt to these changes are exacerbating the impacts – snow making machines use large amounts of water in areas already affected by changes in water availability due to melting glaciers and use large amounts of energy, thus increasing the carbon footprint of these forms of tourism. Similarly, increased use of air conditioners in hotels during heat events have the same negative effect.

 Read how winemakers in Australia are responding to climate change: www.abc.net.au/news/2016-06-05/ rising-temperatures-spark-winemakers-move-to-tasmania/7371262

The follow-on impacts from these direct effects are disruptions to transport systems, damage to infrastructure, impacts on agriculture, fisheries and thus food supply, and changes in water availability as well as increasing incidence of vector-borne diseases such as malaria and dengue fever. For example, above average snow and ice shut down roads, airports, trains and even the underground system in the UK in December 2017, while bad weather led to a major P&O ferry running aground in Calais. (**http://www.abc.net.au/ news/2017-12-11/snow-disrupts-road-air-travel-in-england-wales/9245302**)

The costs of repairing infrastructure damage, delayed or cancelled services and other business interruptions, higher operating expenses (e.g. air conditioning or snowmaking), the requirement to invest in developing and training for additional emergency preparedness, increased costs within the supply chain (e.g. food and water), as well as rising insurance costs will all take their toll on tourism as we now know it.

But the story does not end there. The changes described by the IPCC above will also mean increased geo-political insecurity in many destinations, as well as much slower economic growth across the world. At best, climate change is likely to mean a higher cost of living for most of us, less discretionary income available for tourism, as well, and in all likelihood, some form of carbon tax, which will also be applied to tourism – which, at present accounts for between 5% and 14% of the world's carbon emissions (Lenzen et al., 2018). The direct cost of travel is likely to change dramatically.

These changes also raise questions about the future legitimacy of travel for leisure, with its present carbon footprint.

Review

This chapter has tried to capture some of the challenges that have hampered efforts to make tourism more sustainable. It does so in the spirit of pragmatism; that to understand the challenges helps us identify them when they are present, and work with and around them. It also urges caution in using the 'green is gold' argument that so often pops up when discussing ways to make business more sustainable. While the argument may hold true in some cases, in many others, the relationship between profit and sustainability actions is not so clear.

It helps to think of the relationship as bidirectional, or as a virtuous cycle; engaging in sustainability is likely to develop new skills and resources, which in turn may create new opportunities to invest those skills and resources into sustainability actions. A note of caution was also raised around framing sustainability as a money-saving activity versus a pro-environmental and pro-social activity; Steinhorst et al.'s (2015) study warns of potential unintended spill-over consequences of particular framing approaches.

Moreover, the tourism sector has its own quirks and peculiarities that make it in some ways more amenable to sustainability if harnessed correctly, and certainly more resistant if not. Throughout this section (and in Chapter 1), I have made reference to tourism as a complex, interrelated and dynamic system – and managing it requires what is known as systems thinking. To fully explain systems thinking is beyond the scope of this book, it challenges the way we typically break complex wholes into their composite parts and try to control linear, direct relationships between two or maybe three of those parts. Hopefully as the chocolate example in Chapter 1, and the issues raised in this chapter have shown, tourism simply does not work like that.

This issue of complex systems is compounded by the nature of the tourism sector: Garay & Font (2012) urge us to remember that tourism businesses are frequently SMEs with a "lack of structured decision-making and control, financial instability, greater risk exposure mixed with a strong need for independence and also a great importance of owners' values and a strong identification between owners and their values" (p.331).

The issue of leadership and responsibility is key for many reasons and will be discussed in more detail in Chapter 5. Of the six challenges presented in Section 2.2., five of them will benefit directly from strong leadership, be it from government in the case of public-private partnerships, the footloose nature of much of the sector and the need for multi-disciplinary, contextually-specific technical experience, or from the tourism sectors/hosts in the case of the inseparability of the tourism experience, the infrequent nature of tourism purchases, and the relationship between SME and large, multi-national businesses.

Finally, this chapter address the elephant in the room – tourism's relationship with climate change. It poses the question that given tourism's reliance on a stable climate and its contribution to the destabilising of that climate, what direct and indirect impacts does tourism face moving forward. The answer is worrying, and will be picked up again in subsequent chapters on tourism's impact on the natural environmental (Chapter 3) and the regulatory framework for tourism (Chapter 4).

Questions and exercises

1   Tourism for Tomorrow lists the sustainable tourism award winners and finalists on their website – www.wttc.org/tourism-for-tomorrow-awards/winners-and-finalists-2018/#beyond

2   See if you can identify whether they are using one of the 'green is gold' business case arguments for sustainability, and outline which one they are using.

3   Research the main local tourism attractions in your own local area. Who owns and/or governs them? And how do tourists access them? Is there a possibility of 'tragedy of the commons' situation arising? Justify your answer.

4   Review the Measuring Sustainable Tourism documents released by the UNWTO. What are some of the key points in these documents with regards to the scale of tourism and its measurement and its impact on sustainability?

5   Hares et al. (2010) report that the five most common factors considered by travellers when booking holidays tend to be price, weather, the wishes of family and friends, travel time and activities. Clearly sustainability-oriented

characteristics of tourism do not feature here. Explore this further by polling your friends and family about their decision-making factors. Take note of how you feel when having those conversations (we'll return to this in Chapter 6)

Multiple choice questions

1   Which of the following is NOT one of the reasons given for the inclusion of sustainability-related behaviours within a business:

   a) To gain public support for their activities

   b) To leverage government grant opportunities for green business

   c) To prevent tighter regulations of their performance

2   The phrase 'green is gold' is accurate across all business contexts: True or false

3   The fact that many tourism attractions are publically owned is a challenge for sustainability for which of the following reasons?

   a) The so-called tragedy of the commons.

   b) There is not enough public funds to manage them efficiently

   c) There are too many stakeholders involved

4   The best way to measure tourism's carbon footprint is to extrapolate using a lifecycle assessment approach: True or false

5   What does inseparability refer to in tourism sustainability?

   a) Tourists' behaviour directly contribute to the sustainability (or otherwise) of a destination or business

   b) Tourism's impacts cannot be separated from other industrial impacts in a destination

   c) Destination managers must work closely with all stakeholders to develop a holistic approach to sustainability

Further reading

Dodds, R., & Kuehnel, J. (2010). CSR among Canadian mass tour operators: good awareness but little action. *International Journal of Contemporary Hospitality Management*, **22**(2), 221-244.

Font, X., Walmsley, S., Cogotill, S., McCombes, L. & Hausler, N. (2012). Corporate Social Responsibility: the disclosure-performance gap. *Tourism Management*, **33**(6), 1544-1553.

Inoue, Y. & Lee, S. (2011). Effects of different dimensions of corporate social responsibility on corporate financial performance in tourism-related industries. *Tourism Management*, **32**(4), 790-804.

Pulido-Fernández, J.I., Andrades-Caldito, L. & SánchezRivero, M. (2015). Is sustainable tourism an obstacle to the economic performance of the tourism industry? Evidence from an international empirical study. *Journal of Sustainable Tourism,* **23**(1), 47-64.

Scott, D. (2011). Why sustainable tourism must address climate change. *Journal of Sustainable Tourism,* **19**(1), 17-34.

References

Ajzen, I. (1991). The theory of planned behaviour. *Organisational Behaviour and Human Decision Processes,* **50**, 179-211.

Barr, S., Shaw, G. & Coles, T. (2011). Times for (Un)sustainability? Challenges and opportunities for developing behaviour change policy. A case-study of consumers at home and away. *Global Environmental Change.* **21**, 1234-1244.

Becken, S. (2007). Tourists' perceptions of international air travel's impact on the global climate and potential climate change policies. *Journal of Sustainable Tourism,* **15**, 351-368.

Buckley, R. (2002). Tourism ecolabels. *Annals of Tourism Research,* **29**(1), 183-208.

Budeanu, A., Miller, G., Moscardo, G., & Ooi, C. S. (2016). Sustainable tourism, progress, challenges and opportunities: an introduction. *Journal of Cleaner Production,* **111**, 285-294.

Coles, T., Zschiegner, A-K., and Dinan, C. (2014). A cluster analysis of climate change mitigation behaviours among SMTEs. *Tourism Geographies,* **16**(3), 382-399.

Dolnicar, S. & Grün, B. (2009). Environmentally-friendly behaviour: can heterogeneity among individuals and contexts/environments be harvested for improved sustainable management? *Environment and Behaviour,* **41**(5), 693-714.

Garay, L. & Font, X. (2012). Doing good to do well? Corporate social responsibility reasons, practices and impacts in small and medium accommodation enterprises. *International Journal of Hospitality Management,* **31**, 329-337.

Gössling, S., Scott, D. & Hall, C.M. (2015). Inter-market variability in CO_2 emissions-intensities in tourism: Implications for destination marketing and carbon management. *Tourism Management,* **46**, 203-212.

Gössling, S., & Buckley, R. (2016). Carbon labels in tourism: persuasive communication? *Journal of Cleaner Production,* **111**, 358-369.

Gunn, C. A. (1994). *Tourism Planning: Basics, concepts, cases* (3 ed.). Washington, D.C: Taylor & Francis

Henderson, R. (2015). Making the business case for environmental sustainability. In R. Henderson, R. Gulati & M. Thusman (eds). *Leading Sustainable Change: an organisational perspective,* pp.22-50. Oxford: Oxford University Press.

Juvan, E. & Dolnicar, S. (2014). Can tourists easily choose a low carbon footprint vacation? *Journal of Sustainable Tourism,* **22**(2), 175-194.

Hares, A., Dickinson, J., & Wilkes, K. (2010). Climate change and the air travel decisions of UK tourists. *Journal of Transport Geography,* **18**, 466-473.

IPCC (2014). *Climate Change 2014: Synthesis Report*. Contribution of Working Groups I, II and III to the Fifth Assessment Report of the Intergovernmental Panel on Climate Change [Core Writing Team, R.K. Pachauri and L.A. Meyer (eds.)]. IPCC, Geneva, Switzerland.

Lavelle, M.J., Henrike Rau, H & Frances Fahy, F. (2015). Different shades of green? Unpacking habitual and occasional pro-environmental behaviour. *Global Environmental Change*, **35**, 368–378.

Leiper, N. (1979). The framework of tourism: Towards a definition of tourism, tourist and the tourist industry. *Annals of Tourism Research*, **6**(4), 390-407.

Lenzen, M., Sun, Y.Y, Faturay, F., Ting, Y.P., Geschke, A. & Malik, A. (2018). The carbon footprint of global tourism. *Nature Climate Change*, **8**, 522–528.

McKercher, B., Mak, B. & Wong, S. (2014). Does climate change matter to the travel trade? *Journal of Sustainable Tourism*, **22**(5), 685-704.

Mill, R. C., & Morrison, A. M. (1998). *The Tourism System: An introductory text* (3 ed.): Dubuque, Iowa: Kendall/Hunt

Miller, D., Merrilees, B. & Coghlan, A. (2015). Sustainable urban tourism: Understanding and developing visitor pro-environmental behaviours. *Journal of Sustainable Tourism*, **23**(1), 26-46

Moisander, J. (2007). Motivations complexity of green consumerism. *International Journal of Consumer studies*, **31**(4), 404-409.

Rodriguez, F.J.G. & del Mar Armas Cruz, Y. (2007). Relation between social-environmental responsibility and performance in hotel firms. *Hospitality Management*, **26**, 824-839.

Steinhorst, J., Klöckner, C.A. & Matthies, E. (2015). Saving electricity – For the money or the environment? Risks of limiting pro-environmental spillover when using monetary framing. *Journal of Environmental Psychology*, **43**, 125-135.

Simpson, M. C., Gössling, S., Scott, D., Hall, C. M., & Gladin, E. (2008). *Climate Change Adaptation and Mitigation in the Tourism Sector: Frameworks, tools and practices*. Chatelaine, Switzerland; United Nations Environment Programme (UNEP).

Singal, M. (2014). The Link between Firm Financial Performance and Investment in Sustainability Initiatives. *Cornell Hospitality Quarterly*, **55**(1), 19-30.

UNWTO – UNEP (2008). *Climate Change and Tourism: Responding to global challenges*. (prepared by Scott, D., Amelung, B., Becken, S., Ceron, J.P., Dubois, G., Gössling, S., Peeters, P., and Simpson, M.C.). UNWTO, Madrid, and UNEP, Paris.

Van Mai, T. (2010, August). Systems thinking approach as a unique tool for sustainable tourism development: a case study in the *cat ba* biosphere reserve of Vietnam. In *Proceedings of the 54th Annual Meeting of the ISSS-2010*, Waterloo, Canada(Vol. 54, No. 1).

Warren, C., Becken, S., Nguyen, K., Stewart, R. (2018). Transitioning to smart sustainable tourist accommodation: Service innovation results *Journal of Cleaner Production*, **201**, 599-608.

Wearing, S., Cynn, S., Ponting, J. & McDonald, M. (2002). Converting environmental concern into ecotourism purchases: a qualitative evaluation of international packbackers in Australia. *Journal of Ecotourism*, **1**(2-3), 133-148.

Weaver, D. (2006). *Sustainable Tourism: Theory and Practice*. Oxford: Butterworth: Heinemann.

Weichard, R. S. (1992). *Travel Marketing: an introduction*. McGraw-Hill

3 Impacts of tourism

Introduction

An impact is considered to be the change in a given state over time, resulting from an external stimulus. It is important to distinguish internal and external stimuli: a change in state from internal drivers, e.g. the maturing of an ecosystem and the successional changes in species (e.g. from grasses to trees) as a result, would not be considered an impact, under that definition.

To best understand the impacts of tourism, it is easiest to examine economic, social and environmental impacts as separate categories from each other. The caveat here, is that the boundaries between categories are generally fuzzier in any given tourism context. As we become better at understanding tourism impacts, we will start to see relationships between social, environmental and economic impacts.

For example, increased tourism development might generate more waste, use more natural resources, and impact negatively on biodiversity, at the same time as generate more jobs and a higher standard of living. When these negative environmental impacts and positive economic impacts are weighed up against each other, what is the likely outcome on social, e.g. wellbeing, outcomes? Those are the types of questions that impacts studies of tourism seek to answer, and that sustainability initiatives will seek to address.

This chapter will therefore outline each different category of impact, highlighting both negative impacts and positive impacts, then move on to an example where one researcher has incorporated all these different impacts into a model, where the relationships between these can be assessed both in terms of their strength and their direction with a more realistic, holistic system. In addition, in taking a systems approach, it also becomes clear that it is difficult to separate the impacts of tourism from other activities and events that occur within destinations and tourism-generating regions. This chapter will open with this point so that a realistic understanding of impacts can be developed.

> **Key words and concepts**
>
> - Fuzzy boundaries
> - Multiplier effect
> - Leakage
> - Linkage
> - Cultural commodification
> - Authenticity
> - Cultural appropriation
>
> - Front and backstage
> - Emotional labour
> - Irridex model
> - Demonstration effect
> - Culture shock
> - Interpretation

3.1   Issues of with identifying tourism impacts

Because of the nature of tourism and its fuzzy boundaries, as well as the scale issues discussed in Chapter 2, our ability to understand tourism impacts and attribute impacts them to specific actions can be a challenge. Even more so, as the study of impacts only has a 40 year history or so (the equivalent of the professional lifetime of one researcher), and is even more recent in tourism research. Furthermore, tourism impact research tends to focus on destinations, and at very localised levels, e.g. an attraction, and often in very similar environments, e.g. recreation ecology as a sub-discipline devoted entirely to the scientific study of environmental impacts arising from recreational activities in protected natural areas, has been developing since the 1960s.

Another issue of understanding tourism impacts is that they cannot easily be distinguished from impacts of other activities. With the exception of tourism development undertaken as part of a growth strategy, tourism itself is often one element of a suite of development initiatives. This means that infrastructures such as roads and airports may be constructed for the purpose of transporting cargo as well as facilitating tourism. As another example, are changes in gender roles or fashion tastes related to a so-called demonstration effect of outsiders visiting a community and their behaviours and possessions leaving a marked effect on local culture, or can these changes be attributed to what is shown on TV and other media within those same host communities?

Moreover, for cities and towns, the traits that make the place appealing to tourism may also make it appealing to live in, and so issues such as crowding, rising amenities costs, increased pollution, even increased petty crime may be attributed to both the presence of more tourists as well as the growth of a city or town through inward migration. The relationships between tourism and place are complex and interwoven, not easily separated into distinct categories.

Indeed, as tourism is best understood as a system of interrelated elements, and tourism impacts will general transcend various sectors, activities and categories. Hall and Lew (2009) present a Venn diagram of impacts, showing overlaps between economic, social and environmental areas (Figure 3.1). By way of example, environmental economic impacts would include a changes in the valuation of biodiversity, while socio-economic changes could be changes to income distribution as new tourism-related jobs are created.

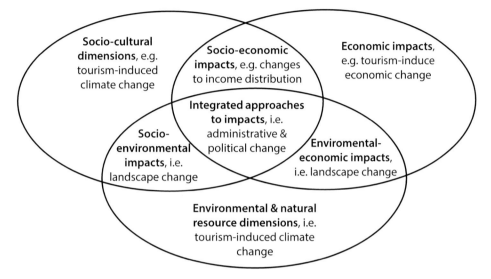

3

Figure 3.1: The overlaps between the three pillars of sustainability, their goals and how these overlap.

To anyone wanting to study impacts, it is important to understand whether impacts can be related to sub-systems within tourism, i.e. relationships between elements which are only weakly tied to the broader, open tourism system. This will help to determine the scale of analysis required. It is also important to understand the relationships between elements as flows (people/tourists, goods, capital and resources/energy), causal relationships and feedback loops.

A final issue that will need to be carefully considered is that we have little understanding of the progression of impacts. To start with, we have relatively few longitudinal studies of tourism impacts. In cases where changes over time can be identified from a range of sources, the different methodologies used to collect data and the different metrics used to measure impacts can make direct comparisons difficult. We also have little idea of baseline data – what was a place like before tourism, compared to now.

3.2   Economic impacts of tourism

In Chapter 1, I introduced the various platforms of tourism. One of these was the Advocacy platform, where tourism is seen as a means of economic development for areas where other industries are in decline, generate low returns or simply do not exist. It is certainly a large economic sector, accounting for around 10% of jobs (directly and indirectly) around the world, and punches well above its weight for a sector that is dominated by SMEs (see Chapter 2). A recent benchmarking study by the WTTC found that it is only smaller in size than the global construction sector, financial sector and global retail – all of which are dominated by large multinational corporations.

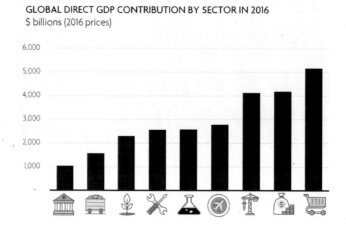

GLOBAL DIRECT GDP CONTRIBUTION BY SECTOR IN 2016
$ billions (2016 prices)

Figure 3.2: WTTC's 2017 benchmarking report, showing tourism's global direct contribution to GDP. Download the report here: www.wttc.org/-/media/files/reports/benchmark-reports/regional-reports-2017/world.pdf

The same report also makes the claim that one tourism job will lead to the creation of two additional jobs in the tourism supply chain (e.g. taxi, laundry, agriculture, and so forth). This is referred to as the multiplier effect, and as we will see shortly is one of the primary economic benefits of tourism. This section unpacks some of these claims, which are of course, positive economic impacts, and also examines some of the less positive economic impacts associated with tourism.

Negative economic impacts of tourism

In this section, we will review both the costs of tourism (not *per se* a negative impact – just a feature of 'doing business') as well as the indirect costs that arise from tourism and finally, some of the more unintended negative economic impacts of tourism development.

As with any other economic sector, tourism requires investments in order to deliver returns. These are important to note when considering the positive economic impacts, so that the latter accurately reflects true gains. This is particularly relevant in tourism. As we have already mentioned in Chapter 2, the tourism sector is a hybrid of public and private entities, often working in partnership, and often associated with different costs and returns from tourism. For example much as the destination marketing and upkeep of national and regional attractions falls within the remit of the public sector. These costs will be associated with wages and salaries, advertising, promotion and publicity, research and development activities, departmental costs as well as grants and prizes, and other capital grants, subsidies, training programs, familiarisation trips to attract potential large conventions or events, and provision of infrastructure at public expense to entice the investment of private capital into tourism development.

In a similar vein to tourism accounting, which relies on a composite satellite account to calculate the size of the sector, much of this expenditure will fall across several government departments – e.g. the cost of upgrading a road to an attraction will fall to a state department of Main Roads and Infrastructure, while the provision of extra security cameras within a tourism precinct of a city will fall to local town councils. This makes it difficult to calculate the costs of tourism to the public sector, particularly as these are rarely approved with only visitors in mind, and so serve the local interest as well.

On the other hand, costs directly associated with the promotion of a destination, through a national destination marketing organisation are more easily accessible, and often account for tens to hundreds of millions of dollars. Visit Scotland's 2016 campaign is reported to have cost $5.6 million, whereas Tourism Queensland pulled off a marketing coup with their Best Job in the World Campaign.

Watch the Spirit of Scotland video: <u>https://www.youtube.com/watch?v=otEcULXOpGc</u>

Figure 3.3: Tourism Queensland's 2009 marketing campaign that generated significant public relations value and destination awareness globally.

Test
yourself

There are also indirect costs associated with tourism. Opportunity costs are one example, where opportunities for revenue from sectors such as mining, forestry or fisheries (mostly extractive industries) are foregone in favour of tourism, which relies on intact nature resources and aesthetic value of a landscape. Another important term to remember here is 'revenue leakages' – if you think of a destination as a bucket and tourism revenue as water, then every hole in that bucket is allowing water to leak out. Of course the water is still going somewhere and benefitting someone, but the general idea is for the economic benefits of tourism to go to the destination, which bears most of the social, environmental and economic costs of tourism. In as much as possible, we want the costs of tourism to be balanced out by the benefits, in order to drive the sustainability of the sector – this means retaining the economic benefits of tourism within the destination.

Leakages will occur through several mechanisms, primarily through imported goods and services for tourism. For example, if the food provided for tourists is sourced from outside the region, this would create a leakage. Similarly for construction materials, furnishing, forms of transport, fuel, souvenirs, as well as guides, consultancy fees (e.g. for developing an attraction or facilitating community workshops). Other forms of leakage would include factor payments abroad, e.g. hotel management fees, repatriated wages and profits in the case where hospitality workers (often senior management positions) are not locally hired. Induced imports may also constitute a form of leakage if suppliers to the tourism industry are importing their goods and services.

Enclave tourism represents perhaps the most extreme forms of leakage, where resorts are commonly foreign owned and managed, rely heavily on imported goods and services, and discourage tourists from exploring the local area and spending on local produce and so forth. In its worst forms, severe revenue leakages can lead to local, small-scale producers being outcompeted on price and quality, dissuade local entrepreneurship, exacerbate the so-called 'demonstration effect' (see Section 3.3) where foreign imports start to replace locally-produced goods as more desirable, and finally lead to a high dependency on external players and undermine the destination's self-governance. Revenue leakages are also hard to quantify and difficult to address once established.

Other economic costs of tourism relate more to the variable nature of the sector: for example, tourism is often seasonal, either through climate-related conditions (think of 3S tourism or winter sports) or through holiday-related factors (school holidays, public holidays or the timing of pilgrimages such as the Haj). The result is that tourism-related jobs may often be seasonal in nature – only a few months of the year, and not enough to sustain a family on an on-going basis. This is particularly pronounced in alpine destinations, for example (Figure 3.4).

Moreover, tourism demand can often fluctuate rapidly and substantially. Think of a volcanic eruption, flood or terrorist attack within a destination and the ensuing booking cancellations. Similarly a weak economy in a major source market will also affect jobs in the destination market. As with seasonality, the result is often the casualization of tourism jobs, which again means that they are not always a good source of reliable and stable incomes for workers.

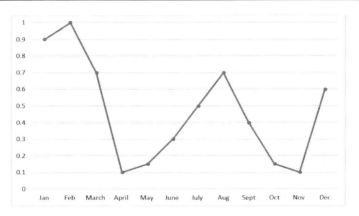

Figure 3.4: A typical seasonal pattern of visitation for alpine regions, with a peak for winter sports, and a second summer peak for hiking and other outdoor recreation.

The issues with tourism-related jobs do not end there, however. These are often seen as low-skilled jobs, as the emotional labour that goes into them is generally under-recognised and under-valued. Management jobs are often earmarked for ex-patriots, and local jobs are often paid at minimum wages with few opportunities for upward movement within the business, or upskilling through training. With the exception of some countries (notably Fiji), tourism workers' unions and collective bargaining abilities are weak, and in some cases, the absence of alternative sources of employment further drives wages downwards. The result is that while tourism may indeed generate a lot of employment opportunities, there are often low paying, seasonal, part-time or casual jobs with few opportunities for advancement or upskilling.

Positive economic impacts of tourism

The most obvious benefit of tourism is its direct revenue. By welcoming visitors into a destination, that destination is attracting revenue from outside the local economy; in effect tourism is the 'export'. This impact is perhaps most easily calculated at the international level, where figures on tourist visitation are more readily available than at national or regional levels. International tourism receipts include all consumption expenditure, payments for goods and services made as part of trips by international tourists for their own use or to give away, accruing to the destination itself (UNWTO, 2013). Direct tourism receipts remain heavily skewed towards traditional, well-established destinations such as the USA, Spain, France, Italy and the UK, but with the notable inclusion of countries such as Thailand and China in the more recent figures compiled by the UNWTO (2016).

The major categories of expenditure include food and drink, accommodation, transport and shopping. The former two categories usually account for up to 50% of expenditures, while tours and entertainment may typically account for less than 10%. In addition, a portion will often be paid in advance, especially where package tours are involved. Different groups of tourists will have notably different expenditure patterns. Backpackers are commonly associated with lower spending on food and accommodation, with a greater proportion of their expenditure going towards entertainment and attractions. Another group with a distinct spending pattern are international students. Education fees for international tourists can form a substantial source of revenue within a destination, although they only apply to a small percentage of tourists. Cruise ship tourists are another interesting category here, although not covered in this book.

Rank	Region	International tourism receipts (2016)
1	United States	$205.9 billion
2	Spain	$60.3 billion
3	Thailand	$49.9 billion
4	China	$44.4 billion
5	France	$42.5 billion
6	Italy	$40.2 billion
7	United Kingdom	$39.6 billion
8	Germany	$37.4 billion
9	Hong Kong	$32.9 billion
10	Australia	$32.4 billion

Table. 3.1: Top 10 international tourism receipts for 2016 (source UNWTO)

Taxation represents another form of positive economic impact derived from tourism. For international visitors, a departure tax is usually payable at ports leaving the country. These are most commonly included in the total price of a package tour, airline ticket or cruise ship cost. Other commonly used taxes include bed taxes applied to hotel rooms, hostels, B&Bs and other formalised types of accommodation (the informal sector and shared economy sectors such as Airbnb often fall outside of these established taxes, at least for the present time). Permits and entry fees for attractions, e.g. a national park permit, as well as the cost of visitor visas represent another form of direct economic benefit for tourism, while goods and services taxes often apply as well, although some countries may allow tourists to claim these upon departure through a tax rebate program.

Based upon these figures it is possible to calculate the contribution of tourism to Gross Domestic Product (GDP). The contribution of tourism to GDP reflects both the revenue from tourism as well as the diversity of the destination's economy. Some destinations, particularly Small Islands Developing States (SIDS), may display a form of hyper-reliance on tourism, with up to half of the GDP generated through tourism, or in the extreme case of Macau, 98%. Meanwhile, nations with highest revenue from tourism, the USA, Spain and France, only attribute around 1-2% of their GDP to tourism, reflecting the diversity of their economies. Strategies to increase direct contributions from tourism will usually involve one or several of the following:

1 Increase visitor numbers

2 Increase visitor spending

3 Increase visitor length of stay.

It is also possible to increase indirect revenue from tourism, by understanding and maximising the multiplier effect of tourism. This focusses on how the tourism supply chain is managed to benefit the local economy. As the revenue flows through the supply chain, and the extended supply chain, a cascade of indirect economic impacts occur. These are classed as first-round indirect impacts, second-round indirect impacts, etc., depending on where in the supply chain the revenue is being spent. The multiplier effect impacts the number of people benefiting from that initial input of tourism revenue into a destination.

One effect of the multiplier effect of tourism is that destinations with more diverse economies (i.e. a lower percentage of their GDP directly attributed to tourism) will usually have more sectors that are able to supply the goods and services required in the tourism supply chain, therefore relying less on foreign imports. This is referred to as backward linkages, and reflect a desired degree of integration and diversification between tourism development and the rest of the local economy, e.g. agriculture, construction, manufacturing and so forth.

This leads us to the two final economic benefits of tourism: (i) direct employment in tourism, and the induced benefits associated with it, and (ii) regional development opportunities through tourism. The latter relates to the type of backward linkages described above, and is particularly relevant to destinations that may have few other economic development opportunities, but are considered attractive tourist destinations, e.g. 3S destinations. Finally, the creation of jobs is another oft-cited economic benefit; tourism is indeed a labour-intensive service sector, and can provide paid employment to groups that may not otherwise have access to wages, e.g. women in many developing nations. However, as we have seen in the section on economic impacts of tourism, the employment figures associated with tourism must be analysed with care, as these are more often than not casual or part-time positions, and may lack career-advancement opportunities.

3.3 Socio-cultural impacts of tourism

Test yourself

As a reminder, the UNWTO's definition of sustainable tourism as it relates to social impacts is that sustainable tourism must:

> *"respect the authenticity, traditional values and cultural heritage of host communities and contribute to cross-cultural understanding; and, ensure viable businesses, and distribute economic benefits to all stakeholders equitably "*

(UNWTO-UNEP, 2008).

In this definition, social and cultural impacts of tourism are considered together, and both will be included in this section. One way of understanding the distinction between culture and society is provided by Geertz (1973) who defines society as the arrangement of social relationships in a group and culture as that group's shared beliefs and symbols. Culture is:

> *"the set of distinctive spiritual, material, intellectual and emotional features of society or a social group"* (UNESCO, 2001).

The socio-cultural impacts of tourism refer to how tourism impacts community structures, lifestyles, values, collective and individual behavioural patterns, and ultimately quality of life. Hall and Lew (2009) remind us that the factors that will contribute to social wellbeing and quality of life include economic security, employment, health, personal safety, housing conditions, physical environment and recreational environment.

As with economic and natural impacts, tourism can and will have both positive and negative impacts upon the social environments in which it operates. The next sections first look at negative impacts, followed by positive impacts. First, however, some overarching rules of thumb are that the social impacts of tourism will be influenced by:

☐ The extent of cultural and economic similarities between hosts and tourists.

☐ The ratio of tourists to hosts.

☐ The socio-economic status and educational levels of host communities.

☐ The level of dependency upon tourism as an economic driver within the host community.

☐ The prominence of tourists and the tourism industry in the host community and the existence of backstage areas for locals.

☐ The political and social makeup of the host region.

Where one or several of these factors come to dominate the host community, we might expect to see significant (and usually negative) social impacts of tourism on the host community. These can be identified at macro-scales (the global level), meso-scale (the level of regional and national relations) and micro-scale (communities and individuals).

Let's explore these in a bit more detail.

Negative social impacts of tourism

At its broadest and global level, a number of academics have raised concern over the neo-colonial and neo-liberal nature of tourism. Far from encouraging the lucky few to discover new cultures and places, the argument here is that tourism encourages globalisation and homogenisation of cultures according to Euro-centric guidelines, and a direct response to capitalism's need for expansion and the creation of new markets.

The result, according to Hall and Lew (2009) is that "the unique characteristics of different places are disappearing, local traditions are weakening and consumerism is becoming the defining value of people and places" (p.147). If you are not convinced, think of the last time you took a holiday and were relieved to find a familiar tasting beer, coffee, pizza, or breakfast cereal, or wifi connection or even a hot shower. At its extreme, a process of acculturation and/or assimilation occurs, when local traditions and values become replaced by those of dominant culture, which gain their dominance from their economic, and often political, reach and power.

Commodification of culture and heritage at national and regional levels is also a commonly cited socio-cultural impact of tourism. This occurs where traditional arts, crafts, music, costumes and performances are changed to suit the tastes and needs (e.g. smaller and lighter artefacts for packing) of outsiders, allow them to become more marketable to bought and sold in a way that was not the original intention, and can subvert their original meaning. Sometimes this occurs in minor ways, a cultural performance is explained in advance so that its meaning is more easily understood by foreigners, signage or guides are used to ensure that outsiders do not transgress any cultural norms.

Studies of cultural commodification (e.g. Van der Veen, 1995, cited in Hall and Lew, 2009) have identified at least four ways in which cultural commodification occurs:

1 **Aesthetic**: designs are modified to meet the artistic tastes of tourists.

2 **Practical**: items are redesigned to provide more practical value.

3 **Uniformity**: either a greater or lesser variety of designs are introduced to suit the tastes of tourists.

4 **Quality**: the materials and/or skill used to make items is often watered down to suit the larger volumes sold to tourists (at the upper end of the market the opposite may also occur).

One example that covers all four of these commodification changes is the Hawaiian *lei*, the flower garland commonly used to greet visitors to Hawaii. Traditionally, the garlands were worn by ancient Hawaiians to beautify themselves and distinguish themselves from others, and often presented as a symbol of a peace agreement between tribes. In ancient Hawaii, wearing a lei represented wealth, royalty, and rank, and had strong associations with hula, religion and geography. The garlands would be constructed of flowers, leaves, shells, seeds, nuts, feathers, and even bone and teeth of various animals. Today leis are commonly given to all arriving visitors at attractions, events and accommodation around Hawaii, and are less likely to be handmade.

Sometime cultural commodification may occur in ways that are considered offensive to cultural groups – co-opting rites, performances and so forth, can lead to what is known as cultural appropriation. Simply put, it is the adoption of the elements of a minority culture by members of the dominant culture.

Test yourself

It inherently contains elements of colonialism and power imbalances, as it involves the use of another culture's dance, dress, music, language, folklore, cuisine, traditional medicine, religious symbols without permission. This can be contrasted to more power-neutral cultural exchange which will be discussed in the positive socio-cultural impacts of tourism.

An example of this is provided in the following essay: "Why white people need to stop saying namaste":

> *[…] hearing namaste chanted by the white yoga instructor to a predominantly white class was unsettling. Really? If the yoga class itself wasn't white-centric enough, she really had to place the appropriative cherry on top.*

Read the essay here: https://www.smh.com.au/lifestyle/why-white-people-need-to-stop-saying-namaste-20160401-gnw2xx.html

The adoption of Hindu or Buddhist practices and religious symbols is undergoing its second Western revival, and as the article above suggests, one that can raise questions about how it is being used by people outside of those religions. On personal note, I took a group of students on a field studies tour to India, and invited them to take a yoga class in the school of a well-known local yogi. The class was full of stops and starts (from a Western perspective) involving stories and elaborations and side notes, often mid-posture/pose. To my surprise, rather than appreciating an Indian yoga class, my students came out of the class bewildered and somewhat disappointed that it wasn't a 'real' yoga class.

Another form of this subversion of culture and history may come about as national governments, regional and even sometimes international authorities (e.g. UNESCO or ICOMOS) choose which aspects of place to highlight, and by extension, to suppress. Adopting certain ceremonies, festivals and cultural practices to form part of a destination image may serve to depoliticise them, and suppress contested views of history – an issue that is particularly salient with the selection and (re)presentation of certain heritage tourism, and the official narratives that accompany them, and the complete absence of other sites that are therefore less likely to influence collective memory.

All of the above leads us to the topic of **authenticity** – perhaps one of the most slippery terms in tourism studies, as it refers to both objectivity and measurable authenticity of an object, as well as the personal and subjective authenticity of experiences and ways of life. It is a difficult concept to pin down in tourism and Hall and Lew (2009) provide the following definition: "authenticity is derived from the property of connectedness of the individual to the perceived, everyday world and the environment, the processes that created it, and the consequences of the one's engagement with it".

Test yourself

Authenticity matters because for many travellers, it is the holy grail of travel. It is seeing the 'real' place – be it Thailand, Cuba, Italy, and Australia. It is seeing behind the scenes, reaching a deeper level of understanding, meeting the locals – it permeates the marketing of much youth travel, and is at the heart of travel giants such as Airbnb. And as result, the authentic becomes highly marketable, and prone to the issues of commodification listed above.

THECONVERSATION.COM

Airbnb, social media and the quest for the authentic urban experience

Figure 3.5: How the 'authentic' is at the centre of Airbnb's story. <u>theconversation.com/airbnb-social-media-and-the-quest-for-the-authentic-urban-experience-48889</u>

From a sustainable tourism management perspective, manipulating authenticity can have its advantages. For example, creating replica artefacts, performances or heritage spaces can both relieve visitation pressure on the originals and create more defined frontstage and backstage spaces that define the boundaries between tourism performance and everyday lives. Examples of these types of spaces can be perhaps be best appreciated in the crowded centre of Venice, while just across the canal remains much more local in feel. This is the "one block back" effect, where tourism just dissipates not far from its main hub.

Taking this idea further, researchers of authenticity describe four authenticity states in the form of a matrix (Table 3.2). On the one hand is the production of the experience, either real or staged, on the other is the consumption of the experience, again either staged or real. An experience that is both perceived to be real in its experience (consumption) and in production is authentic. An experience that is staged in production but is believed to be real in its consumption is known as 'staged authenticity'. This allows cultural performances to be re-created in highly structured, quickly produced settings, that are often enough for tourists to sample culture as part of a leisure experience.

Table 3.2: The varied perceptions of authenticity (adapted from Weaver & Lawton, 2014)

		Tourists' perception of an attraction	
		Genuine	Contrived
Residents' perception of attraction	Genuine	Both parties appreciate the authentic nature of the attraction	Tourists under-appreciate the authentic nature of the attraction
	Contrived	Tourists are misled, creating a negative impact	Both parties accept the contrived nature of the attraction

Where both the production and the consumption of experiences are staged, this becomes a contrived experience. This is not necessarily problematic, as the performance maybe enjoyable without requiring a deeper engagement. Finally, it is possible to get cases where the production of the experience may be real, but the tourist may believe it to be staged – in this case, authenticity is (falsely) denied.

A concept that has been raised a couple of times already is this idea of backstage. A tourist-host encounter can be thought of as a performance, where both parties have a role to play which is scripted: host and guest, buyer and seller, guide and visitor. While this may appear to go against the spirit of authenticity, such scripting can actually serve the tourism experience well. It allows greater predictability for the tourist, reducing stress for them in novel situations. It also allows hosts to limit their emotional labour to the frontstage or performance area of the tourism experience, and maintain a separate back-stage space where they do not need to perform any emotional labour.

The term **emotional labour** refers to the process of managing feelings and expressions to fulfil the emotional requirements of a job, particularly interactions with customers, in this case tourists. Emotional labour is a key aspect of hosting in tourism, whereby a welcoming, helpful, warm and accommodating interpersonal skills are essential to a positive tourism experience, combined with the ability to model desirable behaviours to minimise the negative social and environmental impacts described in this chapter. The research into emotional labour suggest that it can lead to burnout and cynicism if the correct forms of support and management are not implement.

One form of training that has proven to be particularly successful is the use of deep acting techniques. Deep acting allows service providers to match their emotions felt to the emotions portrayed; a portrayed willingness to help the 100th day tripper to find the toilets is underpinned by a genuine pleasure in assisting people to have a more comfortable and enjoyable day. Deep acting asks the service worker to 'psych themselves' into the desired mood. The alternative is surface acting, where the service-related emotions (being warm, welcoming, helpful, etc.) are simulated at a surface level, and not matched to a genuine emotion (Hochschild, 1983). The latter is much more likely to lead to burnout, cynicism, and potential hostility towards tourists.

Doxey (1975) captures these various processes (the need for regulated emotional labour, the development of "performance front and back stages" for tourism experiences, the management of authenticity in experiences and the intercultural exchanges) at a community-level in the Irritation Index, or Irridex model (Figure 3.6). This traces the attitudes of locals towards tourists, over time. The model proposes five stages, from initial euphoria to eventual antagonism. When tourist numbers and tourism development are still low, local communities may feel positive towards visitors and the opportunities that they bring. This turns to apathy as locals become used to tourism, and annoyance as negative impacts start to be felt. Eventually, if no efforts are made to manage the negative impacts of tourism, we may witness overt or covert forms of antagonism towards tourists.

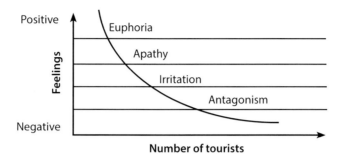

Figure 3.6: Doxey's Irridex Model shows how locals' feelings of irritation towards tourists will grow as tourist numbers increase.

Crime against tourists is a particular concern for tourism, as tourism-related crimes are often highly publicised and reflect badly on the destination. Weaver and Lawton (2014) list six reasons why tourists might be more susceptible and vulnerable to crime:

1 Tourists stand out, through conspicuous differences in race, clothing, language, and behaviour.

2 They tend to carry objects of value on themselves.

3 They are more likely to stray into unsafe areas, and/or get lost in unfamiliar places.

4 They are more vulnerable as no one is likely to quickly raise the alarm if they go missing, and they often do not know the numbers to call for emergency services.

5 They are likely to be in holiday mode, and less alert to dangerous situations.

6 They are not as aware of local culture and services, and can be taken advantage of more easily.

Other impacts that might occur at a micro-level that may reinforce the Irridex stages are increased littering, crowding, vandalism, theft, removal and sale of cultural artefacts and natural products due to the presence of tourists. Doxey also discusses the impact of the demonstration effect as a negative social impact of tourism. Tourists tend to display more relaxed behavioural norms in host communities for a variety of reasons, and may often introduce new behaviours and different values into a destination. Where locals' (especially youth) beliefs, values and behaviours become influenced by visitors, changing traditional social structures, and encouraging the acculturation effects (see above), this is known as the *demonstration effect*.

Positive socio-cultural impacts of tourism

Not all socio-cultural impacts of tourism are bad. The employment and development opportunities that are created through tourism were discussed in Section 2.2. Other positive social and cultural effects of tourism are also noted, when these are investigated through impact studies (see Chapter 7). Perhaps one of the most obvious is the preservation of culture as it becomes sought after by tourists, and becomes a tourist attraction (of course, we must also be mindful here of the risks of commodification). Historic precincts may be protected from redevelopment, heritage sites may be able to attract enough funding through visitor entrance fees, merchandising, and changes in use, that are able to be better conserved, and traditional arts and crafts may be revitalised thanks to the renewed interest from tourists.

To illustrate this, we use the example of Maori performances. The *haka* is a type of ancient Māori war dance traditionally used on the battlefield, as well as when groups came together in peace. Haka are a fierce display of a tribe's pride, strength and unity. It's an impressive performance of foot-stamping, tongue protrusions and rhythmic body slapping to accompany a loud chant, and is much sought after as a form of cultural expression by visitors. This showcasing of cultural performances has led to the popularisation of cultural dance championships, which in turn have led to the revitalisation of skills in body art painting by the performers.

For more about the haka: https://www.newzealand.com/au/feature/haka/

Perhaps one of the more contested outcomes of tourism is what is known as 'soft diplomacy', where destination branding can be used to showcase the positive, warm and non-threatening aspects of a country. Japan, for example, has invested heavily in its brand as a peaceful, non-threatening nation, promoting its cultural and natural attractions as symbols of sophistication and balance. (http://hir.harvard.edu/article/?a=13059)

Two-track diplomacy through unofficial face-to-face encounters between hosts and visitors from nations that are on not on the best of terms can also be a positive outcome from tourism. Weaver (2006) uses the example of the 2004 cricket test match between India and Pakistan, two countries that have fought three wars since they split from each other in 1947. Hosted by Pakistan, the Test Match series consolidated the stabilising of some diplomatic relations between the two countries (e.g. the civil aviation links), and the Pakistani government issued 10,000 visas to Indian cricket spectators. The successful hosting of Indians in Pakistan, and the incident-free matches are believed to have contributed to furthering goodwill between the two countries.

As an extension of this, positive inter-cultural experiences are believed to foster positive social outcomes, such as better cross-cultural understanding, mutual empathy and tolera nce. A fully immersive experience that allows visitors to witness first hand and engage directly with very different cultural norms can have lasting effects once the visitor returns home as well. For example, students returning from a field studies course in India realised that bartering is a common part of trade in India, and were less impatient when foreign tourists asked for discounts in shops where these students worked back in their home country.

For many of us, however, this valuable form of cross-cultural understanding comes as the result of a difficult process of cultural shock. An immersive experience into a different culture can lead to confusion over what is appropriate and inappropriate behaviour (c.f. the roles described earlier). Often tourists experiencing cultural shock will pass through three stages; the honeymoon stage, where tourists are excited to explore a new culture, followed by a negotiation stage, where differences become highlighted for their unfamiliarity, and may be judged for their differences (and this can be as simple as longing for pasta or bread in a region where rice is the staple food). At this stage, some may find themselves shutting off from local culture, seeking out familiar types of bars, or cafes, spending increasing time on social media, and becoming increasingly worried about hygiene, etc. The final, and desirable stage, is assimilation, where differences become accepted and normalised, part of the everyday routines.

Another major positive impact of tourism within destinations is improved quality of life for the hosts. Many destinations will invest in greater security to protect tourists from petty theft and crime. These measures will also improve security for local residents. Infrastructures such as roads and paths, street lighting, parking, rubbish collection, water availability and improved health standards (e.g. preventative measures against diseases such as malaria) as well as the improvement of leisure amenities for visitors, such as viewing platforms and benches and even wifi availability, have spill-over effects for local residents.

An influx of tourists is also likely to result in more cafes and boutiques and other leisure opportunities as well as other essential services such as pharmacies, doctors, mini-marts, and so forth. For example, Australia's first bike sharing venture was launched on the Gold Coast, just in time for the influx of visitors arriving for the 2018 Commonwealth Games, while benefiting locals by creating new ways to move around the city (See Fig. 3.7).

Figure 3.7: Mobike Gold Coast. https://mobike.com/au/blog/post/mobike-gold-coast

Ultimately, if managed correctly to minimise negative impacts (see Section 3.2. and Chapter 8), tourism can lead to greater civic pride within a destination. The combination of economic development prospects, higher employment and training opportunities, positive social encounters between hosts and guests, new and improved infrastructure and amenities, and a showcasing of their cultural heritage and general sense of place (often accompanied by investments to improve both of these) as well as a clear financial marker of the value of their place, can lead to greater community pride and civic engagement within a destination. We'll discuss civic engagement in Chapter 5, but in the words of Hall and Lew (2009) "an involved citizenship will have a greater sense of ownership and more positive attitudes towards tourism" (p.162).

As a last point in this section on socio-cultural impacts of tourism: it is important to note that the tourism experience will impact individual tourists as well. The tourism experience is one of liminality – at the edge of the known and unknown where new possibilities are created, including new experiences and even identities. The break from everyday life and its structure creates a space where tourists are freer to recreate or reinvent themselves.

A number of specific forms of tourism, most obviously wellness tourism, but also tourism associated with spiritual or religious pilgrimages, volunteer tourism, nature-based and ecotourism are commonly associated with the higher levels of Maslow's hierarchy of needs, in particular affiliation (more positive relationships with others, and a greater sense of belonging) and self-actualisation (the realization of one's full talents and potentialities). Volunteer tourism, in particular, can (although not always) lead to "value change, changed consciousness" for participants (Wearing, 2002, p. 239), with cathartic effects influences values and attitudes regarding material possession, the value of human beings, family life and finally a sense of justice and individual responsibility towards society (McIntosh and Zahra, 2007).

TOURISM.AUSTRALIA.COM
No Leave, No Life - Our Campaigns - Tourism Australia

Fig. 3.8: Focussing on the positive benefits of tourism on tourists, as part of Tourism Australia's No Leave, No Life campaign. http://www.tourism.australia.com/en/about/our-campaigns/past-campaigns/no-leave-no-life.html

Leisure is also associated with a number of mental and physical health benefits. A full review of the relationship between tourism and health benefits is provided by Chen and Petrick (2013). The benefits of holidays include decreases in work stress, burnout and exhaustion and absenteeism. Respite travel for careers might have significant health benefits, as well as for those who may not have equal access to vacations (low income earners, people with disabilities, patients). Similarly, it has been found that travel can positively impact cardiac health, as well as perceptions of self-identity, skill development, and social relations for those with mental health issues. These types of findings led to the 2005 Tourism Australia's No Leave No Life campaign.

3.4   Environmental impacts of tourism

3

The environmental impacts of tourism are perhaps the most pervasive, yet most difficult impacts to quantify. They range from the global systems impacts such as climate change, to localised habituation and/or aggression of wildlife towards tourists. However, as mentioned in the introduction, where we have little knowledge of baseline conditions of the natural environment, it is difficult to attribute changes to tourism to the exclusion of other human activities, and impacts may be incremental, cumulative, and non-linear and/ or occur at different temporal and spatial scales.

Even more challenging, the definition of a natural environment is often contested. Various regions have their own definition, focussing on air, land/ soil, air and atmosphere as well as flora and fauna, and the interactions between these elements. The presence of humans in these definitions of the natural environment varies. Some definitions do not reference humans, while others include human beings as category alongside flora and fauna. Others, e.g. Australia, go further and include people and communities, the heritages values of places, and the social, economic and cultural aspects of any of the above (Commonwealth Environmental Protection and Biodiversity Conservation Act 1999).

The latter type of definition makes it difficult to defend the rights of nature as separate from vested human interests. As a result, the Rights of Nature movement has emerged to provide Nature with equal legal rights to humans in deciding the fate of natural environments. This movement is still young and emerging, but where adopted, has had significant legal implications for development activities including tourism development proposals and will be reviewed in more detail in Chapter 4.

Test yourself

One seminal paper that reflects how we think about tourism and nature is Budowski's (1976) paper on tourism and environmental conservation. He outlines three positions between tourism and the natural environment:

☐ **Conflict**: where tourism has a detrimental impact on the environment

☐ **Coexistence**: where tourism and the environment have little contact

☐ **Symbiosis**: where tourism can support the protection of the natural environment, which in turn enhances the quality of the tourism experience.

The following two sections will examine these three conditions in more detail. It is worth highlighting that the impact of the natural environment on tourism was covered in Chapter 2, and reminding ourselves that the relationship between the environment and tourism works both ways; we now know that changes in climate, for example, will have significant impacts on tourism in ways that were not covered by Budowski in 1976.

Negative environmental impacts of tourism

The most obvious impact of tourism on the natural environment is its carbon emissions. The first comprehensive study of tourism's carbon footprint was delivered by the UNWTO in 2008, and found that tourism accounted for 5% of the world's greenhouse gas (GHG) emissions. The second major study was published a decade later (Lenzen et al., 2018), and found that this figure had risen to 8%. This increase confirms what was predicted: more people are travelling, and are travelling further and more frequently. The aviation industry accounts for nearly 2% of all GHG emissions, ranking 12th if it were a country, and approximately 80% of the aviation industry is tourism-related (Gossling et al., 2015). The figure is also higher than the 2008 figure, as it claims to a world-first look at the full life-cycle analysis of tourism, calculating the carbon footprint of all tourism-related activities, from growing the food required, to supplying souvenirs, and disposing of tourists' waste.

Worryingly, neither tourism nor aviation are currently covered by the 2015 Paris climate treaty, to keep global warming below a 2 ° increase in temperature rise. The tourism sector has set its own targets for a 50% reduction in GHG emissions by 2035, from a 2005 baseline. However, Gossling and his colleagues (2013) are quick to point out that no mechanisms to achieve these reductions have been put forward. The climate change impact of 1 billion tourists is equal to 4.5 gigatonnes of carbon-dioxide equivalent, while the average Australian household emits approximately 3.5 tonnes of carbon-dioxide equivalent each year. A back of the envelope calculation suggests that one international trip is the equivalent of an entire year's household emissions.

Travelling less frequently, and staying closer to home are two obvious options, but these would buck current trends and would require significant reshaping of travel behaviours. Given the trend towards more frequent, more exotic and more remote travel, we are unlikely to see this occurring. Instead, forecasts predict a quadrupling of air travel between 2005 and 2050 (Gossling et al., 2015).

Carbon offset programs would appear to be a softer target for travel-related behaviour changes. These effectively neutralise the carbon emissions of flying by investing in carbon reduction measures in other areas (tree planting being a classic example). Yet, the uptake of these programs have been stunningly low.

Studies have shown that only 1 in 100 people buy carbon offsets on international flights. Next time you board an Airbus A380 (the double decker planes), think to yourself, only 5 people – 10 at most – on that flight have chosen to offset the climate change impact of their travel. Are you one of them?

 Listen to this discussion of airines' carbon offset programs:
www.abc.net.au/radionational/programs/archived/rnafternoons/
airlines27-carbon-emission-programs/6747408

Gossling et al. (2015) present one interesting decarbonisation strategy for tourism. They develop their strategy on the basis that different forms of tourism have different carbon footprints, e.g. cruises have a much higher footprint than any flight-based holidays, which will have a bigger footprint than train or cycling holidays; and that carbon emissions are also affected by the number of tourists travelling, the distance that they are travelling based on their country of origin and their destination country, as well as the type of flight (as not all flights are equal in their emissions). They argue that governments who pro-actively want to reduce their country's tourism-related GHG emissions could run a marketing approach that integrate emission-intensity in their campaigns and actively target lower emission markets, and demarket themselves to higher emissions market. For example, swapping British for Chinese tourists would reduce New Zealand's tourism's GHG emissions by 6% (Gossling et al., 2015).

The environmental impacts of tourism do not end with the climate change, however. Other impacts include:

- ☐ Substantial increases in resource use, e.g. water, energy, food, building materials;
- ☐ Changes in land cover and land use;
- ☐ Issues of waste disposal and pollution;
- ☐ Physical impacts of erosion, site hardening and/or trampling;
- ☐ The spread of disease and invasive species;
- ☐ Species loss and wildlife disturbance (e.g. through corridor fragmentation) and/or conflict.

Some of these impacts are more difficult to quantify than others. With the focus on climate change, the energy use of tourism has received the most attention. We already know that transport accounts for up to 75% of all energy use in tourism, with accommodation responsible for the next highest use. The latter can be highly variable in total emissions, varying between 0.1 to 260kg CO_2 per night. This not only reflects the type of accommodation (camping versus luxury hotels) but also the wide range of energy-saving strategies employed by various types of accommodation provider. For those interested in this area, Warren and Becken (2017) provide a comprehensive review of the research on energy and water conservation measures in tourism accommodation.

Water usage is another area that has received some attention. Water usage by tourists tends to dwarf that of locals in many developing countries. For example, tourists in the Philippines use up to 981 litres/guest-night, in China 956 litres/guest-night and in Malaysia 914 litres/guest-night (Becken et al., 2014). In Bali, Indonesia, for example, tourism reportedly consumes 65% of local water resources, and conflict between the hotel industry and local communities is evident (Cole, 2012).

This intense level of water usage is an outcome not only of guest behaviour (long and frequent showers and baths), laundry requirements for linen and towels, but also in landscaping, pools and other water features within the accommodation. Golf courses are particularly problematic; Tourism Concern states that an average golf course in a tropical country such as Thailand uses as much water 60,000 rural villagers. Gossling and Peeters (2015) add up all water usage for tourism (including that associated with energy use, biofuels, food production etc.) and reach an average of 6,575 litres per guest night (note that the average domestic use of water in Australia is 4,50l/day – but this does not include all the factors that form part of Gossling and Peeters' calculation).

Much less is known about food consumption, land use and use of materials for buildings, etc. Not surprisingly, a similar pattern is detected for food consumption. While the average Brit may consumer 1.2kg of food per day, the few studies of food consumption in hotels suggest that it is up around 2.2kg to 3.1kg. Meanwhile, use of raw materials for construction is likely to be context-based, but has not been quantified at a global scale.

Direct use of land for tourism includes airports, roads, railways, paths and trails, shopping areas, parking, campsites, vacation homes, marinas, ski areas, as well as land used for the disposal and treatment of waste and areas required for the production of goods used in tourism. Again Gossling (2002) worked out rough estimates of land use, calculated on existing data about the number of golf courses, theme parks, convention centres, traffic infrastructure and accommodation inventories around the word. That study suggested (albeit underestimated figure) 515,000km^2 of land set aside for leisure-related activities – just a little more than the size of Spain.

The changes in land use and in particular, urban sprawl along coastlines can be particularly problematic. In 2018, rangers at the protected nesting sites of Mon Repos in Queensland, noticed for the first time, that baby turtle hatchlings were travelling along the beach from their nests (rather than across and down the beach), making for distant lights from second home housing developments and beach resorts. The increase in marina development has also been heavily criticised for its impact on coastal environments, limiting natural habitats in those areas, changing ecosystems and altering water movement patterns.

This article illustrates how coastal development can affect marine wildlife:

https://www.npsr.qld.gov.au/parks/mon-repos/pdf/mrcp-lights-marine-turtles.pdf

Figure 3.9: Bundaberg's appeal to local residents to limit night lights to help turtle hatchlings.

3

Pollution is another key issue. This include noise pollution from aviation and other forms of transport, as well as littering, sewage, oil and chemical pollution and arguably visual pollution. Noise pollution by planes is heavily regulated but still problematic for those living near flight paths. Other forms of noise pollution include jetskis, snowmobiles and recreational vehicles, which can be significant in some natural areas, such as marine reserves and national parks.

One Yellowstone National Park study found that snowmobiles could be heard 90% of the time at 8 of 11 sites surveyed. The increase in sewage and rubbish can be highly problematic for destinations in developing regions that do not have the infrastructure to dispose of them. Cruise ships also face similar problems, with 4 million litres of greywater produced (approximately two Olympic-sized swimming pools' worth) and dumped during a 7 day cruise, and 400,000 litres of blackwater (sewage) legally dumped in the high seas.

Trampling, erosion and other physical impacts are problematic. These are usually studied under the discipline of recreation ecology. Trampling of vegetation is likely to cause breakage and bruising of plant material, reduced plant vigor and regeneration, loss of ground cover, and changes in species composition, while trampling on soils will lead to a loss of organic matter, reduction in soil macro porosity, decreases in air and water permeability and increase in water run-off and subsequent erosion. These will not only occur in terrestrial environments but also in marine environments, particularly in fragile systems such as coral reefs, where anchor damage can be significant, or the breakage of live corals as snorkelers and divers get too close to corals. The creation of navigation channels or the construction of a pier for boats will also have major impacts on the movement of water, erosion and the deposition of suspended material.

Diseases can often be spread through tourism, e.g. in the ballast water of cruise ships and recreational vessels, but also through the movement of tourists. The outbreak and spread of foot and mouth disease in 2001 in the UK was probably one of the most shocking cases. It took only 2 weeks for the disease to spread throughout the whole country, travel in affected areas was almost completely prohibited, and up to six million sheep, cattle and pigs had to be slaughtered. There was widespread concern that the popular recreational activity of walking through farming areas facilitated the spread of the disease. Many entry ports enforce strict quarantine measures to ensure that local species are not subject to invasive diseases.

The removal of species can also be significant; one trekking tourist in Nepal can use four to five kilograms of local wood a day as firewood. The removal of shells and other marine species in the guise of souvenir collection also has significant negative localised impacts.

Finally, animals that routinely come into contact with tourists are also likely to show changes in behaviour that can be detrimental to them. Feeding wildlife habituates wild animals to human presence – eliminating the natural fear and/or avoidance behaviours that wild animals have for humans – and creates expectations of an easy food source. This, not unexpectedly, leads to aggression sooner or later. This has been reported with bears in North America or dingos in Australia. At the time of writing, a debate around taking selfies with wild animals was going strong on social media.

Is that selfie really worth it? Why face time with wild animals is a bad idea

https://theconversation.com/is-that-selfie-really-worth-it-why-face-time-with-wild-animals-is-a-bad-idea-96272

The presence of tourists will also disturb animals which may be resting, feeding or breeding. Tourists approaching nesting birds, e.g. penguins, are likely to cause birds to temporarily leave the nest and its chicks, and if this happens often enough, the chicks (and therefore the population as a whole) will suffer. Similarly, whalewatching boats approaching whales and dolphins will disturb them at the surface and cause them to dive – again creating a stress response. These stress responses can actually be measured; studies of tourism-related changes of the stress hormone cortisol have been measured in macaques. Another area that we will address in Chapter 6, is the specific issue of using wildlife in tourism, e.g. elephant rides, as an ethical issue.

Positive environmental impacts of tourism

Despite what has been said above, not all tourism is bad for the natural environment. Negative impacts will have to be managed, as is the case for all tourism. However, if designed well and with forethought, it is possible to leverage positive environmental benefits from tourism, through direct conservation outcomes or through pro-environmental behaviours of tourists.

Generally, discussions of positive impacts of tourism on the environment focus on five main areas:

1 Tourism can provide an economic justification for the conservation and preservation of natural heritage, and/or provide direct revenue for conservation.

2 Tourism can create a new constituency for conservation.

3 Nature-based or ecotourism creates a captive audience for environmental education opportunities, and engage tourists with nature and conservation in direct and impactful ways.

4 Tourism may provide opportunities for direct conservation activities, e.g. through volunteer tourism.

5 Tourism can deter wild animal poaching, by merely having a continuous presence in areas where poachers would normally be active.

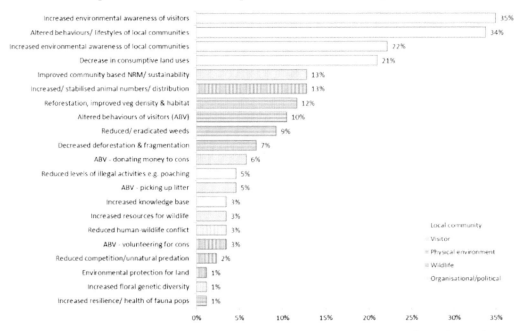

Figure 3.10: Conservation impacts identified in the tourism literature (Wardle et al., 2018)

The research has largely focussed on tourism's impact on the environmental awareness of visitors, or the behaviours and awareness of local communities, and changes in the consumption of natural resources as a result of tourism

(Figure 3.10). Direct impacts on wildlife, gene flow between populations, resources for wildlife and ecosystem health and resilience, as well as reductions in poaching, etc, are much less well understood and recorded (Wardle et al., 2018).

In fact, all five of the proposed beneficial relationships between tourism and the natural environment are difficult to quantify, with little large scale empirical research to fill in the gaps. Meanwhile, case studies invariably end of up being of the "yes but" variety when examining the positive impacts of tourism on the natural environment.

Recognising the importance of tourism as both a deterrent to poaching as well as a contributor to poaching, through the souvenir trade, the World Travel and Tourism Council has made poaching and tourism one its priority areas. In April 2018, WTTC launched its Travel and Tourism declaration on Illegal Wildlife Trade. The action centers on the adoption of a zero tolerance policy for International Wildlife Trade, but could also look at sector-wide training on how to engage with poaching issues when they are identified so these can be effectively reported and stopped. Anectodally this is one area where many national park visitors that I speak to say that tourism can have an important role in promoting conservation.

 Find out more about the WTTC's Illegal Wildlife Trafficking campaign here: https://www.wttc.org/priorities/sustainable-growth/ illegal-wildlife-trade?wvideo=89uok6uyku

Relatively little is known about the positive impacts of tourism on whole ecosystems. The impact of ecotourism on forests, for example, has been the most studied, representing just under half of all the research on tourism's environmental impacts (Wardle et al., 2018). Of 111 studies on the links between ecotourism and forest protection, only 17 had empirical approaches, generally using satellite imagery of forest cover as a proxy measure for ecosystem health (Brandt & Buckley, 2018). The 17 studies produced mixed results, with ecotourism sometimes creating a mechanism to protect forests, and other times, leading to further degradation. However, three distinct trends were apparent:

1 The forests must have their own formal government protection, e.g. as a national park, in order for tourism to provide benefits through community support, direct revenue and jobs.

2 There must be a clear delineation of the conservation areas, often surrounded by a buffer zone.

3 There must strong enforcement and monitoring of the zone, with significant community engagement, participation and support for the monitoring.

Where these conditions were not present, forests continued to be degraded, highlighting the need for a symbiotic relationship between tourism and conservation, rather than the reliance on tourism as a conduit to conservation.

A similar pattern has been detected when it comes to species conservation, with net conservation gains arising from tourism only where tourism is combined with other regulatory factors such as habitat restoration, management of alien species, anti-poaching initiatives and the creation of protected areas (Buckley et al., 2016).

Areas that are listed as a form of natural heritage, in particular if they are listed as a World Heritage Area, are more likely to receive attention with regards to tourism. Again, however, finding actual numbers on the revenue generated from tourism for the protection of wildlife and ecosystems is challenging. Generally, where tourism relies on permits to access a natural area, revenue for conservation can be generated through visitor entry fees, increased land values (and therefore land taxes), mobile tour operating permits or licences, concession fees, and fixed-site developments, again with associated taxes. In most cases, these returns go into consolidated revenue for the government, their relationship to conservation is largely unquantified, and most cases is far less than the funds required to maintain the protected area (Buckley, 2011 and 2018).

The constituency argument is also complex. Buckley (2018) suggests that it is rare for the tourism sector to provide political support for conservation unless it has financial investment under threat from another industry, e.g. Australian tourism peak bodies have lobbied against fracking, car racing and logging in protected areas, but these are the exception rather than the rule. It wasn't until May 2018 that the tourism sector associated with Great Barrier Reef started to lobby for action on climate change, the major threat to the reef (Figure 3.11) – over a decade after scientists started warning of the impact of major bleaching events caused by a warming climate.

CLIMATE CHANCE ALLIANCE FORMED

A NEW alliance has formed between dive operators and a major green group, who are calling upon the Federal Government to take stronger action against climate change.

Figure 3.11: A new alliance between the tourism industry and environmentalists to tackle climate change impacts on the Great Barrier Reef. (Source: Cairns Post)

Far more studies focus on local communities and tourists. In the former case, the relationship is relatively straight forward: direct local benefits from tourism are more likely to generate local community support for tourism. In the case of tourists, however, the longer-term impact of tourism on their pro-environmental attitudes or behaviours is less clear. Environmental education in the free learning context of tourism is called *interpretation*, and generally serves to relate the environment to the tourist at a more personal level, often through story-telling. Interpretation can be effective at modifying immediate, on-site behaviours, e.g. picking up litter, not straying from a designated path, approaching wildlife with care (e.g. Kim & Coghlan, 2018). However, its longer-term impacts on off-site behaviours, e.g. lobbying for the protection of the Great Barrier Reef for example, are much less clear. There are examples of pledges that have worked in some cases to encourage tourists to perform pro-environmental behaviours once they return home (Mann, Ballatyne & Packer, 2018).

The broader tourist behaviours, as well as changes in attitudes, intentions, motivations, ethical perspectives, linked to global environmental change are much harder to quantify and as yet, no empirical study has been able to capture these positive impacts. Anecdotally, however, many of us are content to believe that visiting a protected area, and having a good experience there, is more likely to lead us to value and protect those sites, than not.

Thus, the evidence for the environmental benefits of tourism is at best piecemeal and difficult to quantify. Buckley (2011) summarises the conditions necessary for the environmental benefits of tourism as follows:

1 **A facilitative commercial setting:** an appealing and accessible attraction, and sufficient industry experience to market, package and provide environmentally sensitive activities.

2 **Strong social support:** a supportive local, who receives some financial (and other) benefits from tourism.

3 **An adequate legal framework**: formal title over land and/or wildlife and conservation status are required and must allow the landowner to generate either income or capital gain.

Review

The introductory chapter asked you to think about sustainable tourism as a juggling act, keeping three balls in the air. This chapter has looked at those balls in more detail, and the various aspects of them, of which there are many. The simple rule of sustainable tourism – move towards that which enhances relationships, and away from what undermines relationships – is evident here. We want tourism to enhance local employment opportunities: to do this we must understand the casual, low skilled nature of tourism, and the issue of leakages, and deliver jobs that are offer some economic security and capacity-building prospects, as well as create opportunities for backward linkages and strong multiplier effects. Wider scale issues such as taxation, visas, infrastructure development and so forth, must be addressed in consultation with all stakeholders, e.g. government ministers who hold portfolios removed from tourism concerns. Tourism's susceptibility to external shocks must also be considered, and again relies on strong partnerships with all stakeholders.

Similarly, the capitalist imperative for growth must be weighed up against community capacity for hosting visitors – thresholds of visitor numbers that can be accommodated by a destination (c.f. Butler's Tourism Area Lifecycle and Doxey's Irridex model). How authenticity is affected by tourism must be identified and discussed, to avoid unintended commodification and appropriation, and instead support cultural revival or survival and the protection of cultural heritage. Moreover, issues of tourist safety and quality of their experience can be leveraged to create better living conditions for local communities, where these are balanced, and one is not subservient to the other. If done well, the desired outcomes of greater inter-cultural understanding may also become a reality. At an individual level, we may also want look at opportunities to leverage leisure and tourism activities for personal wellbeing.

Finally, the environmental impacts of tourism require the greatest attention. Nature cannot speak for herself, and if we ignore the signs of nature in distress it is usually to our own detriment. Chapter 2 presented climate change as the elephant in the room – and this was again picked up here. Tourism cannot and will not be sustainable until we have found effective ways to reduce its carbon footprint – the current trend does not hold much promise for this outcome, but we'll look at this in more detail in Chapter 9. Other environmental stressors must be identified on a case by case basis. This chapter has given you an idea of what impacts to look for, and has given you some ideas of how tourism can benefit the natural environment.

This chapter is the longest in the textbook – and well done for sticking with it! To move tourism towards greater sustainability, you must be aware of the negative impacts of tourism as well as its positive impacts, look for these a broad scale and a localised scale, be able to identify them, recognisedthat managing them will be effortful and require a partnerships approach, and finally, have the tools to track these impacts and minimise the negative ones, and maximise the positive ones. This chapter on impacts concludes the opening section of the textbook, and now we'll move on to the issues of operationalising sustainable tourism, ethical decision-making, setting up good governance structures, working with partners, and creating your own tool box for sustainable tourism (Section 2).

Questions and exercises

1   Think back to your last travel experience, what positive impacts on the environmental and local community did you trip have? Are there any areas where you feel your travel could have a larger positive impact and how would do about it?

2   Why does interpretation have a limited impact on people's pro-environmental attitudes and behaviours? How does taking a pledge change its impact?

3   List five reasons why tourists are more vulnerable to crime when they are on holidays.

4 Explain the concepts of leakage and linkage in your own words. Explore these within the context of two destinations of your choice, comparing a destination with a high reliance on tourism for its GDP (e.g. the Maldives) and a low dependence on tourism (e.g. the USA).

Multiple choice questions

1 An opportunity cost is a direct economic cost in tourism: True or false ?

2 The multiplier effect in tourism results in:

a) More money being created through tourism

b) More local jobs being created through tourism supply chains

c) More investment into tourism

3 Which of the following are ways in which cultural commodification can occur?

a) Aesthetic change and uniformity change.

b) Quality change and practical change

c) All of the above .

4 Tourism encourages the globalisation and/or homogenisation of cultures: True or false?

5 Environmental impacts of tourism are complex to identify and understand because they are often incremental, cumulative, and non-linear and/or occur at different temporal and spatial scales: True or false?

Further reading

Buckley, R. (2013). To use tourism as a conservation tool, first study tourists. *Animal Conservation,* **16**(3), 259-260.

Gössling, S., & Buckley, R. (2016). Carbon labels in tourism: persuasive communication? *Journal of Cleaner Production,* **111**, 358-369.

Jamal, T. & Dredge, D. (2014). Tourism and community development issues. *R. Sharpley and D. Telfer, Tourism and Development. Concepts and Issues, Second Edition.* London: Channel View, 178-204.

McKercher, B. (1993). Some fundamental truths about tourism: Understanding tourism's social and environmental impacts. *Journal of Sustainable Tourism,* **1**(1), 6-16.

Mowforth, M., & Munt, I. (2015). *Tourism and Sustainability: Development, globalisation and new tourism in the third world.* Routledge.

Sharpley, R. (2015). *Tourism and Development.* Sage publications.

References

Becken, S., Garofano, N., McLennan, C.L., Moore, S., Rajan, R. & Watt, M. (2014). *From Challenges to Solutions 2nd White Paper on Tourism and Water: Providing the business case*. Griffith Institute for Tourism Research Report Series Report No 1 March 2014

Brandt, J.S. & Buckley, R.C. (2018). A global systematic review of empirical evidence of ecotourism impacts on forests in biodiversity hotspots. *Current Opinion in Environmental Sustainability* **32**, 112-118.

Buckley, R. (2011). Tourism and the environment. *Annual Review of Environment and Resources*, **36**, 397-416

Buckley, R. (2018). Tourism and natural World Heritage: A complicated relationship. *Journal of Travel Research*, **57** (5), 563-578

Buckley, R.C., Morrison, C. & Castley, J.G. (2016) Net effects of ecotourism on threatened species survival. *PLoS ONE*, **11**(2),doi:10.1371/ journal.pone.0147988

Budowski, G. (1976). Tourism and environmental conservation: conflict, coexistence, or symbiosis?. *Environmental Conservation*, **3**(1), 27-31.

Chen, C.C. & Petrick, J.F. (2013). Health and Wellness Benefits of Travel Experiences: A Literature Review. *Journal of Travel Research*, **52**(6), 709-719.

Cole, S. (2012). A political ecology of water equity and tourism. A case study from Bali. *Annals of Tourism Research*, **39**(2), 1221-1241.

Doxey, G. V. (1975). A causation theory of visitor-resident irritants: Methodology and research inferences. In *Travel and tourism research associations sixth annual conference proceedings* (pp. 195-98).

Geertz, C. (1973). *The Interpretation of Cultures* (Vol. 5043). Basic books.

Gössling, S. (2002). Global environmental consequences of tourism. *Global Environmental Change*, **12**(4), 283-302.

Gössling, S. & Peeters, P. (2015). Assessing tourism' global environmental impact 1900-2050. *Journal of Sustainable Tourism*, **23**(5), 639-659.

Gössling, S., Scott, D. & Hall, C.M. (2013). Challenges of tourism in a low carbon economy. *Wiley Interdisciplinary Reviews: Climate Change*, **4**(6), 525-538

Gössling, S., Scott, D. & Hall, C.M. (2015). Inter-market variability in CO_2 emission-intensities in tourism: Implications for destination marketing and carbon management. *Tourism Management*, **46**, 203-212.

Hall, C.M. & Lew, A.A. (2009). *Understanding and Managing Tourism Impacts: an integrated approach*. Oxon: Routledge.

Hochschild, A.R. (1983). *The Managed Heart: Commercialization of the human feeling*. Berkeley: Berkeley University Press.

Kim, A. & Coghlan, A. (2018). Promoting site-specific versus general pro-environmental behavioral intentions: the role of interpretation. *Tourism Analysis* **23** (1), 77-91

Lenzen, M., Sun, Y. Y., Faturay, F., Ting, Y. P., Geschke, A., & Malik, A. (2018). The carbon footprint of global tourism. *Nature Climate Change*, **1**.

Mann, J.B., Ballantyne, R. & Packer, J. (2018). Penguin promises: encouraging aquarium visitors to take conservation action. *Environmental Education Research*, **24** (6), 859-874.

McIntosh, A. J., & Zahra, A. (2007). A cultural encounter through volunteer tourism: Towards the ideals of sustainable tourism? *Journal of Sustainable Tourism*, **15**(5), 541-556.

Wardle, C., Buckley, R., Shakeela, A. & Castley, G. (2018). Ecotourism's contributions to conservation: analysing patterns in published studies. *Journal of Ecotourism*, 1-31

Warren, C., & Becken, S. (2017). Saving energy and water in tourist accommodation: A systematic literature review (1987–2015). *International Journal of Tourism Research*, **19**(3), 289-303.

UNESCO (2001), *UNESCO Universal Declaration on Cultural Diversity*. http://www. unesco.org/new/fileadmin/MULTIMEDIA/HQ/CLT/pdf/5_Cultural_Diversity_ EN.pdf (accessed March 2019)

UNWTO (2016). *UNWTO Annual Report 2016*. http://media.unwto.org/publication/ unwto-annual-report-2016 (accessed March 2019)

UNWTO – UNEP (2008). *Climate Change and Tourism: Responding to global challenges.* (prepared by Scott, D., Amelung, B., Becken, S., Ceron, J.P., Dubois, G., Gössling, S., Peeters, P., and Simpson, M.C.). UNWTO, Madrid, and UNEP, Paris.

Weaver, D. (2006). *Sustainable Tourism: Theory and practice*. Oxford: Butterworth: Heinemann.

Weaver, D. & Lawton, L. (2014). *Tourism Management*. Milton: John Wiley & Sons.

Section 2: Managing for Sustainability

4

4 Sustainable Tourism Policy Frameworks

Introduction

Having looked at the external and internal challenges facing the move towards more sustainable tourism, and the impacts of tourism, you should now be wondering how sustainability in tourism can be turned into more than an ideal.

Perhaps one of the most obvious way to achieve this is simply to regulate the sector. After all regulation worked for the ozone layer: scientists raised the alarm in the 1970s that a hole was appearing in the atmosphere's ozone layer, caused by Ozone Depleting Substances or ODS (most notably CFCs) and resulting in adverse effects on human health and the environment. By 1987 the Montreal Protocol was established to phase out the use of ODS, and by June 2015, all countries in the United Nations, the Cook Islands, Holy See, Niue and the supranational European Union had ratified the original Protocol. The result was a 98% drop in ODS since ratification, and the hole is expected to have fully repaired itself by 2050. A significant achievement in terms of international cooperation, based on scientific advice.

Can such an approach be replicated in tourism? Well, the situation is perhaps more complex, as you've hopefully come to realise in Chapters 1-3. Sustainable tourism means different things to different people; there are significant external drivers (outside the direct control of tourism stakeholders) that hinder the move towards greater sustainability; there is relatively little coordination between the different decision makers, who often have competing agendas; there is a lack of data and understanding about the impacts of tourism at various scales; and moreover tourism can have both positive and negative impacts in equal parts – often providing development opportunities where no others exist, or where other alternatives are more harmful than tourism itself.

> ## Key words and concepts
>
> - Wicked problem.
> - Sustainable development goals
> - Human rights act
> - Paris Agreement
>
> - Rights of Nature
> - Supply chain management
> - Organic, incremental and induced path to sustainable tourism

4.1 Tourism as a wicked problem

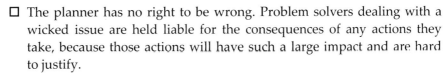

These characteristics have led some to label the move towards greater sustainability in tourism a 'wicked problem' – not a moral judgement, or simply slang, or even hyperbole, but a specific term used to describe highly complex issues possessing several characteristics in common. Rittel and Webber (1973) describe these characteristics as follows.

☐ There is no definitive formulation of a wicked problem, unlike an ordinary problem.

☐ Wicked problems have no stopping rule – the search for solutions is ongoing, as the problem is never fully resolved.

☐ Solutions to wicked problems are not true or false, but are largely a matter of judgment.

☐ There is no immediate and no ultimate test of a solution to a wicked problem, and there are likely to be unexpected consequences over time, making it difficult to measure solutions' effectiveness.

☐ Every solution to a wicked problem is a 'one-shot' operation. There is no trial and error, as every implemented solution has consequences that cannot be undone.

☐ Wicked problems do not have an exhaustively describable set of potential solutions.

☐ Every wicked problem is essentially unique – experience does not help you address it.

☐ Every wicked problem can be considered to be a symptom of another problem, and is entwined with other problems, meaning there is no one root cause.

☐ A wicked problem can be explained in numerous ways, and each stakeholder will have different ideas about what the problem really is and what its causes are.

☐ The planner has no right to be wrong. Problem solvers dealing with a wicked issue are held liable for the consequences of any actions they take, because those actions will have such a large impact and are hard to justify.

Test
yourself

Figure 4.1: The characteristics of a wicked problem.

The upshot is that there is no one way to regulate for greater sustainability in tourism.

4.2   Overview of policy and planning in tourism

Because there is no one way of regulating tourism, we rely instead on a number of international declarations on issues ranging from Human Rights, Rights of the Child, and International Labour to the Protection of the World's Cultural and Natural Heritage, Convention on Biodiversity, on the Environment and Development, and Climate Change. The more relevant ones will be briefly outlined in Section 4.3., with more detail on the significance of Agenda 21 (Environment and Development) and the Paris Agreement (Climate Action). The emerging area of Rights of Nature will also be explored here as will the Sustainable Development Goals (SDGs) which are an important discussion of any form of sustainable development.

There are also a number of more specific tourism-related international frameworks, such as the Warsaw Convention on Air Transport (1929), the Manila Declaration on World Tourism (1980) and on the Social Impact of Tourism (1997), as well as the various Resolutions of the World Tourism Organisation's General Assembly. The rights of movement, including visas and migration, also has an important impact on sustainable tourism development. These will be addressed in Section 4.4.

In addition, the International Organization for Standardization is an independent, non-governmental organization and largest developer of voluntary international standards, and facilitates world trade by providing common standards between nations. Over 20,000 standards have been set, covering everything from manufactured products and technology to food safety, agriculture and healthcare. Many of these will also impact on the tourism sector, both directly and indirectly, through its supply chain. Other supply chain management initiatives exist, specifically for the tourism sector, e.g. the UNEP's Global Reporting Initiative (GRI). It's worth touching on a number of additional regulations that will affect the delivery of tourism services, e.g. building codes, food production, health and sanitisation, waste disposal, zoning regulations, and so forth. These will be covered in Section 4.5.

Finally, destinations, at a national or regional scale, will develop tourism policies and plans to guide the development of sustainable tourism. These are specifically designed to integrate concerns of economic viability of tourism, local prosperity, employment quality, social equity, community wellbeing, physical integrity, protection of natural heritage, resource efficiency, local control and visitor fulfilment. How these are developed will be discussed and some case studies of how they are applied will be covered in Section 4.6.

4.3 International frameworks related to sustainable tourism

As mentioned in Section 4.2., there are a number of international agreements, on issues much broader than tourism, that will have a bearing on progress towards sustainable tourism. At a fundamental level these include the 1948 Declaration of Human Rights – which businesses are encouraged to take leadership in fulfilling as human rights relate to direct activities, supply chains, and communities where companies operate. As a sector, tourism has both 'spheres of influence' and 'spheres of responsibility', and must usually abide by domestic legislation designed to protect human rights at a national level.

Some of the key human rights issues that relate to tourism include:

☐ Labour conditions and a living wage

☐ Land rights and forced displacement

☐ The rights of indigenous peoples

☐ The right to water and sanitation

☐ The right to life and health

☐ The right to dignity and privacy

☐ Economic exploitation

- ☐ Cultural exploitation
- ☐ Child labour
- ☐ Sexual exploitation
- ☐ The right to participate

Chapter 3 already highlighted some of the impacts resulting from tourism development that relate to the list above (e.g. the casualization and seasonality of jobs in tourism) but these issues can become particularly apparent where local landholders are moved on from lands to make way for enclave tourism.

Tourism Concern provides one case study of Bekal, in the Indian state of Kerala – an area popular for domestic and international tourism. In their report, they claim that many local people were threatened with eviction if they refused to sell their land, and often ended up selling for much less than the land was worth. Alternative housing was provided, but in areas prone to flooding, in low quality rentals, often in arrears. Traditionally livelihoods focussed on fishing became impossible as the new homes were much further from the sea, and promised tourism-related jobs did not materialise. The right to water and sanitation has also been undermined, as the communities must travel 1.5 kilometres to obtain safe drinking water, meanwhile the propensity to flooding during heavy rains, exacerbates the already poor sanitary conditions and undermining the right to health.

In this example, 8 of the 11 human rights listed above have allegedly been violated (Labour conditions and a living wage; land and rights and forced displacement; the rights of indigenous peoples; the right to water and sanitation; the right to life and health; the right to dignity and privacy; the prevention of economic exploitation).

Bekal Special Tourism Zone, Kerala, India[14]

Bekal, in the southern Indian state of Kerala, became India's first Special Tourism Area (STA) in the 1990s. The Bekal Resorts Development Corporation Ltd (BRDC), a government agency formed to facilitate the development, has since acquired 250 acres of land for six resorts. Whilst the BRDC claims to be environmentally sensitive and socially responsible, the reality has seen lack of transparency and consultation with communities, violations of coastal regulations, and aggressive land acquisition.

Many local people claim to have been threatened with eviction if they refused to sell their land, often with little notice. This includes very poor fisher families who were forced into selling for as little as 25 per cent of the market rate. Women were allegedly threatened whilst their husbands were at sea. More than a year after their forced displacement, promises to rehabilitate them are unfulfilled. Land for building new homes remains flooded, the rental accommodation provided is of poor quality, and rents BRDC said it would pay are in arrears. The right to a livelihood has been undermined as the distance to the sea makes fishing unviable, while promised jobs at the resorts have not materialised. The right to water and sanitation has also been undermined, as the communities must travel 1.5 kilometres to obtain safe drinking water. The houses are subject to flooding during heavy rains, exacerbating the already poor sanitary conditions and undermining the right to health.

The BRDC and developers have allegedly violated various national laws, including the Coastal Regulation Zone (CRZ) notification, the Wetland Conservation Act and the Environment Protection Act. The developers have reportedly destroyed mangroves, reclaimed wetlands, diverted rivers and appropriated agricultural land.

Because of the alleged human rights abuses and legal transgressions, the Bekal development has attracted significant civil society opposition. This has included public campaigning and mass protests. Social tensions and resentment even led to some local people reportedly issuing warnings to tourists to stay away.

Families displaced by tourism development in Bekal

Figure 4.2: Tourism Concern's case study on tourism and human rights (Source: https://www.tourismconcern.org.uk/wp-content/uploads/2014/10/TourismConcern_IndustryHumanRightsBriefing-FIN-4.pdf)

To ensure that this type of situation does not arise, and that business are aware of their human rights obligations, a number of tools and packages exist to guide business practice and policy .

Read Tourism Concern's industry briefing on human rights: https://www. tourismconcern.org.uk/wp-content/uploads/2014/10/TourismConcern_ IndustryHumanRightsBriefing-FIN-4.pdf

The International Standards Organisation (ISO) now includes human rights as one of seven core aspects of social responsibility, identified as ISO 26000. Some tourism companies have embraced human rights into their core business strategies, e.g. Marriott International has a human rights policy statement that makes direct reference to the Universal Declaration on Human Rights.

Business should also be aware of other, similar frameworks such as the International Covenant on Economic, Social and Cultural Rights (ICESCR), International Covenant on Civil and Political Rights (ICCPR), the Rights of the Child, and the International Labour Organisation's labour law standards. For example, the main aims of the International Labour Organisation are to promote rights at work, encourage decent employment opportunities, enhance social protection and strengthen dialogue on work-related issue, again key topics for the working conditions in the tourism sector.

Another key international framework that has facilitated the development of tourism is the 1995 General Agreement on Trades and Services (GATS), which covers market access and trade for services, including tourism. As GATS focusses more on the liberalisation of trade in tourism services, and does not have a direct sustainability focus, it is not covered in detail here. However, Wood (2009) provides a good overview of GATS and tourism in his chapter on Tourism and International Policy.

Areas of cultural heritage, including build heritage, tend to be protected under Protection of the World's Cultural and Natural Heritage managed through United Nations Educational, Scientific and Cultural Organization (UNESCO). UNESCO has a rather broad mandate seeking to "build peace through international cooperation in Education, the Sciences and Culture". Of relevance to tourism is that UNESCO preserves 1073 World heritage Sites in 167 countries (a land area of 10 million square kilometres, virtually the size of China), many of which are major tourism attractions – e.g. the pyramids of Egypt, the Taj Mahal in India, the Great Barrier Reef in Australia.

Read about UNESCO's tourism program here: https://whc.unesco.org/ uploads/activities/documents/activity-669-7.pdf

Because of the relationship between World Heritage listed status and tourism appeal, as well as tourism's ability to meet the requirement in the *World Heritage Convention* to present World Heritage properties, and as a means to realise community and economic benefits through sustainable use, UNESCO pro-actively develops plans and policies to facilitate their management and the development of sustainable tourism, through fostering increased aware-ness, capacity and balanced participation of all stakeholders in order to protect the properties and their Outstanding Universal Value. This includes a plan to protect UNESCO sites of high tourism value from climate change impacts, a theme we will return to many times in this book.

As well as UNESCO listed World Heritage sites, the natural environment is further protected by a number of international frameworks and treaties. Examples include the Convention on Biodiversity, on the Environment and Development (Rio Declaration/Earth Summit), the Protection of Wetlands (RAMSAR), the Convention on International Trade in Endangered Species of Wild Fauna and Flora (CITES) and perhaps most importantly, climate change (United Nations Framework Convention on Climate Change).

The relationship between some of these international environmental frameworks and tourism may appear more obvious than others. CITES for example, may not immediately be obvious, but these two personal examples can perhaps illustrate their real world implications.

In the first case, I was returning from Africa to Australia with a number of wooden carvings that would need to be checked at Australian Customs. I had completely forgotten that my traveling companion had gifted me a wrapped item during the trip, and told me not to open it until I arrived home. To my horror, the unwrapping of the gift revealed a tusk, and many animals bearing tusks, e.g. elephants, are on the CITES list. After a lengthy inspection, the tusk was deemed too small to be from an elephant, and identified as being from a warthog (I have a soft spot for Pumba) – which prompted a 20 minutes search of the CITES list by customs to determine whether or not I would be issued with a fine (I wasn't). The second case stems from a local market in Papua New Guinea, where the stall owner tried to barter with me around the sale of 'genuine' black coral jewellery. Black coral is listed under CITES, and its sale is definitely illegal. Just those two examples should hopefully demonstrate that it can happen easily and to anyone.

In terms of larger issues of sustainable development and tourism, the Rio Declaration is the most influential international framework. The Declaration is implemented through Agenda 21. Part of Agenda 21 was to encourage sus-tainable development to be operationalised at an international level, but more importantly at a national, regional or local level. Indeed many national and state governments who agreed to the resulting conference documents have legislated or advised that local authorities devise strategies to implement Agenda 21 locally, as well as formulated policy at the national level.

In adopting a strategic policy and planning approach, three core features were noted as important to move from the broad rhetoric to a localised imple-mentation of sustainability principles. According to Bennett (1997), these are:

Test
yourself

1 A long-term comprehensive, integrated and inclusive strategy

2 Extensive collaboration and participation of all relevant actors

3 A move towards cross-sectoral harmonisation of policy and decision-making processes for improved integration.

One example of a successful implementation of this approach is the Netherlands National Environmental Policy Plan (NEPP). It is considered one of the most successful, innovative and advanced plans for positive environmental action to achieve sustainability within one lifetime (25 years). It is revised every four years, to take into account new objectives and challenges, as well as lessons learned. It is supported through a reliable fiscal commitment by the Dutch government to the plan's implementation, and strategic governance held to account by a participatory citizenry. Measures of its success suggest that over 70% of the original goals have been achieved, largely from a deliberate decoupling of economic growth and environmental pressure, and the application of an environmental ethic as part of decision-making processes. The Netherlands is perhaps the exception rather the rule, with most countries still struggling to successfully implement Agenda 21 in their development decision-making plans.

Perhaps the biggest area where an international framework is required to drive sustainability is in the area of climate change. The United Nations Framework Convention on Climate Change (UNFCCC) is an international environmental treaty adopted on 9 May 1992 and opened for signature at the Earth Summit in Rio de Janeiro. It currently has 165 signatories and has been ratified by 50 states. The UNFCCC's objective is to "stabilize greenhouse gas concentrations in the atmosphere at a level that would prevent dangerous anthropogenic interference with the climate system", which is generally represented by a global warming of temperatures by no more than 2° centigrade (2DS) compared to the pre-industrial era (c.f. Chapters 2 and 3).

The framework sets non-binding limits on greenhouse gas emissions for individual countries and contains no enforcement mechanisms. Instead, the framework outlines how specific international treaties (called 'protocols' or 'agreements') may be negotiated to specify further action towards the objective of the UNFCCC. The Kyoto protocol and the Paris Agreement are examples of these. The Kyoto Protocol in 1997 established legally binding obligations for developed countries to reduce their greenhouse gas emissions in the period 2008–2012. A later amendment, the Doha Amendment, was proposed to extend these reductions to 2020, but was never entered into force. The Doha Amendment has since been superseded by the Paris Agreement in 2015, which governs emission reductions from 2020 on through commitments of countries in their Intended Nationally Determined Contributions (INDCs), which become NDCs once ratified.

The Paris climate agreement: key points

Temperatures
2100

- Keep warming "well below 2 degrees Celsius"

- Continue efforts to limit the rise in temperatures to 1.5 degrees Celsius"

Financing
2020-2025

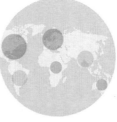

- Rich countries must provide 100 billion dollars from 2020, as a "floor"

- Amount to be updated by 2025

Specialisation

- Developed countries must continue to "take the lead" in the reduction of greenhouse gases

- Developing nations are encouraged to "enhance their efforts" and move over time to cuts

Emissions goals
2050

- Aim for greenhouse gases emissions to peak "as soon as possible"

- From 2050: rapid reductions to achieve a balance between emissions from human activity and the amount that can be captured by "sinks"

Burden sharing

- Developed countries must provide financial resources to help developing countries

- Other countries are invited to provide support on a voluntary basis

Review mechanism
2025

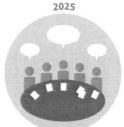

- A review every five years. First mandatory world review: 2025
- Each review will show an improvement compared with the previous period

Climate-related losses

- Vulnerable countries have won recognition of the need for "averting, minimising and addressing" losses suffered due to climate change

© AFP

Figure 4.3: Graphic representation of the key points of the Paris Climate Agreement (Source: AFP.com)

These NDCs occur at a national level, and according to some experts, are unlikely to be met by all countries and are actually insufficient to achieve the UNFCCC's 2DS objective. Of even greater concern is that they exclude the international aviation and maritime sectors, i.e. international commercial flights and cruise ships. Instead these fall to the International Civil Aviation Organisation (ICAO) and the International Maritime Organisation to manage, which some argue have done little to address their sectors' emissions, preferring to focus on soft targets such as the development of biofuels and more energy efficient vessels (Gossling, 2013).

Test yourself

This is problematic as Chapter 3 indicated that tourism not only has a large carbon foot, being almost entirely dependent on fossil fuels, but that aviation and cruise ships are two significant contributors to tourism's carbon footprint.

Instead the tourism sector has developed its own set of targets, which aim to bring tourism's carbon emissions into line with the INDCs to cut global emissions by -40% to -70% by 2050. These will be reviewed in Section 4.4. below.

Before we move onto the tourism-specific frameworks, it is worth touching on two areas that have been mentioned in Chapters 1 and 3. These are the Sustainable Development Goals and the emerging area of Rights of Nature.

Returning briefly to Chapter 1, you may remember mention of the UN Development Programme's new 17 Sustainable Development Goals (SDGs), replacing the previous Millennium Goals, to address most aspects of sustainability setting specific targets for 2030. Goal 12 (of 17 SDGs) is to promote Responsible Consumption and Production, forming the umbrella for the *One Planet – Sustainable Tourism Programme* for greater sustainability in tourism through "efficiency, innovation and adaptability".

The Programme lists four objectives:

1 Integrating sustainable consumption and production (SCP) patterns in tourism related policies and frameworks.

2 Collaboration among stakeholders for the improvement of the tourism sector's SCP performance.

3 Fostering the application of guidelines, instruments and technical solutions to prevent and mitigate tourism impacts and to mainstream SCP patterns among tourism stakeholders.

4 Enhancing sustainable tourism investment and financing.

Figure 4.4: The Global Goals. Watch the video on Tourism and the SDGs: https://www.youtube.com/watch?v=6bX6iah_4Ec&feature=youtu.be

Test
yourself

Through its One Planet programme, the UNWTO also sees the potential for sustainable tourism to also contribute to SDG8 focusing on decent work and economic growth, SDG13 addressing climate change or SDGs14 (sustainably use and conserve marine resources) and SDG15 (sustainably use and conserve terrestrial resources). The links to the international frameworks listed above and the impacts of tourism described in Chapter 3 should now put the UNWTO's One Planet – Sustainable Tourism Programme into a wider context for you.

Question

In Figure 4.4, how many of the SDGs can be facilitated through the effective implementation of sustainable tourism? List them, and explain how.

Rights of Nature is a movement to "legally recognise the rights of the natural world to exist, thrive and evolve" (AELA, 2018). It recognises the place of humans as only one part of a wider Earth community, and that we must co-exist with, and depend upon, a complex system. Advocates seek to secure the highest legal protection for ecological health, recognising their inherent worth and providing a mechanism to protect that worth. It fundamentally changes the way that we, as humans, interact with nature, and radically transforms the way in which citizens defend and restore nature. It places economic development in balance with nature, rather than at the expense of the latter.

Under Rights of Nature laws:

☐ Nature is empowered to defend and enforce its own rights;

☐ People are empowered to defend and enforce the Rights of Nature; and

☐ Governments are required to implement, defend, and enforce the Rights of Nature.

While this concept might be novel to some countries, several countries have embraced this concept; the rights of nature were enshrined in Ecuador's 2008 Constitution, Bolivia's 2010 'Rights of Mother Earth' Act, as well as some local laws in the USA and in New Zealand, where the Whanganui River and the Urewera Forest are recognised to have legal rights. The European Citizen's Initiative on the Rights of Nature is looking for ways to introduce the Rights of Nature into Europe as well.

Adopting a Rights of Nature approach would fundamentally shift the balance of sustainability away from environmental sustainability as an afterthought and place it firmly at the centre of our legal system.

4.4   Tourism's sector-specific international frameworks

In addition to the international frameworks listed above, the tourism and travel sectors have also devised a number of policies and plans at an international level that aim to make tourism more sustainable. These include the Manila Declaration on World Tourism (1980) and on the Social Impact of Tourism (1997), the Quebec Declaration on Ecotourism (2002) as well as the various Resolutions of the World Tourism Organisation's General Assembly, including the WTO's Code of Ethics for Tourism (c.f. Chapter 6).

The **Manila Declaration on World Tourism** (1980) (http://www.univeur.org/cuebc/downloads/PDF%20carte/65.%20Manila.PDF) resulted from the World Tourism Conference convened by the WTO *"to clarify the real nature of tourism in all its aspects and the role tourism is bound to play in a dynamic and vastly changing world, as well as to consider the responsibility of States for the development and enhancement of tourism in present-day societies as more than a purely economic activity of nations and people"*. This Declaration recognised the systems-like nature of tourism, the breadth of its stakeholders, and the resulting widespread nature of its impacts, both positive and negative.

The WTO has continued to develop a range of documents to promote tourism development, e.g. the Tourism Bill of Rights and Tourism Code (1985) which focuses on tourists' freedom of movement, and the Declaration on the Facilitation of Tourist Travel (2009) as well as ones that focus more specifically on sustainable tourism development, e.g. the **Manila Declaration on the Social Impact of Tourism** (1997) (http://www.univeur.org/cuebc/downloads/PDF%20carte/70%20Manila.PDF). The latter focusses on the impacts on local communities, and encourages greater involvement of local people in the planning and implementation and evaluation of tourism policies, to ensure that the heritage and integrity of destinations remain intact, and protect those who may be particularly vulnerable to negative impacts of tourism.

The **Quebec Declaration on Ecotourism** (2002) (http://www.univeur.org/cuebc/downloads/PDF%20carte/72.%20Quebec.PDF) represents the outcome of the first International Year of Ecotourism as designated by the UN and the World Ecotourism Summit held in Quebec. It sets out a preliminary agenda and set of recommendations for the international development of ecotourism activities in the context of sustainable development, and builds on the World Summit on Sustainable Development in 2002 in Johannesburg that specifically called for sustainable tourism as one strategy to manage the natural resource base of economic and social development.

The Quebec Declaration was very much a multi-stakeholder approach, referring directly the roles and responsibilities of:

1   National, regional and local governments, e.g. that they develop destination-level tourism development policies and strategies that are in line with sustainable development;

2 The private sector, e.g. that they ensure that their activities minimise negative impacts on their local environment;

3 Non-governmental organizations, community-based associations, academic and research institutions, e.g. that they provide technical and educational support to other stakeholders;

4 Inter-governmental organizations, international financial institutions and development assistance agencies, e.g. that they incorporate multi-stakeholder dialogue processes into policies, guidelines and projects at the global, regional and national levels for the exchange of experiences between countries and sectors involved in ecotourism;

5 Local and indigenous communities, e.g. that they strengthen, nurture and encourage the community's ability to maintain and use traditional skills in a sustainable manner.

The most recent tourism-specific international frameworks with a sustainability focus look at the carbon footprint of tourism. The first of these is the 2003 Djerba Declaration on Climate Change and Tourism, followed by the 2007 Davos Declaration, a combined effort from the WTO and World Meterological Organisation which asked tourism to "rapidly respond to climate change, within the evolving UN framework and progressively reduce its greenhouse gas emission". The Declaration specifically recognised tourism's need to develop strategies to allow tourism to adapt to climate change, as well as ensure that resources are made available to poorer regions and countries (who are most vulnerable) are also able to meet the recommendations.

The World Travel and Tourism Council (2009) has also offered a set of aspirational carbon emission reduction targets specifically for the tourism sector, to reduce its emissions by 50% by 2035 (on 2005 levels). Achieving these targets has been explored using a combination of technological advancements to reduce energy use, shifts to lower carbon fuels and changes in tourism consumption patterns (e.g. longer stays, closer to home, focused on lower-carbon intensive activities). Scott et al. (2016) provide a comprehensive review of potential scenarios to reach these -50% targets, and conclude that these targets will be very difficult achieve, and require strong frameworks (which currently do not exist) to drive carbon abatement programs within the tourism sector. The alternative, relying on the purchase of carbon offsets, will be more expensive in the longer run and leave tourism vulnerable to the likely introduction in future of carbon policy changes.

4.5   Supply chain policies that shape sustainable tourism

Alongside these international frameworks exist a number of national laws and initiatives that will affect the sustainability of tourism. These may apply directly to tourism business, or alternatively may influence tourism's supply chain.

Key legislation & initiatives

Legislation often plays a large part in how you run your business, so it's important to be aware of the laws that apply to your industry. Key legislation that may affect businesses in the tourism industry includes:

- Competition and Consumer Act 2010
- Australian Consumer Law (ACL)
- Commerce (Trade Descriptions) legislation
- National marine safety laws
- State tourism legislation
- State liquor licensing
- State restricted trading days
- Anti-Money Laundering and Counter-Terrorism Financing Act 2006
- State gambling & gaming legislation
- Interactive Gambling Act 2001
- State wildlife management laws.

Mandatory industry codes & standards

- Food Standards Code
- Mandatory safety standards
- Franchising code of conduct.

Environment

Tourism businesses often rely heavily on the environment to explore and showcase the natural wonders of Australia, so they can have a potentially large impact on the environment including the local flora and fauna. The main environmental concerns that businesses in the tourism industry should be aware of include:

- Protection of national parks, forests or marine parks
- Protection of whales, dolphins and other marine life
- Protection of waterways including rivers, lakes, estuaries and wetlands
- Protection of threatened species
- Protection of aboriginal heritage sites and land
- Protection of world heritage and other heritage listed sights
- Waste management and reduction
- Sustainability.

See specific advice from the Department of Environment for tourism operators. Go to environmental management for advice on how you can manage your impact on the environment.

Figure 4.5: Examples of legislation and initiatives that apply to tourism in Australia, with reference to the Environment and sustainability. .

These national laws may both facilitate and hamper sustainability in practice, and should be checked individually for your local country, region or city.

Chapter 2 discussed the complex nature of the tourism supply chain, and Chapter 3 looked at opportunities to increase the linkages between tourism and suppliers in a region and, conversely, reduce leakages. When it comes to making tourism more sustainable, what happens in the supply chain will also affect the sustainability outcomes of the tourism sector. Greening the supply chain can be either deliberately managed by the tourism sector, or more often than not, various elements within the tourism supply chain are subject to their own sustainability standards.

Table 4.1: Global reporting initiative: supply chain management indicators (SCM) for tour operators. Taken from Weaver (2006), reproduced with permission from GRI (2002).

SCM1	Describe the supply chain management policy, objectives and targets on environmental, social and economic performance
SCM2	Describe the processes through which suppliers, by type, are consulted during the development and implementation of the supply chain management policy, described in SCM1
SCM3	Describe issues identified through supplier consultation and actions to address them
SCM4	Describe processes through which suppliers, by type, are engaged in the implementation of the supply chain management policy, described in SCM1
SCM5	State joint actions taken with suppliers by type, subject to support improvements in suppliers' own environmental and social performance
SCM6	Describe progress in achieving objectives and targets related to supply chain policy
SCM7	Indicate percentage of suppliers, by type, subject to supply chain management policy
SCM8	Indicate percentage of suppliers, by type, subject to supply chain policy that have a published sustainability policy, implemented a sustainability management system and/or have a staff person with management responsibility for corporate sustainability
SCM9	State types of information requested from suppliers, by type, on their: (a) environmental practices and performance, (b) social practices and performance
SCM10	Indicate percentage of suppliers, by type, subject to supply chain management policy that provided the requested information
SCM11	Indicate percentage of suppliers, by type, subject to supply chain management policy whose environmental, social and economic performance has been reported.
SCM12	State actions taken by the reporting organisation in response to suppliers' reported performance (as per SCM11), by type of suppliers.
SCM13	State actions taken to inform suppliers of customer requirements
SCM14	State contracting policy and how it is communicated to suppliers
SCM15	Describe joint initiatives with suppliers to improve environmental, social and economic conditions in destinations.
SCM16	State benefits for the reporting organisation from implementing the sustainable supply chain policy

In the first case, Weaver (2006) reports on the Global Reporting Initiative's standards on supply chain management indicators for tour operators. Sixteen items are listed for tour operators to consider and report on when choosing their suppliers; the procurer (the tour operator) is asked to report on their own standards set for their suppliers, and how they work with suppliers to raise their (the supplier's) social, environmental and economic performance with regards to sustainability. This approach is a good starting point for thinking about managing a supply chain for greater sustainability outcomes.

If the task appears daunting (which it probably does), it can be useful to break it down into first level and second level suppliers. First level suppliers include those directly supplying tourism services to tourists or their intermediaries (e.g. tour operators and travel agents). These will include accommodation providers, transport providers, food suppliers and so forth. Second level suppliers, on the other hand, supply tourism service providers with products and services, e.g. energy and water service providers, food and drink manufacturing, waste recycling, and so forth.

As first level suppliers are all directly involved in tourism, they ought to be responding the WTO's Manila Declaration on the Social Impact of Tourism (1997) and the 1999 Code of Ethics (covered in more detail in Chapter 6). Suppliers can be questioned directly about the actions they take to adhere to WTO's standards, using the types of questions set out by the Global Reporting Initiatives on supply chain management.

The second level suppliers are the ones who are most likely to be adhering to their own sectors' standards and codes of best practice that ought to include sustainability issues. Secondary suppliers are best broken down into categories and examined one by one: food production, building materials, energy supply, water, transport, infrastructure, waste management, and so forth.

It's worth searching for best practices in each of these, often spread across many countries. France, for example, is leading the way in minimising food waste; in 2015 it passed a law prohibiting supermarkets from throwing out food. Large supermarkets now donate unsold food to charity, provide it for animal consumption or compost left over waste. This simultaneously tackles SDGs 2 (zero hunger), 1 (no poverty), 12 (responsible consumption ad production) and 13 (climate action).

Read more here: www.policy-shift.com/single-post/2016/03/24/ To-Market-To-Market-Implementing-Frances-antifood-waste-law

When it comes to transport and urban infrastructure, many cities are moving away from cars as their primary mode of transport, and increasing infrastructure for cyclists, pedestrians and public transport. Many of these cities include major tourist destinations, including London and Paris: **www.businessinsider.com.au/cities-going-car-free-ban-2017-8?r=US&IR=T**

This extract from a TED talk describes how New York city planners have changed transportation achieve health benefits, economic benefits, tackle climate change and so forth: https://www.ted.com/talks/janette_sadik_khan_new_york_s_streets_not_so_mean_any_more#t-826766

When it comes to building codes, insulation is one area that is heavily regulated. Switzerland, a country known for doing things that just make sense, have taken this a step further, and the Swiss city of Basel is has mandated that, from 2002, all new and renovated flat roofs must be greened and also stipulates associated design guidelines under the City of Basel's Building and Construction Law. The city also provides subsidies for green roof installations. This approach targeted energy savings through insulation, but also became a haven for wildlife as well.

Figure 4.6: Basel's local council has mandated that all new buildings include a green roof as part of its climate change response

Opportunities for searching out and encouraging best practice in secondary level suppliers goes on and is worth spending some time researching. Alternatively a number of supply chain management companies are prepared to do it on behalf of big business: Marriott Hotels, for instance, outsourced the job to MindClick in 2013, and committed to spending 75% of their furniture budget on suppliers who completed a greenhouse gas emissions check. The result was that, of the hundred suppliers in the program, 56% are measuring their energy consumption and 40% are measuring GHG emissions, and this has led to an estimated 3,072,132.26 MT CO2e reduction through the supply chain, "the equivalent of removing 646,765 passenger vehicles from the road".

Read more here: mindclick.com/engine/wp-content/uploads/2015/05/Case-Study_Marriott-GHG-Emissions.pdf

Question

What are some of the ways in which Marriott's furniture suppliers could have reduced the carbon emissions of tourism? Which other areas of Marriott's supply chain (or any other hotel's supply chain) could also be very effective at reducing the carbon emissions of tourism?

4.6 Developing regional sustainable tourism strategic plans and policies

The international frameworks for sustainability in general (Section 4.3) and sustainable tourism in particular (Section 4.4), and examples of best practice in supply chains (Section 4.5) form a good launchpad for making specific destinations and attractions more sustainability, but as the old saying goes:

Failing to plan, is planning to fail.

It is vital for each destination, attraction and business to have its own sustainability plan, parts of which we will cover in other sections, but an overview of which will be provided here. In fact, one of the leading experts on sustainable tourism, Prof. Dave Weaver, sums up the journey towards sustainable tourism like this (paraphrased for brevity):

For tourism to be sustainable, we must bring together the economies of scale provided by mass tourism, and the ethical imperatives of alternative tourism. This synthesis can be achieved through one of three convergent paths:

1 **An organic path**, with little planning, responding to changes in context, e.g. market needs and resource restrictions.

2 **An incremental path**, whereby core alternative tourism principles are accompanied by careful management of carrying capacities as the tourism destination increases in popularity.

3 **An induced path**, involving a deliberate regulatory approach that embraces growth and a sustainability-focussed ethic.

This section will present several cases which represent these three pathways: (i) an induced path for Bhutan, (ii) an arguably incremental path for the Cocos Islands, and finally (iii) an organic path for Nuie, where tourism is struggling to grow beyond small-scale forms of nature-based, adventure tourism.

And while it is true that this summation of how tourism does, if at all, reach a level of sustainability, it is obvious that the second and third paths are the more desirable pathways if tourism activities are to minimise their negative impacts and maximise their positive ones.

So we'll start this section with a quick overview of tourism planning for sustainable destinations. There are a number of good handbooks on tourism policy and planning for destinations, e.g. Tourism Australia's *The Guide to Best Practice Destination Management*. The WTO/UNEP's joint publication on making tourism more sustainable is a good starting place, although a little dated now (UNEP/UNTWO), 2005). In this handbook, the authors lay out three guiding principles for any plan:

1 Setting the course

2 Developing the approach

3 Ensuring ongoing progress.

Setting the course involves ensuring that a holistic view of tourism as part of a wider system is adopted – competing use of resources, and mutual support between sectors should all be given consideration, as well as the law of unintended consequences between various tourism impacts and how these are managed (c.f. systems-thinking, Chapter 2). Multi-stakeholder engagement will be important, both through formalised partnerships as well as informal arrangements, and actions to strengthen democratic participation of interested parties should be reinforced (c.f. partnerships, Chapter 5). Long-term planning should be encouraged over short-term approaches, and both global and local impacts should be considered (c.f. issues of scale, Chapter 2). Tourists themselves should be invited to participate in the sustainability of the sector, promoting the links between sustainability and quality of experiences (c.f. experience design, Chapter 8).

Developing the approach starts with a 'polluter pays' mentality and adopts a precautionary principle (c.f. Chapter 7). A life cycle approach is encouraged for all tourism-related products and services, and functional alternatives with best impacts should be considered wherever possible (c.f. circular economies and management plans, Chapter 7). Finally, limits on tourism growth and visitor numbers should be given serious consideration and applied to destinations to avoid issues of overtourism (c.f. Chapter 3).

Ensuring on-going progress requires adapting to changing conditions (c.f. Chapter 7), as we know that tourism is highly sensitive to external conditions and changes, particularly in the case of a disaster and/or crisis and future risks must be considered during planning (c.f. Chapter 9). And finally, indicators should be used to monitor specific impacts, and progress towards desired goals (c.f. indicators, Chapter 7).

How these principles come together in a mature, well-resourced, and attraction-rich destination can be viewed on Destination Queensland's website (read the snapshot version of the plan here: https://www.destq. com.au/_data/assets/pdf_file/0009/1257858/destination-success-snapshot. pdf), as well as the research and data sourcing activities that went into the

final tourism plan, through a tourism research report (https://globaleco.com. au/Publications/Megatrends%20-%20tourism%20CSIRO.pdf) delivered by Australia's independent Australian federal government agency responsible for scientific research, the CSIRO (Hajkowicz, Cook, & Boughen, 2013).

A list of other examples of tourism plans for destinations has been put together by The Hong Kong Polytechnic University: www.polyu.edu.hk/htm/ academy/documents/nto_policies.pdf

Let's also look at how three smaller, and less well-resourced, destinations have applied (or not) these principles in developing their sustainable tourism. These cases are all taken from Hughes, Weaver and Pforr (2015) on sustainable tourism and illustrate Weaver's three alternative pathways to sustainable tourism: organic, incremental and induced.

First case: Nuie

Nuie is situated in the South Pacific Ocean, between Fiji, Samoa and Tonga, and is one of the world's smallest independent nations, with a surface of only 260km² and 64km of coastline, and a population of 1,600 residents (based on figures from 2016). The island is linguistically and culturally different to any other Polynesia island, and whilst self-governing, retains strong ties with New Zealand.

In terms of resources, Reiser and Pforr (2015) describe Nuie as having:

- poor accessibility and high transport costs
- a limited human and non-human resource base
- a small domestic market with strong dependency on export to and high import levels from New Zealand
- a lack of infrastructure
- a limited capacity to govern
- limited local financial capital for development, and a high reliance on New Zealand for aid.

Tourism in Niue remains small-scale, with 6,000 tourists in 2011. The sector is relatively new to the island, as the first hotel only opened in 1975. Tourism development in Nuie can arguably be viewed as socially and environmentally sustainable, but not economically viable. It is largely focussed on nature-based and adventure tourism products such as whale watching, diving and snorkelling, hiking and caving. Other attractions such as entertainment (nightlife), historic building and monuments are lacking in Nuie.

Tourism development has been slow to date, and has a dual ambition to boost economic performance, whilst recognising its dependency upon its pristine natural resources. The most recent plan at the time of writing the chapter, the *Nuie National Strategic Plan 2009-2013* (Nuie Government 2008, p.3) pledges to protect the "environment through sustainable environmental practices" and to grow tourism in a sustained and responsible manner by increasing visitation by 10% each year.

However, in addition to the issues associated with being a small island state, Nuie also has a lack of skilled labour and human resources, with only 663 residents in the labour force in 2011, many of whom work in the public sector, and the remaining number is probably not sufficient to sustain the labour-intensive tourism sector. Access is also restricted with only one weekly flight from New Zealand, mainly carrying Nuieans, and as the island has no natural harbour, sea access remains problematic.

Nuie suffers from limited water supplies and agriculture, as the rocky surface of the island can be difficult to cultivate. The island is also confronted with additional future challenges from climate change, increased frequency of extreme weather events, sea level rise, and coral bleaching (i.e. the degradation of one of its key natural attractions). Finally, Nuie remains heavily dependent on New Zealand for foreign aid, raising concerns about its ability to self-govern and as foreign developers can only lease the land, with long-term leases very difficult to obtain, foreign investment in tourism is limited

As you can see, the list of challenges facing Nuie is substantial. Tourism development remains small-scale and slow, representing what the authors call "small is beautiful and sustainable" (p.154) in its most literal sense. Reviews of the tourism sector on the island appear to indicate that it is indeed sustainable from an environmental and social perspective, it is the third dimension, its economic sustainability that is failing. It represents a case of organic sustainability, with visitor number and tourism development being constrained more by resource restrictions, than by deliberately planning and careful consideration.

Figure 4.7: Nuie's official tourism logo

Second case: Cocos Islands

The Cocos Islands are located in the Indian Ocean 2,760km north west of Perth in Western Australia. With the assistance of an Australian tourism researcher, Carlsen (2015), all of the key variables that represent the economic, social and ecological inter-relationships associated with tourism development were mapped out for the island, and the strength and type (positive or negative) of the relationships between each variable – an activity that is only possible because the Cocos Islands effectively represent a closed system for many of these variables.

By placing tourism development at the centre of the influence map, it become possible to visualise what would happen with increased tourism development in the Cocos Islands. For example, there would be increased waste generation, land clearance, water use and fishing effort, which will in turn have a negative impact on island biodiversity. Meanwhile, increased island biodiversity (negatively impacted by increased tourism) would have a positive impact on tourism development. On the other hand, increased tourism development will increase employment, in-migration and therefore island population and standard of living and so forth.

The idea was to anticipate the changes that result from feedback between the different variables, and suggest appropriate indicators that could track the impacts and sustainability of tourism development on the island, allowing adjustments to be made where necessary. According to Carlsen (2015), this would require ongoing monitoring of tourist flows, tourism expenditure, tourism investment, household income and living standards, employment, population and in-migration, resource exploitation, water use, land use and so forth. This incremental approach would help generate planning and policy recommendations, and advise the stakeholders (community, developers, etc.) on the implications of change, planning and policy actions.

Third case: Bhutan

Bhutan presents a fairly unique case of sustainable tourism development, as we noted in Chapter 1. We return to it here to take a closer look.

Bhutan's commitment to Gross National Happiness (GNH), as an alternative to Gross Domestic Product (GDP), has informed the development of tourism in that small country. GHN represents an alternative development paradigm that value its people's happiness over material wealth. It is founded on four pillars, namely:

1 The conservation and preservation of the natural environment

2 Cultivation and promotion of culture

3 Good governance

4 Sustainable and equitable socio-economic development (Ura and Galay, 2004).

The resulting GNH index is measured across nine domains, for example, psychological wellbeing, health, education, ecological diversity and resilience, and the 33 indicators of GNH progress associated with these nine domains. One key aspect of the GNH is the governance domain, represented by indicators of government performance, fundamental rights, services, and political participation. In particular, Bhutan's governance approach focuses on the rational of achieving happiness and wellbeing for its people through operationalising the four pillars of GNH described above.

The GNH Tourism Model has often be used to illustrate Weaver's 'deliberate alternative tourism' – small scale tourism based on strong regulatory frameworks. Bhutanese tourism began in the 1970s, and was originally state-owned and highly regulated. Privatised tourism operations began in 1991, and was estimated to include around 55,000 international tourists by 2012, mainly seasonal (spring and autumn), to avoid monsoons and excessive snow.

Tourism has been regulated through a number of mechanisms to reach its *high value, low volume* desired outcomes. These regulations focus on the high tariff system (around US$200/night/person) designed to deter backpackers, a royalty fee (US$65/night/person), physically limited access to Bhutan, either overland or through limited flight capacities. In addition, itineraries within Bhutan follow restricted routes, with approved drivers and guides. Accommodation and food choices are also regulated.

These measures have all been used to limit the number of tourists arriving in the country, encourage high yield tourists, control the distribution of visitors around the country and ensure that the benefits of tourism, through the royalty fee, support the rest of Bhutan's GNH plan. However, it is important to note that the regulations only apply to international tourists, not to regional tourists from India, Bangladesh and the Maldives. These regional tourists do not require a visa to enter Bhutan and numbers are therefore not controlled, and their impacts are not quantified.

4

Despite efforts to manage the number of tourists entering the country and focus on high value, Bhutan faces a number of issues that raise questions about the high value nature of its tourism offerings. These include:

- Tourist overcrowding
- Overall poor service quality
- Poor quality of infrastructure, particularly roads, toilets and hot water supply
- Problems with waste management, including litter at iconic tourist sites
- Local social habits, e.G. Littering
- Howling stray dogs at night

(Teoh, 2015, p.9)

Questions were raised about the future development of tourism in Bhutan and whether the country's social-economic development could be accelerated through a new tourism strategy. The new strategy, developed by an American consultancy group, advocated moving from "maximising foreign exchange earnings whilst minimising the adverse cultural and environmental consequences", i.e. *high value, low volume,* to "high yield with low negative impact in terms of social, cultural and environmental impacts", i.e. *high value, low impact* (Teoh, 2015, p.122, citing Brunet et al, 2001, p.254).

This move has proven controversial as there is an impression that the lure of economic benefits are compromising the GNH philosophy, and local tourism stakeholders believe that Bhutan is already struggling to meet the demands of existing tourists under the low volume model, without any additional expansionist programs. The new tourism strategy would therefore represent a move away from the previous induced pathway towards sustainable tourism, to an incremental pathway at best, or at worst, a move towards less sustainable mass tourism.

Review

Although it may sometimes feel that way, the sustainability of tourism does not sit in a vacuum. We already know that tourism is very much part of an open system, and is highly intertwined with other systems at local and global levels. This means that its delivery is accountable to a number of international frameworks designed to safeguard human wellbeing, the integrity of natural systems, the protection of cultural, built and natural heritage. All of these frameworks can assist planners in determining how tourism should be developed in ways that are sustainable, and apply as much to tourism itself, as to the secondary level suppliers that make up the tourism supply chain and which can have their own very interesting and effective approaches to sustainability.

To further assist tourism planners, a range of tourism-specific international frameworks are provided, highlighting areas worthy of particular consideration in destination planning, and focussing on stakeholder involvement – a topic that will be discussed in more detail in Chapter 5. The most challenging of these is, of course, managing the carbon footprint of tourism – an issue that goes beyond any single destination, and is a concern for all tourism providers. The highest GHG emitters of the tourism sector are currently exempt from any international frameworks on climate change, and the WTTC's aspirational goals of cutting tourism's GHG emissions by -50% by 2035 is proving challenging to say the least.

Developing a tourism plan that offers the best chance at creating a sustainable sector is essential, and largely context-specific. Weaver suggests that destinations can reach a state of sustainability through three different pathways – organic, incremental and induced – reflecting different levels of proactive planning, and government intervention in that space. This chapter has provided a few examples of destination-level plans and strategies. No matter which approach is adopted, the guiding principles of planning for sustainable tourism remain the same: a course needs to be set, the approach needs to be developed, and on-going progress needs to be ensured. The knowledge to achieve this is provided to you across the entire textbook, not just in this one chapter.

Finally, it is important to think of the sustainability of tourism as a wicked problem; many will argue that the even the term 'sustainable tourism' is outdated because in 30 years of talking about it, we have made so little progress towards achieving it. It's true that progress has been slow, painfully slow at times, and we've already discussed several reasons for this in Chapter 2. But progress is also slow because of the characteristics of wicked problems – there is no stopping rule, no definitive formulation, no immediate and ultimate test, no describable set of potential solution, each situation is essentially unique, linked to a number of other problems, and a one-shot operations, in that every implemented solution has consequences that cannot be undone.

To return to the juggling ball analogy, it is going to take a certain level skill and lots of on-going practice, balls will sometimes be dropped, but is essential to pick them back up again and keep trying. Which takes us to the next chapter… on building and maintaining partnerships for sustainable tourism.

Questions and exercises

1   Thinking about tourism as a tool for regional development, how might it be considered a wicked problem?

2   Find your local tourism destination management plan (or review the examples given in the text), what aspects of sustainability are included in the plan?

3   Bhutan has a unique tourism model, in your view is it sustainable?

4   Explain in your own words why the Paris Agreement is an important factor in the sustainability of tourism and what impacts it might have on the future of tourism.

Multiple choice questions

1 Which of the following is one of the characteristics of a wicked problem?

   a) They arise from deliberate acts of bad governance

   b) They are impossible to solve

   c) They are essentially unique to their circumstance and context.

2 Following the lead of ISO many companies are now including human rights as part of their social responsibility policies: True or false?

3 Agenda 21 should be applied by all signatories at a regional level: True or false?

4 The Paris Agreement covers all sectors that are major carbon emitters: True or false?

5 Which of the following is not part of the UNWTO One Planet Program?

   a) Encouraging greater stakeholder engagement and partnerships around sustainable consumption.

   b) Reviewing and directing sustainable tourism investment and financing

   c) Regulation of the tourism industry at an international level

Further reading

Fodness, D. (2017). The problematic nature of sustainable tourism: Some implications for planners and managers. *Current Issues in Tourism*, **20**(16), 1671-1683.

Hall, C. M. (2008). *Tourism Planning: Policies, processes and relationships*. Pearson Education.

Ruhanen, L. (2010). Where's the strategy in tourism strategic planning? implications for sustainable tourism destination planning. *Journal of Travel and Tourism Research (Online)*, , 58-76

UNESCO World Heritage Sustainable Tourism Toolkit, available from http://whc.unesco.org/sustainabletourismtoolkit/how-use-guide

References

Bennett, G., (1997). Niederlande, the Dutch National Environmental Policy Plan. In *Nationale Umweltpläne in ausgewählten Industrieländern*, edited by M. Jänicke, A. Carius and H. Jörgens. Berlin: Springer. pp.73-85.

Carlsen, J., (2015). Island Tourism: Systems modelling for sustainability. In Hughes, M., Weaver, D. & Pforr, C., *The Practice of sustainable Tourism: Resolving the paradox*, Oxford: Routledge, pp. 83-94.

Gossling, S. (2013). National emissions from tourism: an overlooked policy challenge. *Energy Policy*, **59**, 433-442.

Hajkowicz, S.A., Cook, H. & Boughen, N. (2013) *The Future of Tourism in Queensland. Global megatrends creating opportunities and challenges over the coming twenty years.* Draft for Comment. CSIRO, Australia.

Hughes, M., Weaver, D. & Proff, C. (eds.) (2015). *The Practice of Sustainable Tourism: Resolving the paradox,* Oxford: Routledge.

Nuie Government (2008) *Nuie National Strategic Plan 2009-2013.*

Reiser, D. and Pforr, C. (2015). Sustainable tourism development on Nuie: a catch 22? In Hughes, M., Weaver, D. & Pforr, C., *The Practice of Sustainable Tourism: Resolving the paradox,* Oxford: Routledge.

Rittel, H. W. & Webber, M. M. (1973). 2.3 planning problems are wicked. *Polity,* **4,** 155-169.

Scott, D., Gossling, S., Hall, M. & Peeters, P. (2016). Can tourism be part of the decarbonised global economy? The costs and risks of alternative carbon reduction policy pathways. *Journal of Sustainable Tourism,* **24**(1), 52-72.

Teoh, S. (2015). The governmentality approach to sustainable tourism: Bhutan's tourism governance, policy and planning. In Hughes, M., Weaver, D. & Pforr, C., *The Practice of sustainable Tourism: Resolving the paradox,* Oxford: Routledge, pp-113-132.

Ura, K. & Galey, K. (Eds.) (2004). *Gross National Happiness and Development.* Thimpu: Centre for Bhutan Studies.

Weaver, D. (2006). *Sustainable Tourism: Theory and practice.* Oxford: Butterworth: Heinemann.

Wood, R.E. (2009). Tourism and International Policy: Neoliberalism and Beyond. In Tazim Jamal and Mike Robinson (eds.) *The SAGE handbook of Tourism* Studies. London: Sage.

UNEP & UNWTO (2005). *Making Tourism More Austainable: a guide for policy makers.* UNEP/UNWTO.

4

5 Governance and Partnerships

Introduction

The previous chapter addressed frameworks and regulations that support the move towards sustainable tourism. On their own however, these are not enough. First, they need 'buy-in' from the people who will be affected by them, the stakeholders on the ground. Second, they may not always be fully supported by politicians and governors, who can overturn policies at different opportunities. We don't need to think any further than US President Trump making a shock statement on June 1 2017 that his country would withdraw from the Paris Agreement, jeopardising the whole process, as the US is one of the largest producers of GHG emissions.

These two issues, buy-in from stakeholders and support from managers, can be viewed as:

1 The 'top-down' approach – often starting out as a command and control governing approach which seeks stakeholder buy-in to translate the rhetoric of sustainable tourism into practical, on the ground, outcomes.

2 The 'bottom up' approach – where stakeholders seek to have on-the-ground concerns and actions taken up by policy makers, who are encouraged to consider the social, environmental as well as economic outcomes of their decision-making.

In addition to these two issues, a third issue is the move towards power-sharing and collaborative engagement between governments/regulatory bodies and other stakeholders is also driven by political ideologies and economic interests, labelled variously as the 'New Right', corporatist or neo-conservative agenda.

The idea is fairly simple: the underlying logic is that economic growth is good for society. So in pursuing pubic good, governments are looking for economic growth opportunities, which usually come from the private sector. Which in turn means that governments align with industry and focus on economic efficiencies and investment returns through public-private partnerships. It is then left up to the public, us average citizens, to stand in defence of all other public goods – including protecting the environment and intangible social values – a relatively new role for citizens and one in which we are not (yet) proficient in many cases.

A fourth point, and one that is linked to the idea above, that is very specific to the tourism context, is that the local community itself, as well as the natural environment, are actually part of the tourism 'product' for sale. Tourists interact with the local community in a way that is different and more extensive and intimate than in most development planning settings. This creates an added incentive to have local buy-in with tourism planning.

All of these issues lead to a requirement for a new form of engagement between policy makers and sustainable tourism stakeholders – an integrated approach that is neither top-down or bottom-up.

As a result we are witnessing the growth of a partnership approach, which in the case where it involves joint decision-making by the governors (political leaders) and the governed (citizens/stakeholders) about the exercise of authority and control, and is referred to as a governance approach. This involves multiple stakeholders from the public and private sectors, local community, NGOs and other relevant actors, representing complex, diverse and differentiated values that inform the development decision-making processes.

A governance approach is intended to create a more co-operative, participatory and communicative policy-style, which acknowledges the diverse and differentiated values that must be represented through consensus-based partnership building. It allows the views of stakeholders involved in any sustainable development projects to be represented by government and industry, as well as consumer groups, researchers and other interested parties.

And, as a result of including multiple participants, with their differing views, values, and positions, a governance approach ought to provide greater transparency and accountability as well as a more inclusive decision-making processes and therefore greater social legitimacy for these plans. Another outcome will be policies that are responsive to changing circumstances.

To understand how and why a partnership approach is necessary for sustainable tourism, and what makes up a good partnership, this chapter will consider the principles of good governance, some techniques for developing good governance, as well as some of the pitfalls. Next the chapter will explore one case of governance in practice. The final section will look at other forms of partnerships that can be useful in driving sustainability in tourism.

First though, it is worth making sure that we are starting from the same page, by clarifying what we mean by partnerships.

A **partnership** – the underlying principle of governance – refers to regular, cross-sectoral interactions, based on some agreed norms and rules, to address a common issue or develop a specific policy goal. Some of the common things that we want to look at when thinking about partnerships in this context, are:

☐ What is the problem domain being addressed?

☐ Who are the stakeholders and who do they represent (are they inclusive)?

☐ To what degree is agreement reached about how to act on the problem domain?

☐ What is the outcome and achievements of the partnership?

The final section of this chapter will consider other forms partnerships in tourism and how they can benefit the move towards greater sustainability. These partnerships are not so much concerned with decision-making and power-sharing in governance, but with co-learning for sustainability. We'll revisit this in Chapter 8 on operationalising sustainable tourism.

Key words and concepts

- Bottom up/top down
- Stakeholders
- Governance
- Partnerships
- Transparency
- Accountability
- Inclusiveness
- Explicit, tacit and embedded knowledge
- Enlightened self-interest
- Enterprise defence
- Civic engagement
- Interest-based negotiations
- Appreciative Inquiry
- Groupthink
- Tokenism
- Ladder of civic participation

5.1 Principles of good governance

There are a number of terms with which one must become familiar in order to practice good governance and be able to call out times when governance is poorly practiced. The key terms are:

☐ Transparency

☐ Accountability

☐ Inclusiveness

Transparency means that anyone can obtain information about how a decision was made, what factors went into the decision-making process and how these were weighed up. *Accountability* means that someone is taking responsibility for those decisions and their outcomes – and this must be someone with the power to rectify matters if decisions are poorly implemented or not implemented. *Inclusiveness* means that all stakeholders are represented, and not just those with the most experience at decision-making or the greater ability (in terms of position and resources) to do so.

In addition to these three fundamental principles, good governance should also be responsive to issues of social justice and equity, engaged in ethical behaviour, adopt a precautionary approach, be reflexive, engage in learning and be willing to innovate, encourage integration so that decisions are made with a sense of the system as a whole, and decisions are consistent across multiple departments and levels of government, and finally, should have built-in mechanisms of measurement to track their progress against all these criteria.

As with much of the rest of the material presented in this book, it should be obvious that adopting a successful governance approach is not easy: it requires both the willingness to engage, the interpersonal skills necessary for negotiation, and the knowledge and expertise to make effective decisions about sustainable development. In other words it requires a combination of (i) *explicit knowledge* – codified knowledge about how collaborations function well, decisions are made, policies are created, etc.; (ii) *tacit knowledge* – experience-based knowledge about the sustainability issues likely to arise through different tourism development scenarios; and (iii) *embedded knowledge* – knowledge about the type of community concerned, its values and norms.

It is rare that all three types of knowledge exist in full in any tourism development context, and it strongly recognised that there may be a need for support and capacity building within the local community before strong civic participation can be expected. After all, when was the last time you called or wrote to your local minister about an issue that you were concerned about, answered a call for public submissions about a new development, or how many of us would know where to start when it comes to saving a favourite natural area that we've just discover has been gazetted for development?

We'll return to this issue in Section 5.2. on ways to develop good governance and partnerships.

Another set of requirements have been identified as necessary for partnerships to lead to social responsible action (Spratlen, 1973, cited in Ryan, 2002). These are:

☐ Mutual benefits, which can sustain long-term relationships

☐ Enlightened self-interest, where societal needs are acknowledged and considered over the long-term, rather than short-term.

☐ Ethical awareness, in which a set of moral or social obligations are considered and valued as legitimate.

☐ Power and responsibilities, where the person holding power recognises the responsibilities that come with it.

☐ Enterprise defence, where the autonomy of various stakeholders is preserved.

When it comes to tourism specifically, Bramwell and Lane (2000) outline a number of benefits of partnerships in planning for sustainable tourism development:

5

Test yourself

- ☐ The diffusion of decision-making power and control to multiple stakeholders will support democratic principles.
- ☐ The people affected by changes may well be best placed to introduce change and improvement, and to bring their knowledge, skills and pooled resources to bear on the decision-making, planning and implementation of change.
- ☐ The involvement of stakeholders may increase support for the implementation and enforcement, building social acceptance of changes and greater commitment to see it through.
- ☐ A partnership approach develops its own co-learning dynamic, creating better communication, collaboration and negotiation skills that can serve the partnership in the future.
- ☐ Pooled knowledge and resources can also promote a creative synergy that can lead to new, innovative solutions not otherwise considered.
- ☐ The involvement of a range of stakeholders may lead to greater recognition of non-economic issues and interests under consideration, and strengthen the range of tourism products available.
- ☐ Resulting policies may be more flexible and sensitive to local circumstances and changing conditions.
- ☐ Linkages to other sectors may be explored, broadening the economic base of a given community or region.

Bramwell and Lane (2000) also note a number of issues and challenges that should be considered within the context of tourism collaborations:

- ☐ The range of stakeholders participating in policy-making may be limited in many contexts, under-representing certain groups with less power or experience in civic engagement.
- ☐ The issue of tokenistic partnership engagement may be encountered.
- ☐ Healthy conflict may be stifled or a lack of willingness to negotiate may be encountered.
- ☐ Genuine collaborations may be under-resourced and partners over-stretched.
- ☐ Accountability may become blurred and questions raised over government agents ability to protect the public interest.
- ☐ Vested interests and positioning may stifle innovation and new solutions.
- ☐ Uncertainty around outcomes may lead to reduced investor confidence.
- ☐ The need for information disclosure for decision-making may discourage entrepreneurial development.
- ☐ The complexity of involving a range of stakeholders may be costly and time consuming and lead to fragmentation in decision-making and implementation.

Question

In addition to the pros and cons listed above, can you think of any other benefits or disadvantages of using a governance approach in sustainable tourism development?

One area of key concern is that local community views may often be discounted or not even invited into the discussion, as the local community is not seen to have sufficient knowledge and understanding of tourism systems and their consequences (Moscardo, 2011).

The governance toolkit from UNESCO shows the importance of stakeholder understanding, and engagement as part of the foundations for good tourism planning for UNESCO heritage sites. To help managers achieve these, UNESCO has produced a series of guides to step managers through the process (Figure 5.1).

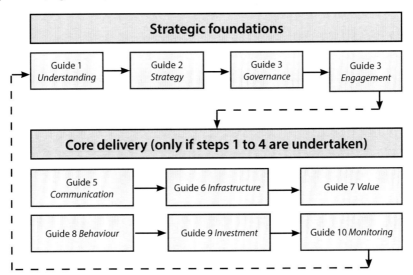

Figure 5.1: The importance of understanding, strategy, governance and engagement as part of managing UNESCO sites. (http://whc.unesco.org/sustainabletourismtoolkit/how-use-guide)

In fact, an analysis of 36 models of tourism planning models found that a third of the models did not mention stakeholders at all, while another third mentioned them as only a generic group (Moscardo, 2011). In fact, only 8 plans of the 36 mentioned residents and local community as major stakeholders. Instead the analysis found that the models were unpinned by five implicit principles:

Test yourself

1 That tourism development is necessary and desirable – effectively excluding an outcome that calls for no tourism development.

2 That tourism development is actually a form of business planning that aims to meet consumer needs.

3   That the focus is on economic and environmental issues, rather than social issues.

4   That the core actors are external agents, businesses and government agencies.

5   That destination residents have a limited role, at best, in planning and decision-making.

5.2   Developing good governance

Section 5.1. highlighted some of the key principles of good governance – most notably transparency, accountability and inclusiveness. But how are these actually practiced, and what do they look like when they are practiced?

The first and perhaps most obvious point is that good governance will combine good people skills with good knowledge about sustainable tourism development. The latter is covered in other chapters of this book, so it is the former that will be covered here. And a good starting place is the advice a business coach once gave me – always begin from a position of "you're OK, I am OK" and aim for a win-win outcome.

If this seems tricky, particularly when you are facing your favourite beach-front park being turned into a hotel complex, take heart that there are a number of negotiation techniques, conflict resolution, collaboration techniques and group-based census decision making theories that can help you out here.

At its most basic level, collaboration models usually include three stages:

1   **Problem setting** – identifying key stakeholders and issues.

2   **Direction setting** – identifying and sharing future collaborative interpretations; appreciating a sense of common purpose.

3   **Implementation**, also referred to as the **empowerment stage** – institutionalizing the shared meanings that emerge as the domain develops.

(Gray, 1989)

It is worthwhile noting here, that different communication styles will be required at different stages. In the first stage, one-way communication is most common, outlining the issue at stake, calling for interested parties to contribute and advising how, when and where this contribution will take place. Where necessary, strategies to build civic engagement capacity should also be implemented at this stage. In the second stage, two-way communication is essential; stakeholders must speak up and share their vision, concerns and so forth. Feedback is an essential part of this stage. In the final stage, two-way communication is also essential as negotiation takes places towards a general consensus on the direction to be taken.

This section will review two of these: interest-based negotiation, and appreciative inquiry. It is worth noting that the second of these, the appreciative inquiry, does not adopt a language of problem-setting. If these two don't appeal to you, many more theories and models exist, and you are encouraged to research these further. The important point is to know that you do not need to reinvent the wheel but that others have already done the thinking for you when it comes to implementing processes of public participation.

Stages	Facilitating conditions	Actions/steps
Stage 1 Problem setting	Recognition of interdependence Identification of a required number of stakeholders Perceptions of legitimacy among stakeholders Legitimate and skilled convener Positive beliefs around outcomes Shared access power Mandate (external or internal) Adequate resources to convene and enable collaboration process	Define purpose and domain Identify convener Convene stakeholders Define problem/issue to resolve Identify and legitimise stakeholders Build commitment to collaborate by raising awareness of interdependence Balancing power differences Addressing stakeholder concerns Ensuring adequate resources to allow collaboration to process with key stakeholders present
Stage 2 Direction setting	Coincidence of values Dispersion of power among stakeholders	Collect and share information Appreciate shared values enhance perceived interdependence Ensure power distributed among several stakeholders Establish rules and agenda for direction setting Organise subgroups if required List alternatives Discuss various options Select appropriate solutions Arrive at shared visions or plan/strategy through consensus.
Stage 3 Implementation	High degree of ongoing interdependence External mandates Redistribution of power Influencing the contextual environment	Discuss means of implementing and monitoring solutions, shared vision, plan or strategy Select suitable structure for institutionalising process Assign goals and tasks Monitor ongoing progress and ensure compliance to collaboration decisions.

Figure 5.2: A collaboration process for community-based tourism planning, based on Gray (1989).

Interest Based Negotiation

Interest Based Negotiation is one technique that has been applied in sustainable tourism planning. The Canadian destination of Banff – known for its nature and national parks as well as events and festivals (e.g. Banff Film Festival) trialled Interest Based Negotiation in the early 1990s, bringing stakeholders together for a 2-year regional tourism planning process (Ritchie, 2000). Briefly, the strengths of this approach were to improve the stakeholders' understanding of the issues involved, arriving at a common vision for the future of the region and facilitating the first steps towards implementation of the consensus-based recommendations (Figure 5.3).

Figure 5.3: Banff's tourism marketing is a reflection of the tourism management plan. https://www.youtube.com/watch?v=majkJmso8Kw

How did it work?

The starting point for this approach was a 'round table' process, where stakeholder groups with an active and proven interest in ensuring the economic, social and environmental wellbeing of Banff National Park were invited to the table. A total of 14 interest sectors ended up at the table, representing culture and heritage; natural environment; local environment; municipal government; federal government; First Nations – Siksika; First Nations – Wesley; Park users; infrastructure and transportation; social/health/education; commercial outdoor recreation; commercial visitor services; tourism and marketing and finally, the study's task force, including a facilitator/technical expert (c.f. explicit knowledge in Section 5.1).

These groups met monthly for a year, where the facilitator implemented the Interest Based Negotiation approach. The aim of this approach is to move away from 'positional bargaining' to focus on basic interests, and seek a 'wise' agreement (c.f. Chapter 6 on ethics). The approach seeks to avoid stakeholders digging into positions, only to have to dig them(selves) back out; looks at all options for mutual gain; uses objective criteria to settle differences of interest (rather than strength of will); and most importantly, separates people from the problem.

At the start of the process, each group was invited to address three sets of questions:

1   What is their authority and accountability: e.g. who do they represent and how do they communicate with their constituents, how are decisions ratified?

2   What are their sector's interests: e.g. what are they negotiating for, what do they hope to gain, what might they lose, what does success look like.

3 What is their sector's vision for the region: e.g. what do they want the region to look like in 10, 50, 100 years, and what kind of place do they want to leave for their descendants?

Next, the professional facilitator prepares a 'Summary of Interests', consolidating the range of interests submitted and identifying common interests, complementary interests, and interests that were apparently in conflict (Phase 1). These became issues for resolution. And this is where the technique starts to differ slightly.

Rather than adopt position statements (preferred solutions to the issues), the process focusses on the sectors' interests, that is, the factors (needs, wants, fears or concerns) that motivated the preferred solutions of the participants. To facilitate the move from positions to interests (Phase 2), groups were invited to ask open-ended questions of three varieties:

☐ **Probing questions** that ask for more information, e.g. *what is it about this that concerns you most?*

☐ **Clarifying questions** that sharpen understanding, e.g. *can you tell me more about what you meant when you used the word....?*

☐ **Justifying questions** that ask for evidence for the view expressed, e.g. *can you tell me how you plan to achieve this?*

Once all positions had been explored and understood, only then was a process to build a common vision started (Phase 3). In this phase, consequential questions were used to 'reality test' all possible solution presented to address the issues apparently in conflict, based on the interests explored in Phase 2. Consequential questions ask groups to look at the possible consequences of a position taken or a solution. The evolving discussion provides the basis for a Core Vision for tourism in the region and a number of supporting themes that will aid this core vision to come to fruition.

The final part of the process is to identify very specific policies and actions that would translate this vision into reality and how responsibilities for these policies and actions will be allocated. In this case, a tourism taskforce has been slowly working at implementing the changes over a number of decades to achieve the final Vision.

Download the Banff plan: https://www.banfflakelouise.com/sites/default/files/business_plan_-_2017.pdf

Appreciative Inquiry

Test yourself

Another approach that has potential usefulness in sustainable tourism planning is the Appreciative Inquiry approach. Commonly practiced in areas that require positive change, the Appreciative Inquiry approach can be understood as a questioning approach that seeks out the best in people and reveals the positive potential in the systems surrounding them. AI differs from a linear problem-based approach (issue → cause → solution) and encourages an iterative process, sometimes referred to as spiralling diagnosis, of "discovery, dream, and design" (see Cooperrider & Whitney, 2005, for further detail on the AI approach).

Essentially, it asks participants to identify examples of success, as well as explore imaginative ideas for the future, and in doing so, becomes an enjoyable process that allows individuals to frame problems in a more positive light. It aligns closely with the Giving Voice to Values approach in Chapter 6, which believes that most of us actually want to find ways to voice and act on our values in a beneficial way.

Instead of seeing something as a problem to be solved, it becomes a mystery to be embraced.

Appreciative Inquiry is most commonly used as a set of management practices to drive positive change by understanding how people construct their subject lives, through the meaning they place on things, the opportunities that they have and the values that they put into action when they are at their best and most effective. *Forbes Magazine*, for example, covers how the correct set of questions – based on AI principles – can lead to greatness.

 Read the article: www.forbes.com/sites/brettsteenbarger/2015/06/21/ appreciative-inquiry-leading-by-asking-the-right-questions/#6abc35fc1609

The approach is underpinned by eight principles.

1 The Constructionist Principle (Words create worlds);
2 The Simultaneity Principle (Inquiry creates change);
3 The Poetic Principle (We can choose what we study);
4 The Anticipatory Principle (Image inspires action);
5 The Positive Principle (Positive questions lead to positive change);
6 The Wholeness Principle (Wholeness brings out the best);
7 The Enactment Principle (Acting 'as if' is self-fulfilling);
8 The Free Choice Principle (Free choice liberates power).

(Whitney & TrostenBloom, 2003).

The way that the AI approach works is to encourage people to talk about past and present capacities: achievements, assets, unexplored potentials, innovations, strengths, elevated thoughts, opportunities, benchmarks, high point moments, lived values, traditions, strategic competencies, stories, expressions of wisdom, and visions of valued and possible futures. Most importantly, it relies on narration, people telling their stories of success.

As shown in Figure 5.4, Appreciative Inquiry is an iterative approach made up of four stages: Discovery, Dream, Design, Destiny – the 4 Ds of Appreciative Inquiry.

☐ In the **Discovery** stage, participants reflect on and discuss the best of what is, (what in this case is the topic under inquiry). It is during this stage that participants share their own stories, best experiences, high points, hopes, and values.

☐ In the **Dream** stage, participants figure out the common aspirations of all stakeholders and the ideal vision for the future, using collective creation techniques (e.g. mapping, drawing, storytelling) to symbolise that common vision.

☐ In the **Design** stage, the 'strategic intent' of the group is built around what can be and what is. This process generates a list of activities necessary to achieve these specific dreams, which are selected and prioritised by stakeholders based on their strengths.

☐ In the **Destiny** stage, actions are set up to support a continuous learning and innovation processes; this causes "what will be" to emerge, and sustains the initial momentum by continuously applying the approach to the systems and procedure in place to make the dream happen.

Activating the destiny phrase brings the organization back full-circle to the discovery phrase, in which continued application of the method may result in new topic choices, dialogues and continue learning.

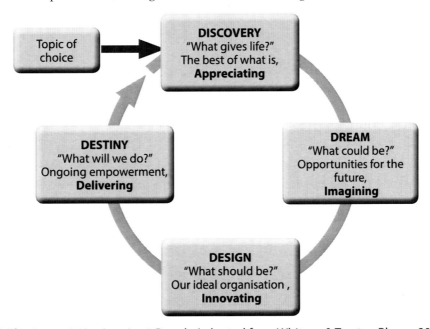

Figure 5.4: The Appreciative Inquiry 4-D cycle (adapted from Whitney & Trosten-Bloom, 2010).

Test yourself

It is most useful in arenas which require 'cooperative capacity' (Barrett & Fry, 2005), and it is this characteristic that make it suited to sustainable tourism planning. It has not yet, however, received much traction in tourism. Some academics have explored the potential for its uses in tourism (e.g. Aziz et al., 2013). It's been used as a research method to investigate best practice in volunteer tourism (e.g. Raymond & Hall, 2008), how tourism can contribute to biodiversity conservation and livelihoods, in particular pro-poor tourism in rural Nepal (Espiner et al., 2017), rural economic development in North America (Ainley & Kline, 2014; Koster & Lemelin, 2009).

The above studies hint at the potential for Appreciate Inquiry to be used a visioning tool as part of sustainable tourism planning, and particularly as a way of engaging with rural communities (although, there is no reason that it shouldn't work as well in urban setting). Raymond and Hall (2008, p.284) view it as an approach that is:

> sympathetic to the goals of community and regionally-based tourism plan-ning, . . . and sustainable development particularly with respect to desires for participation and equity across all members of the community.

The approach does, however, suffer from an image problem, where it can be viewed as a management fad, that is somewhat Pollyanna-ish and too focussed on "warm, fuzzy, group hugs" (Fitzgerald et al. 2001) which can potentially suppress the expression of negative experiences. On this last point, it must be emphasised that it is meant to supplement, not entirely replace, problem-based analyses. It will, nonetheless, be a brave group of people who first apply Appreciate Inquiry to the sustainable tourism planning of a region as a whole.

5.3   Challenges facing governance and partnerships

The case study chosen for this chapter will highlight some of the ways in which governance partnerships, even those with the best of intentions, can be problematic in a live context. There are a number of reasons for this, which we will cover here.

First, it is important to note that many stakeholders, and particularly the host community, may not be naturally skilled, experienced or knowledgeable enough to contribute to partnerships in a manner or time frame expected by planning processes.

This has been identified in the literature as "a lack of institutional struc-tures to support stakeholder engagement, a focus on outcomes rather than processes" (Budeanu et al., 2016, p.288). This may sound more ominous than it actually is, and simply represents the lack of maturity and therefore skills and experience in this space. We're told to involve others in the decision-making process, but we're not really clear on how, and we're not given the time to find out and lay the ground work for this collaborative decision-making process – that often involves giving host communities a complete understanding of the issues, principles and practices of sustainable tourism.

If a lack of experience and skills is one area to be aware of, there are another two (and others, but not covered here) that are slightly more concerning. These are *groupthink* and *tokenism*.

Tokenism

Tokenism has been a concern for as long as the literature on collaboration has existed. Back in 1969, Arnstein proposed a "ladder of citizen participation", where she distinguished between citizen non-participation, i.e. Level 1 Manipulation and Level 2 Therapy, and citizen control, Level 6 Partnership, Level 7 Delegation, and Level 8 Citizen Control. In between these two positions, she describes 'Tokenism', which consist of Level 3: Informing, Level 4: Consultation, and Level 5 Placation.

It is interesting that she places Informing and Consulting only halfway up her scale, and clearly within the 'Tokenism' category, as these are usually some of the terms we would associate positively with governance and partnerships. She makes the point that these are indeed important and valid steps towards genuine citizen participation but that, if they are not accompanied by legitimate power sharing then they are just window dressing.

Arnstein's (1969) use of the word 'Placation' may be less familiar to us. Here she argues that a number of hand-picked 'worthies', carefully selected individuals with limited representation of actual stakeholder groups, may be invited onto committees, allowing citizens to advise or plan ad infinitum. However, true decision-making authority remains with the original power-holders (usually government officials and business investors) who are given the right to judge the legitimacy or feasibility of the advice given by hand-picked representatives of other stakeholder groups.

The difference between these and the higher levels of true citizen control is the genuine sharing of power and access to resources.

Groupthink

The recognition of groupthink as an issue in collaborative decision-making dates back to 1972, where it was described by the social psychologist, Iriving L. Janis. Groupthink has nothing to do with the sharing of power, which may or may not be genuinely present, but instead relates to our tendency as humans to want consensus.

In groupthink, individuals may silence their dissent or concerns about a particular direction that the planning process is taking in order to maintain harmony with the group or avoid rejection by voicing opposition. While it does allow decisions to be made more quickly and efficiently, the downside is that those decision may not always produce the best outcome or even be the most logical!

It is most likely to occur where members of the group are most similar to one another (and this relates to the issue of handpicking stakeholder representatives in Arnstein's Placation level); where a powerful and charismatic leader is present; where the group is under a lot of stress (e.g. in highly contested tourism development situations); or where moral dilemmas exist (c f Chapter 6).

A number of preventative measures to groupthink exist – not least ensuring that if a charismatic leader exists that she or he gives her or his opinion last. Proactively encouraging dissent (and certainly not silencing it) is another useful technique, as well as explicitly assigning one individual with the "role of devil's advocate". These are all valuable techniques in sustainable tourism planning as well.

5.4 Case study: Gold Coast

The Gold Coast in Queensland, Australia, is a city that thrives from tourism, with world famous beaches used by tourists and locals alike for a range of recreational activities. In the mid-1980s the Queensland State Government commissioned a sand by-pass system at the mouth of the Nerang River, to create safe passage for vessels entering the Broadwater, a large expanse of water situated behind a sand isthmus to the south and several islands to the north of the river mouth. Upon completion of the project in 1987 the State Government announced that, as the area was the last remaining open beachfront land on the Gold Coast and was considered an important recreational area for the local community, it would remain as Crown Land, with no development to be approved north and east of Seaworld (the largest development in the area) with existing or future developments south of Seaworld not to be built more than three stories in height. This was ratified in both State Parliament and in successive Gold Coast City Council Town plans.

However, developers both foreign and local, could see the potential in the newly created land area, and different proposals began to emerge, including golf courses, hotels, high-rise developments and large static tourist attractions such as giant statues on Wavebreak Island. While most were rejected outright by the community and the two tiers (state and local) of government, in 2004 the State Government announced a proposal to build a Cruise Ship Terminal (CST) inside the mouth of the Nerang River, on the Spit. Little consultation was undertaken with the local community and businesses prior to announcing the proposal, and it's unclear what feasibility studies existed to see if the site of the project was either feasible or sustainable for the creation and successful operation of a CST. In response, various local community groups were formed and mobilised the local community holding one of the largest rallies ever seen opposing the project, resulting in a petition containing 36,000 signatures being tabled in the State Parliament opposing any development on the Spit. In late 2006, staring at election defeat, the Deputy Premier of Queensland announced that due to many "scientific and environmental reasons" the project was being cancelled, however, the scientific and environmental reports were never released to the public.

In 2012, the local Mayoral Candidate announced 48 hours before the polls closed that if he was elected, he would build a cruise ship terminal inside the Spit. The area was offered to potential developers for $1 in return for an 'operational' cruise ship terminal being built on the Spit. Again, the local community opposed the project. However, this time a community engagement process was initiated and the City of Gold Coast's (GCCC) first online poll as part of their inaugural "Have your say" program asked the question "Do you support a cruise ship terminal at the Spit?" to which 96% of respondents replied in the negative. This result was much debated publicly, and GCCC engaged a research consultancy firm to continue the communication process (P4Group, 2013). There have been a number of questions raised about this process in terms of inclusiveness (did they bias their reference group towards pro-development demographics) and the questions put to the community (there was no option that offered a 'no development' answer in some questions).

Still, the results of the public engagement process showed an overwhelming lack of support for the proposed development. Next a live forum was held at the local Yacht Club, where 175 people attended, however, only 50 attendees completed hard copies of the survey and again a majority "no development" result was recorded, but still did not appear to influence the decision-making process of local council, who argued that local activist community groups influenced the result. It is clear from this flawed previous attempt that the community had grave concerns regarding any future communication around development of the Spit and the Broadwater, when their previous responses have been ignored by both the proponents, the GCCC and the State. However, in January 2015, the State Government in power at the time was defeated at the state election and the incoming Labour government terminated the project, citing a lack of community support as the reason behind the project's demise.

ABC.NET.AU
Gold Coast Spit $3b casino resort canned by Queensland Government

Figure 5.5: Gold Coast Spit. http://www.abc.net.au/news/2017-08-17/queensland-premier-annastacia-palaszczuk-the-spit-qld-gold-coast/8815200

Question

In the case study provided above, which levels of Arnstein Ladder of civic participation do you believe are represented in the actions of the government? Justify your answer.

5.5   Other forms of partnership for sustainable tourism

One of the key characteristics of the tourism sector is that it relies on partnerships – bundling together experiences, services, products and attractions is key to making tourism work. Often these will be covered under destination marketing, and they do not necessarily have to have any form of sustainability focus or aim.

As the last part of this chapter on partnerships and governance, we will cover partnerships that do not have a governance focus but are nonetheless designed to drive tourism towards greater sustainability. These can be identified as sustainability-oriented learning clusters. We'll use the example of Australia's learning clusters as these are some of the best documented ones (McLennan, Becken & Watt, 2016).

We have already identified that much of the tourism sector is made up of small-to-medium sized enterprises or SMEs, which often have little access to information and resources that foster sustainability. A cluster approach, where businesses in concentrated geographical location voluntarily sign up to collectively assist one another to become sustainable, can help business overcome these issues.

Businesses within a cluster can pool their efforts, work together to secure funding support from government programs and gain access to sustainability-focused expertise and assistance. They also learn from one another, forming complex learning systems that support networking, innovation, knowledge creation and learning by sharing practices, processes and experiences (Eisingerich et al., 2010).

These clusters are known to work best when they have:

1   Strong network ties that facilitate knowledge transfer

2   An openness to new members and a reflexive approach to practice

3   Cross-network interactions that provide members with new knowledge, ideas and technologies

4   A source of learning activities

5   A set of socio-cultural institutions that facilitate learning.

In Australia, this approach was encouraged and facilitated through EC3 Global (now called Earthcheck), an international advisory group for tourism enterprises, destinations and community groups. EC3 set up a series of voluntary sustainability clusters around Australia between 2007 and 2012, across three regions (Victoria, Tasmania and Queensland). A total of 307 businesses signed up, representing accommodation providers, clubs, restaurants, visitor centres, event planners, marinas, day spas, tour operators, vehicle hire and attractions.

The businesses were provided with starter kits, information packs, and fact sheets, mostly carrying the 'green is gold' message that we covered in Chapter

Test
yourself

2, i.e. how being more sustainable would save them money. However, the researchers who evaluated the programme (McLennan et al., 2016) found that participating businesses very quickly hit a 'green wall', where small, cost effective sustainability initiatives had been implemented, e.g. insulation, composting, energy efficient appliances, but larger initiatives were still out of reach despite efforts to bulk buy certain sustainability-focussed products and services.

Nonetheless, the participants did show a high willingness to engage and the cluster was found to provide a good way of diffusing sustainability-oriented values across the participants and their communities. It also allowed groups to identify their 'cluster champions' and 'mentors' who would channel external sources of information and knowledge into the cluster through their own high level knowledge and strong networks, 'institutional gatekeepers' who have access to governments and research institutions, as well as 'innovation intermediaries' who act as brokers and enablers of innovation networks, and build credibility and trust in the cluster.

Interestingly, one finding to emerge from the evaluative study was a distinct conflict between the need for a standardised program that everyone could access and was clear to everyone – a one-size fits all approach – and the call for bespoke solutions that could be customised to each business depending on context, resources, orientation and ability. It calls for a "micro-macro framework for tourism sustainability" that can do both collective theorising and individual-level measurements (McLennan et al., 2016, p355).

Again, this reflects that need for that combination of explicit knowledge, tacit knowledge and embedded knowledge, which is difficult for any one person to cover, and in a domain that we have already identified as having the properties of a wicked problem. Not an easy task!

Review

Because the tourism product, service and experience almost always involve a mix of private enterprise, public services, attractions held in the public trust and the host community itself, there needs to be a common vision for tourism planning that encourages each stakeholder to look beyond her or his immediate needs to see a broader picture.

Governance-related partnerships provides the platform or forum to set this vision. If used properly, they can blend top-down and bottom-up approaches to sustainable tourism planning. They are an excellent starting place for any common vision is to get the relevant stakeholders around the table together. There is, however, a certain level of skill, experience and knowledge (think about your juggling!) necessary to move from getting people in the same room, to a shared vision of the future of tourism.

Ryan (2002) raises a number of important overarching questions that need to be considered for governance partnerships to be successful:

1   Who initiates the process? Can community visions be articulated before development proposals are formulated?

2   Do governments have the remit to invite stakeholder interests to be represented, or do stakeholder need to be make their own case?

3   How are the legitimacy of stakeholder claims assessed, who should undertake that assessment?

4   How do governance partnerships interact to other government structures and processes?

5   How can the private sector's sensitive commercial interests be weighed up against their responsibilities to the wider community?

The role of government must be considered in answer to these questions, before even the processes of good governance are drawn upon. These, in turn, should become part of any process of engaging with partners for planning and decision-making. The process should be undertaken with an understanding that conflict will likely arise during the process, and that a successful outcome will require a mix of explicit, tacit and embedded knowledge, unlikely to contained within any one person, and where such knowledge is lacking in one group, time and deliberate effort may need to be invested in building up relevant skills and knowledge in that group.

Failure to do any of the above will result in governance partnerships falling into Arnstein's lower level of civic participation, whether intentionally or unintentionally.

On a final note, it is important to consider how a partnership might wrapped up at the end of its lifespan. Do partnerships have life cycles? Partnerships can end more or less abruptly without any successful conclusion. Or, at a certain stage of the planning and implementation process, one partner may shoulder all further responsibility for the project. The original partnership may spawn further collaborations on other projects. Alternatively, the partnership may be absorbed into larger, regional partnerships and be sustained into future projects, retaining capacity and skills in that area.

Questions and exercises

1   What are the sustainable tourism issues currently happening in your local area? Which stakeholders are involved and using the Ladder of Citizen Participation, what level would you say your area is on when it comes to participation of stakeholders?

2   Think about, or actually do it, writing a submission about this issue. What would you say? Do you feel you have sufficient knowledge and skills to make a submission?

3   If you answered no to Question 2, where would you find more information that you need?

Multiple choice questions

1 In addition to transparency, accountability and inclusion, the book lists how many other necessary requirements for good partnerships?

   a) 3

   b) 5

   c) 7

2 Local communities are often not part of planning and decision-making processes as they do not have/are perceived to lack relevant knowledge of tourism systems: True or false?

3 The interest based negotiation approach uses which type of questions to identify stakeholders' interests?

   a) Descriptive, probing and justifying

   b) Probing, explanatory and clarifying

   c) Probing, clarifying and justifying

4 An appreciative inquiry approach is best used when cooperative capacity building is desirable: True or false?

5 Network-based partnerships work best when?

   a) They are open to new members and cross-network interactions create awareness of new ideas that can be shared through strong internal networks

   b) Strong internal networks are used to generate new ideas

   c) There is an open system where knowledge is generated and shared by anyone

5

Further reading

Bramwell, B. (2013). Governance, the state and sustainable tourism: A political economy approach. In *Tourism Governance*, pp. 59-78. Oxford: Routledge.

Bramwell, B., & Lane, B. (2011). Critical research on the governance of tourism and sustainability. *Journal of Sustainable Tourism*, **19**(4-5), 411-421.

Beaumont, N., & Dredge, D. (2010). Local tourism governance: A comparison of three network approaches. *Journal of Sustainable Tourism*, **18**(1), 7-28.

Hall, C. M. (2011). Policy learning and policy failure in sustainable tourism governance: From first-and second-order to third-order change? *Journal of Sustainable Tourism*, **19**(4-5), 649-671.

Ruhanen, L. (2009). Stakeholder participation in tourism destination planning another case of missing the point?. *Tourism Recreation Research*, **34**(3), 283-294.

References

Ainley, S. & Kline, C. (2014). Moving beyond positivism: Reflexive collaboration in understanding agritourism across North American boundaries. *Current Issues in Tourism*, **17**(5), 404-413.

Arnstein, S.R. (1969). A Ladder of Citizen Participation. *Journal of the American Planning Association*, 35(4), 216-224.

Aziz, R. C., Abdul, M., Aziz, Y. A. & Rahman, A. A. (2013). Appreciative Inquiry: An alternative research approach for sustainable rural tourism development. *Journal of Tourism, Hospitality & Culinary Arts*, **5**(2), 1-18.

Barrett, F. J. and Fry, R. E. (2005). *Appreciative Inquiry: A positive approach to building cooperative capacity*. Chagrin Falls, OH: Taos Institute Publications.

Bramwell, B. & Lane, B. (2000). Collaboration and partnerships in tourism planning. In B, Bramwell, & B. Lane (eds.) *Tourism Collaboration and Partnerships: Politics, Practice and Sustainability*. pp. 1-19.

Budeanu, A., Miller, G., Moscardo, G., & Ooi, C. S. (2016). Sustainable tourism, progress, challenges and opportunities: an introduction. *Journal of Cleaner Production*, **111**, 285-294.

Cooperrider, D. & Whitney, D. (2005). *Appreciative Inquiry: A positive revolution in change*. Berrett-Koehler Publishers.

Eisingerich, A. B., Bell, S. J., & Tracey, P. (2010). How can clusters sustain performance? The role of network strength, network openness, and environmental uncertainty. *Research policy*, **39**(2), 239-253.

Espiner, S., Stewart, E. J., & Lama, L. T. (2017). Assessing the effectiveness of 'Appreciative Inquiry'(AI) in Nepali pro-poor tourism (PPT) development processes. *Tourism Planning & Development*, **14**(3), 369-388.

Fitzgerald, S.P., Murrell, K.L. & Newman, H.L. (2001) Appreciative inquiry: The new frontier, in: J. Waclawski & A.H. Church (Eds) *Organizational Development: Data driven methods for change*, pp. 203–221, San Francisco, CA: Jossey-Bass.

Gray, B. (1989). *Collaborating: Finding Common Ground for Multiparty Problems*. San Francisco: Jossey-Bass.

Koster, R. L. & Lemelin, R. H. (2009). Appreciative inquiry and rural tourism: a case study from Canada. *Tourism Geographies*, **11**(2), 256-269.

McLennan, C.L., Becken, S. & Watt, M. (2016). Learning through a cluster approach: lessons from the implementation of six Australian tourism business sustainability programs. *Journal of Cleaner Production*, **111**, 348-357.

Moscardo, G. (2011). Exploring the social representations of tourism planning: issues for governance. *Journal of Sustainable Tourism*, **19**(4-5), 423-436.

Raymond, M.E. & Hall, C.M. (2008). The potential for appreciative inquiry in tourism research. *Current Issues in Tourism*, **11**(3), 281-292.

Ritchie, B. (2000). Interest based formulation of tourism policy for environmentally sensitive destinations. In B, Bramwell, & B. Lane (eds.) *Tourism Collaboration and Partnerships: Politics, Practice and Sustainability.* pp. 44-77.

Ryan, C. (2002). Equity, power sharing and sustainability – issues of the 'new tourism'. *Tourism Management,* **23**, 17-26.

Whitney, D. & Trosten-Bloom, A. (2003) *The Power of Appreciative Inquiry: A practical guide to positive change,* San Francisco: Berrett-Koehler.

5

6 | Ethics and Values

Introduction

Ethical concerns underpin the sector of sustainable tourism. Ethics is what allows us to make decisions about daily interactions with others and the world around us – it is fundamental to constructing the types of sustainable relationships that we have already discussed in Chapter 1. At its most basic level ethics distinguishes right from wrong.

Its place in sustainable tourism is so important that an ethics-based platform has been suggested as an extension of the advocacy → cautionary → adaptancy → knowledge-based platforms that we reviewed in Chapter 1. Macbeth (2005) calls for a sixth platform in tourism studies, an ethics platform – he places this even after a fifth sustainability platform. An ethics platform provides us with the moral compass to make decisions about all our travel-related decisions, especially the hard ones that we don't like to think about.

Discussions of ethics in tourism are not new; ethics in this case is concerned with moral judgments, standards and rules of conduct, and is usually understood as the ethical behavior of operators and less commonly as the ethical choices and preferences of the tourist. Studies of ethics in the tourism realm have focussed on ethical challenges at an operational level (and associated managerial decision-making), codes of ethics within the industry, the use of ethics as a marketing tool, ethics in tourism education, and finally ethical considerations the development and planning of tourism and related impacts on social, cultural and natural environments (Hultsman, 1995; Weeden, 2002; Yaman & Gurel, 2006).

One common thread to all studies of ethics in tourism is that, compared to other sectors, it is under-studied. One lead author in this area has argued that tourism is more often than not viewed as

> *"a club that bases its ethics on being free to do and say as one pleases [...]:*
> *I paid for it, so I deserve it"* (Fennell, 2006, p.356).

The hedonic nature of tourism means that we do not think about ethics as much as we perhaps should do. Moreover, as we have already discussed in Chapter 2, that relationships in tourism can be tenuous or ephemeral, and

Test
yourself

therefore appear less important or salient than relationships in our everyday lives. In fact, some researchers have stated that "the absence of ethical leadership in the tourism industry has been truly 'astounding'" (Donyadide, 2010, p.429). Indeed, of all the reasons to become more sustainable, ethical and moral arguments are often deliberately excluded as being the least considered factor by most tourism businesses (Hall & Brown, 2006).

On the other hand, Hall and Brown (2006, p.6) outline at least five reasons why tourism would particularly benefit from the application of ethics:

1   It is an activity focussed on human behaviour.

2   It includes several different actors representing a range of perspectives and objectives.

3   It has an applied context.

4   It has social, cultural, economic, ecological and political dimensions.

5   It can create a range of different combinations of impacts in a wide variety of contexts across the globe.

This chapter will introduce some of the basics of ethical thinking and decision-making, how and why these apply to tourism. We'll look at some specific cases where the ethical dimensions of tourism are particularly challenging, why talking about ethics can be uncomfortable and why it is important that we give voice to our values, in a way that acknowledges and diffuses that discomfort. Those stakeholders who do this well, often through the framework of Corporate Social Responsibility, are those most likely to achieve sustainability.

As a little thought experiment, consider that most tourism businesses operate within an interconnected system, facing many of the same challenges, constraints and policies, so why are some clearly more progressive in terms of sustainability than others? This is where the issue of ethical decision-making and giving voice to values may make all the difference in our progress towards greater sustainability.

6

Key words and concepts

- Deontology
- Moral relativism
- Utilitarianism
- Ethics of care
- Virtue ethics
- Phronesis

- Moral dilemma
- Preference projection
- False consensus bias
- Corporate Social Responsibility
- Certification schemes

6.1 Basics of ethics

Many of us are used to operating out of a rational decision-making process – what is sensible, and more often than not, what is sensible according to principles of entrepreneurial self-interest. An ethics-based approach asks instead what is *good* (rather than what is *sensible*), and most importantly what is good for others.

But the question of what is good is also not easy to answer, and is commonly the starting point of an ethical position – the literature lists a range of positions including moral relativism, utilitarianism, rights, distributive justice, communicative ethics, ethics of care, the ethics of difference and the ethics of authenticity (Smith & Duffy, 2003). For the uninitiated the literature is confusing, but this basic understanding is important to distinguish black from white, and question whether grey can ever be better than either.

Four different understandings of what is right form a starting point for ethics:

- ☐ A **deontological** position talks about moral duty; an act is ethical if it adheres to that duty. There are rules established by society that must be abided by, black and white, regardless of your personal sense of what is right based on consequences of that moral duty.

- ☐ A **utilitarian** position does consider the consequences of an action, and tells us that we should act based on securing the greatest good from that action. There is no black and white and each action must be weighed up according to actors, context and consequences.

- ☐ **Relativism** delves even deeper into the shades of grey and says that there is never an absolute moral wrong or right, instead our morals evolve and change with social and cultural norms over a period of time, and it is up to the individual to establish his or her own moral compass (subjective relativism) or act in accordance with their socio-cultural norms of right and wrong (cultural relativism).

- ☐ **Virtue ethics** on the other hand, relates entirely to the individual and her or his virtues, as well as her or his ability to practice those virtues wisely, with– what Aristotle called *phronesis* – discretion and with good intent. There is no codifiable set of ethical principles, based either on moral duty, good consequences or social norms, as such.

These different positions set up how we view right and wrong, and how much we engage with shades of grey, and can heavily influence the outcomes of ethical decision-making.

These starting positions are just that – a starting position. Next we need to act on these positions, through an ethical decision-making process. The starting point for ethical action is the recognition of a moral dilemma – an ethical transgression – where an ethics-based decision-making process needs to be employed.

Rest's (1986) model is perhaps the best known; he described four basic components which are

i recognizing a moral issue,

ii making a moral judgment,

iii establishing moral intent, and

iv engaging in moral behavior or action.

Individuals follow a process of recognizing that a moral dilemma exists, evaluating choices and outcomes, choosing how one intends to act, and lastly taking moral action, the actual behaviour in the situation. If any of these steps in the process are not taken, an ethical decision will not be made. The initial point, recognizing that a moral dilemma exists, relies on engaging with ethical issues in everyday life, and training in ethics of the type usually delivered in Business courses. For example, in our Chapter 1 example of coffee, beer and chocolate, being aware of the social and environmental issues related to the production of chocolate and evaluating the personal impact of choosing Fairtrade chocolate over other forms of chocolate, choosing the latter and finally buying it, are all part of the ethical decision-making process.

However, ethical decision-making will be mediated by a number of other issues. In a study of travel agents who personally support conservation, and perhaps even preferentially sell tours with a conservation-focus (Mossaz & Coghlan, 2017), it was found that five other ethical variables played an important role:

1 Moral intensity of an issue and a sense of moral agency (Jones, 1991),

2 Cognitive effort, i.e. the evaluation of relevant data (Street et al., 1997)

3 Thinking styles (Groves et al., 2007)

4 Preference projection (Brenner & Bilgin, 2011)

5 False consensus bias (Wiltermuch et a.l, 2013)

Moral intensity focuses on risk issues of likelihood, consequences and concentration of effect, temporal immediacy and proximity and social pressures (consensus) regarding the action. That is, moral intensity refers to how likely and severely the decision-maker perceives the effects of the decision upon him or herself. In tourism, this proves tricky, as the impacts of tourism are often firmly removed from the everyday lives of those who create the impacts. Moral agents are described by Jones (1991) as individuals who will make ethical decisions based upon a process of reasoning, through self-reflection, on the ethical dilemma. They must perceive themselves to have some responsibility towards the dilemma and some form of agency towards it – issues that were covered in Chapter 2 as problematic in tourism.

Cognitive effort reflects the degree to which decision-makers are willing and able to expend cognitive effort in resolving ethical issues. It is the diligent evaluation of relevant information (Street et al., 1997).

Thinking styles have also been investigated as an independent variable in ethical decision-making; Groves et al. (2007) found that employees with a balanced thinking style, using both linear (rational, cost-benefit approach) and non-linear (emotional, gut-feeling approach) are the most likely to seek out ethically-relevant information and make ethical and socially responsible decisions. Emotional responses have been found most often to trigger the recognition of an ethical dilemma. Therefore, individuals who are receptive to nonlinear thinking sources such as emotions, feelings and intuitions are more likely to recognize the moral implications of a given dilemma– a finding that is supported in tourism research by Malone et al.'s (2014) study of the role of emotions in choosing ethical tourism.

Two other issues can inadvertently affect our ethical decision-making process: **preference projection** and **false consensus bias**. Decision makers commonly assume that others are likely to share their own preferences, and of course, their own preferences are more salient in their own minds and therefore likely to come to the fore when making decisions for others. As with cognitive effort, unpacking an option, making its characteristics explicit, will also enhance its salience and can help to avoid the process of preference projection. Finally, false consensus bias represents a tendency for people to assume that others hold the same opinions as they do. If we make assumptions about people's travel motivations (pleasure and/or novelty seeking) and their likely response to efforts to curb social or environmental impacts, we already putting the brakes on our progress towards sustainability – false consensus bias can inhibit moral discourse and instead encourages discuss superficial, or socially 'safe', aspects.

Question

Describe in your own words why you think people might not be willing to discuss and act upon ethical issues in tourism. Look at your response and see if it matches any of the six issues listed above (recognising a moral dilemma, feeling the moral intensity of an issue/feeling like one has agency, the cognitive effort that goes with it, our thinking styles, preference projections or false consensus bias).

The result is what has been called 'moral muteness', where professionals, particularly those in a situation of brokering sales and/or information exchanges, will avoid discussing moral issues in a public space in order to maintain harmony and/or authority.

Test yourself

To combat these issues, we need to have a solid understanding of tourism-related issues, covered in Chapter 1 to 4, and in particular in Chapter 3; hone our ability to identify a moral dilemma or ethical transgression; develop our capacity for ethical decision making, knowing what we do about what can get in the way of ethical decision-making; and finally, learn to give voice to our values. Let's focus now, on how these apply in the tourism sector.

6.2   Ethics in tourism

The issue of ethics as a part of sustainability in tourism is perhaps under-developed. In fact, of all the reasons to become more sustainable, ethical and moral arguments are often deliberately excluded as being the least considered factor by most tourism businesses (Hall & Brown, 2006). Matters of ethics in tourism is often described in rather vague terms. They focus on specific areas of concern (e.g. sex tourism, displacement of local communities, subjugation of women, the exploitation of wildlife, c.f. Hall and Brown, 2006) but without really unpacking the ethical issues at stake, how to talk about them, what to do about them or what their relationship is to sustainability.

Another common way that ethics are covered in tourism is through the use of codes of conduct. The World Tourism Organisation's Global Code of Ethics for Tourism (UNWTO, 1999). The latter represents a set of 10 key principles that cover the economic, social, cultural and environmental components of travel and tourism, and are addressed to governments, the travel industry, communities and tourists. These are supported by the World Committee on Tourism Ethics (WCTE), the body responsible for interpreting, applying and evaluating the provisions of the WTO's Global Code of Ethics for Tourism.

Table 6.1: The WTO's 10 Principles in its Global Code of Ethics for Tourism.

Article 1	Tourism's contribution to mutual understanding & respect between peoples & societies
Article 2	Tourism as a vehicle for individual and collective fulfilment
Article 3	Tourism, a factor of sustainable development
Article 4	Tourism, a user of the cultural heritage of mankind and contributor to its enhancement
Article 5	Tourism, a beneficial activity for host countries and communities
Article 6	Obligations of stakeholders in tourism development
Article 7	Right to tourism
Article 8	Liberty of tourist movements
Article 9	Rights of the workers and entrepreneurs in the tourism industry
Article 10	Implementation of the principles of the Global Code of Ethics for Tourism

6

http://ethics.unwto.org/content/global-code-ethics-tourism

As with many codes of ethics, the interpretation of the Articles in the day to day running of tourism proves tricky. These are some of the ways that each Article can be understood in a tourism context.

Test yourself

Article 1 asks that tourists respect the law and take responsibility for acquainting themselves with local laws and characteristics before visiting. It is important that tourists observe local dress codes (e.g. dressing modestly, wearing long pants and sleeves regardless of the temperature, and food habits (e.g. being sensitive to religious customs such as Ramadan in predominantly Muslim countries), and so forth.

Article 2 states that tourism activities promote the human rights of hosts and guests, and particularly those of vulnerable groups (c.f. Chapter 4). This raises important questions such as land reclamation for tourism development – Human Rights Convention Article 17: "No one shall be arbitrarily deprived of his property".

Article 5 is similarly concerned with how tourism can raise the standard of living within a community.

Article 7, the right to tourism, is often debated by those who question the carbon footprint of tourism, and feel that promoting the right to tourism may not be sustainable unless we find ways to lower this carbon footprint to within the bounds of the Paris Agreement (c.f. Chapter 4). Instead the original Human Rights Convention Article 24 might be better employed: "Everyone has the right to rest and leisure, including reasonable limitation of working hours and periodic holidays with pay".

Some authors do provide more guidance in understanding ethics in tourism. In her paper on quality in tourism, Holjevac (2008) lists the types of values that underpin ethical behaviour in tourism, e.g. honesty, justice, fairness, wisdom, kindness, faithfulness, moderateness. A values-based approach such as this one is useful in a number of ways.

To understand how, let's quickly return to the business case for sustainability presented in Chapter 2: 'green is gold' likely reveals a bi-directional relationship between corporate social responsibility and corporate financial performance. This relationship can be explained by one or both of two alternative approaches: the 'slack resources' approach and the 'good management' approach. Here we need to consider the latter of the two: the good management approach, where doing the right thing by others targets the same skills as doing well financially. Interestingly, researchers who unpack this "doing the right thing" element find that it usually comes down to an individual's personal ethic of practicing values such as honesty, justice, fairness, wisdom, kindness, faithfulness, moderateness. In other words, these businesses are practicing virtue ethics within their sustainability efforts.

Garay and Font (2015) describe sustainability as a "value-driven journey, influenced primarily by the development of environmental consciousness and personal, socio-cultural and situational factors of the individual business-owners" (p.336). We see evidence of this in research on why small hospitality operations decide to implement environmental measures in their businesses (Tzschentke et al., 2008). Similar results are reported in studies on transport and personal carbon footprints (Nordland & Garvill, 2003). Meanwhile a sense of moral obligation provides a strong mediating factor in people's engagement in pro-environmental behaviours in general. (van der Werf et al., 2013).

Developing the type of moral compass, being aware of one's own values, knowing when these have been transgressed and how to respond when they have is key part of an ethics-based approach to sustainable tourism – which, as mentioned in the introduction, is not about doing what is sensible (perhaps more akin to the business case for sustainability) but about doing what is right. In a book on ethics and tourism development, Smith and Duffy (2003) suggest that ethics "will not allow us to 'solve' complex equations simply, but it might help us interpret and communicate to other what is it that we think is right or wrong about a certain situation and why" (p.3).

To start us on our journey of identifying tourism ethical dilemmas, the NGO Tourism Concern provides a series of vignettes on various dilemmas from conforming to religious or cultural dress codes, taking photos, haggling, participating in spiritual ceremonies to visiting animal rescue centres:

Find them here: /www.tourismconcern.org.uk/ethical-travel-dilemmas/

Specific cases in tourism

One of the foremost authors in this space, David Fennell (2006) provides a set of illustrative case studies, e.g. sex tourism, all-inclusive mass tourism or ecotourism, where he sets out the basic issue, the specific ethical issue, and the moral decision-making framework that can be (best) applied. We're going to do the same in this chapter, to hone the skills that we discussed above, and go through the various considerations (contrasting ethical decision-making frameworks, moderators influencing decision-making, processes of decision-making) that may influence the final outcome resulting from the ethical transgression. To complete this task we will focus on four areas:

☐ Wildlife tourism

☐ Sex tourism

☐ Medical tourism

☐ Enclave tourism

First case: Animals in tourism

In the case of animals in tourism, the issue is identified as tourists transgressing rules set out to prevent harm occurring to wildlife. In the most minor cases, this transgression can include violating animals' personal space and touching animals, in the more severe cases exploiting animals for entertainment. The latter include zoos, circuses, aquaria, street performers (e.g. cobra dancing), animal rides (e.g. elephants), fights (e.g. bull fights or bear baiting), or killed as part of the souvenir trade and hunting tourism. A number of NGOs have comprehensive guides to animal welfare and tourism; Tourism Concern and Responsible Travel are two NGOs that have guidelines for tourists wanting to know more about animal rights

Read the guidelines here: https://www.responsibletravel.com/copy/ animal-welfare-issues-in-tourism

https://www.tourismconcern.org.uk/wp-content/uploads/2016/02/ Animals-in-Tourism-lWeb-FINAL.pdf

6

Hunting tourism is one area that hit the news in a big way back in 2015. In June 2015, an American dentist paid $54,000 to bow-hunt Cecil, a 13 year old male lion in a national park in Zimbabwe. You or I may (or may not) have an instant reaction to hunting as being wrong or bad. Many would argue that hunting tourism has many positive benefits – the $54,000 paid to shoot Cecil the lion represents a substantial injection of cash into local livelihoods and/ or conservation funds if redirected to the national park. The Africa-based organisation CAMPFIRE (Communal Areas Management Programme for Indigenous Resources) is frequently held up as a flagship project of tourism benefiting local communities and derives 90% of its income from hunting. Its website offers a compelling case in favour of hunting:

Read their case for hunting here: http://www.campfirezimbabwe.org/ index.php/projects-t/14-hunting

These represent arguments that fall into the utilitarian and relativism perspectives of ethics – the killing of one animal achieves a greater good for local people and conservation in general (reducing poaching, setting aside land for wildlife, providing low volume/high yield tourism, delivering environmental education and scientific research programs) and conforming to social norms: "For thousands of years, rural Africans have relied on plentiful supplies of impala and other game animals for meat, clothing and income". Arguments against hunting take the form of deontological ethics: it is wrong to kill another living being (unnecessarily/for sport). A virtue-based ethical approach may rely on the virtue of compassion, taking a position that it is both wrong to kill, and local people should have access to secure livelihoods, and may propose an alternative (photographers and film crews also draw significant revenue for opportunities to view wildlife).

These responses rely on identifying the suffering and death of animal for human entertainment as a moral issue, judging the killing of wildlife to be an ethical transgression, by considering alternative options to avoid harm to animals and support local livelihoods (e.g. catch and release style hunting in a similar manner to fishing or other forms of income generation), and follow through on the ethical-decision making through personal choices, as well as unpacking the issue for others to discuss, increasing its moral intensity, engaging with the cognitive effort to understand the relevant information, allow the emotional response to be heard alongside the rational responses, and avoid issues of preference projection and false consensus.

Second case: Sex tourism

Sex tourism is defined by the WTO as *"trips organized from within the tourism sector, or from outside this sector but using its structures and networks, with the primary purpose of effecting a commercial sexual relationship by the tourist with residents at the destination"*. Some destinations have become associated with sex tourism as part of their organic branding – Thailand is perhaps the best known example, and attracts tourists from the West as well as Asian men from China, Malaysia and Singapore.

Red light districts in Thailand are easily recognised, and centre around bars, gogo-bars, massage parlours and billiard venues. Sex tourism is illegal in Thailand (unlike in some other destinations where it is legal, e.g. Amsterdam or Spain), but the legislation is not strictly enforced in Thailand for a variety of reasons. It is a large industry, with estimates of around 200,000 and 300,000 active female sex workers in Thailand at any given time according to a 2007 report compiled by the Institute for Population and Social Research at Mahidol University.

The Lonely Planet, one of the world's leading guidebook series, highlights the sex tourism sector in Thailand in one of its 'destination in detail' snapshots.

Read the article in the sex industry in Thailand:
https://www.lonelyplanet.com/thailand/bangkok/background/
other-features/b9e4d08a-a917-4bbb-8329-656c5e62bdd6/a/nar/
b9e4d08a-a917-4bbb-8329-656c5e62bdd6/357640

From a deontological perspective, there are several arguments against sex tourism: the first is simply that is illegal in Thailand, but mostly the arguments stem from the fact that many sex workers are coerced into the job, and coercion is a violation of human rights. Prostitution is commonly associated with human trafficking, slavery and other human rights violations, including the rights of children. From a utilitarian perspective, the issue become more hotly debated: the issues raised above are weighed up against the opportunity for earning an income and secure the livelihoods of families of these women as well as the women themselves. Many argue that a majority of Thai women are not coerced in the strictest meaning of the word and, having chosen sex work as a form of income, cannot be said to have their rights violated.

From a relativism perspective, many simply argue that prostitution is the oldest job in the world, and others present socio-cultural perspectives that "Buddhism is not regulating sexual behaviour as Christianity or Islam, and therefore sex is not seen as a sin [...] For Thai girl her intentions mean much more than what she actually does, and prostitution is not seen as a questionable form of income as she is usually working to support her family" (Peltonen, 2016, p.8). The argument here is that prostitution is part of society, and in cultures where sex is not associated with sin, there is less taboo around the nature of the transaction being paid for.

From a virtue ethics perspective, Fennell offers this argument: "sex tourism exists as perhaps one of the most explicit examples of bad vices [greed, selfishness and thoughtlessness], which to some extent returns to Peltonen's (2016) argument around different cultural attitudes towards sex. That argument aside, it is not clear whether sex tourism can lead to positive self-identities for all parties involved, which would thus mean that sex tourism would fail the virtues test – indeed placing a monetary value on people always diminishes

6

the other's moral identity, and opens the way to treating others as objects over which to exercise control, and therefore possibly exploitation.

This is perhaps the core of the ethical dilemma: while in some circumstances sex tourism may be argued to do little harm – in situations where there is no possibility of coercion, positive self-identities are not denied, and so forth – investigations into the sector repeatedly encounter behaviours that can only be described as immoral (trafficking, slavery, and so forth), which are an undeniable product of the 'little harm' sex tourism, argued by proponents of this sector. Once again, we need to go through the process of (i) recognizing a moral issue, (ii) making a moral judgment, (iii) establishing moral intent, and (iv) engaging in moral behavior or action.

Third case: Medical tourism

Medical tourism is defined as the process of traveling outside one's country of residence for the purpose of receiving *medical* care. The World Health Organisation (WHO) estimates just under half of international patients receiving medical care are medical tourists (the remainder being expatriates seeking medical care in their country of residence and emergency visits for other tourists).

Mapping these medical tourists' movements is a complex affair (Figure 6.1): medical tourism includes both travellers moving from less developed countries in order to seek highly specialised medical treatment not available in their own country, as well as travellers from developed countries seeking medical procedures that are cost-prohibitive (or simply more expensive) in their own country, or are not provided under insurance or have prolonged waiting lists for procedures.

Seeking out more advanced technology as well as better quality care for medically necessary procedures accounts for almost three quarters of medical tourism, while quicker access for medically necessary procedures represents 15% of trips, lower-cost care for medically necessary procedures 9% of trips and lower-cost care for discretionary procedures (4%). (Figure 6.1)

The drivers of medical tourism are equally complex: health provision has become a globalised market through the restructuring of health systems (e.g. privatisation), private sector investment, the deregulation of health services, large differentials in efficiency and quality standards due to differences in funding for health provision, as well as individual trends in health care requirements and preferences (in the case of cosmetic interventions). These health trends are occurring at the same time as travel has become easier, and technological advances makes it possible to seek out and connect with health providers overseas.

The most common procedures sought through medical tourism are dental care, elective surgery and fertility treatment. And the ethical issues that go hand in hand with medical tourism are as varied as the types of procedure sought. In some cases, the revenue from medical tourism has been contributed directly to the provision of higher level health care for locals. For example, Singapore is an important medical hub within its region, and medical tourism has allowed economies of scale in specialised equipment and and helped to prevent brain drain of its medical experts that also benefit Singaporeans. Indonesia is trialling a similar approach, while the Turks and Caicos Islands have developed an interesting private-public partnership between the local government and Interhealth Canada (international provider of healthcare services) to fund the national health care.

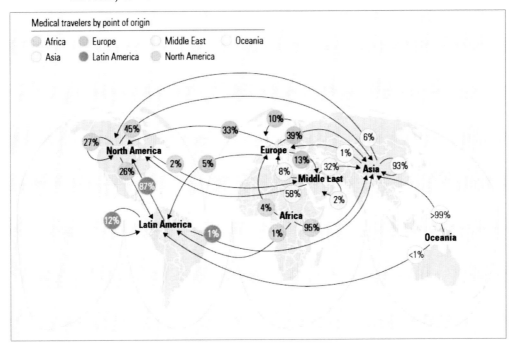

Figure 6.1: The patterns of medical tourism travel around the world (Source: WHO, https://www.who.int/global_health_histories/seminars/kelley_presentation_medical_tourism.pdf).

There are some generic ethical (and legal) concerns around medical tourism, however, such as the impact on the fair distribution of medical resources, contract of services (what happens if follow-ups are needed or complications arise), addressing malpractice issues, as well as giving informed consent at a distance prior to travel, standards of safety and hygiene, and post-procedural care. In Australia, it's been estimated by researchers at Monash University that travelling overseas for budget breast enhancements cost the Australian health system an average AU$12,600 to fix complications when the surgery goes wrong. International agreements on how to regulate medical tourism are only just being worked out.

In addition to these issues, more severe ethical issues are reported around illegal organ donations and maternal surrogacy. As in sex tourism, the ethical concern here centres on issues of exploitation due to a power differential, both as medical experts are likely to be viewed as authority figures and as recipients of organs and surrogate babies have significantly greater resources than the donors, who need the funds.

Read the WHO report on organ trade and medical tourism:
http://www.who.int/bulletin/volumes/85/12/06-039370/en/

Fourth case: Enclave or all-inclusive tourism:

The following text is taken from Tourism Concern's *Guidebook to Ethical Tourism*, written by Polly Pattullo.

A morality tale:

Once, when Europeans went on holiday to the Gambia, they all stayed on the coast near the capital, Banjul. With its wide, sandy beaches bordering the Atlantic Ocean, the 'Smiling Coast', as it was known, welcomed tourists to its manicured resorts. The hotels looked like any other hotel the tourists might have visited in, say, Florida or Spain, and provided food just like the tourists ate at home. The visitors rarely left the beach. Sometimes they complained about the young men, the bumsters who chatted up the women; sometimes they bought carvings from the endless craft stall clustered around the resorts, alongside bars advertising road beef specials. They would never see anything that was 'real' about the Gambia although once a week, they would get a bizarre glimpse of reality when their hotels offered an 'African buffet' and put on folkloric evening of drumming and dancing.

Much money was spent, but Gambians rarely saw it. From airport to hotel, to trips on the river or to Joffre, the ancestral home of Roots author Arthur Haley, the package-greedy, foreign-controlled tourist industry retained an iron grip.

When local people tried to break into the tourism industry, they found their paths blocked; the foreigners had it all sewn up. No one bought their products or their services – the big boys would not take the risk. They tried to leaflet the hotels but no one seemed interested; they went to the airport to find business but the arriving package-tour visitors would be hustled away by the tour reps.

It not difficult to see how this form of tourism goes against the code of ethics set out by the WTO (see Table 6.1). It does little to address:

☐ **Article 1**: Tourism's contribution to mutual understanding and respect between peoples and societies

☐ **Article 2**: Tourism as a vehicle for individual and collective fulfilment

☐ **Article 3**: Tourism, a factor of sustainable development

☐ **Article 4**: Tourism, a user of the cultural heritage of mankind and contributor to its enhancement

☐ **Article 5**: Tourism, a beneficial activity for host countries and communities

☐ **Article 6**: Obligations of stakeholders in tourism development

☐ **Article 9**: Rights of the workers and entrepreneurs in the tourism industry

The ethical issues under consideration here are subservience and marginalisation. Subservience in this case refers to the condition of being less important than something else. Here the economic development opportunities of local people are considered less important than those of foreign investors. Marginalisation refers to the treatment of a person or group as insignificant or peripheral. I will leave you to work through the different ethical positions that relate to this type of tourism, and in doing so, suggest that you refer back WTO's code of ethics and the UN's Declaration of Human Rights.

Question

Can you go through the same process of identifying a deontological, utilitarian and relativism position for the ethics of enclave tourism?

6.3 Positioning your business ethics

Corporate social responsibility

In a business context such a tourism enterprise, one of the first places that we can look for the ethical position of the enterprise (small or large) is in its CSR statements. In today's society, no reputable brand would be without one, but the concept of CSR only really took off in the 1990s, and has now proliferated into a wide area of research and practice. (One research paper alone presented 37 definitions of CSR – c.f. Carroll, 2015.) It is briefly summed up as our expectations of business: economic, legal, ethical and discretionary (philanthropic). The former two are requirements, the latter two are expected and/or desirable – how an enterprise should conduct its business in a way that is just and moral, thereby acting as a good corporate citizen that contributes to a better society and a cleaner environment.

Although 37 definitions of CSR might exist in the literature, a closer analysis of them shows that they all include five dimensions, building on the Triple Bottom Line approach common to all issues of sustainability, focussing on stakeholders (c.f. Chapter 5 on partnerships), and perhaps most notably:

☐ **Economic**, ensuring sustainability in business profits while being mindful to avoid issues of exploitation

☐ **Environmental**, to ensure best practice in resource use, waste disposal, etc.

☐ **Social**, including labour practices, human rights, society and product responsibility towards consumers.

☐ **Stakeholders**, involving proactive sustained long-term healthy relations with employees, suppliers, customers and other secondary stakeholders

☐ **Voluntariness**, activities which are over and above what is expected by law; maintaining positive relations with stakeholders; doing what is right; and increasing brand capital as a 'good enterprise'. (Dahlsrud, 2008)

6

In tourism, the WTO, as part of its push for adoption and implementation of its Code of Ethics, has encouraged tourism enterprises to articulate a CSR position with particular reference the Sustainable Development Goals. At the time of writing, the WTO showcases 13 examples of CSR practices, from airlines to tourism education provider and of course major hotel groups:

Access the WTO's examples of good practice here:
http://ethics.unwto.org/content/corporate-social-responsibility-initiatives.

Each case study indicates which SDG its CSR strategy relates to, provides an overview of the strategy, how its progress and success is measured and finally a call to action for others in the same field. The case studies are also accompanied by videos illustrating relevant CSR practices.

To find the CSR strategy of any company that you might be interested in, you will usually have to search at the bottom of that company's website, under the 'About us' section.

Question

How easy is it to find the CSR program of a tourism company? Pick one travel company and have a look and match it to an SDG.

Labels representing some form of certification scheme are another way of identifying how enterprises relate to their natural and social environments. We'll talk more about these in Chapter 7, as certification schemes can (but do not always) provide useful guidelines on how to make business practices more sustainable; provide indicators for how to measure progress towards greater sustainability; as well as often (but again not always) providing third party validation of business practices, including advice and expertise to guide businesses who might be willing, but inexperienced, at tackling certain areas of sustainable practices.

The other reason for having certification, their marketing appeal for ethically-aware, 'green' consumers, has been heavily criticised by a number of researchers in this area, not least for the crowding in this space and the low level of consumer awareness (or indeed faith) of labels and their meaning. If you have never noticed whether your last holiday attraction was eco-certified or not, you could be forgiven as you are not alone!

Greenwashing and greenhushing

Any time a conversation starts up about CSR and business ethics, someone will eventually raise the issue of greenwashing. This is the act of misleading consumers regarding the environmental and/or sustainability practices of a company or of a product or service. It's basically pulling the moral wool over consumers' eyes, and some estimates reckon that it occurs in up to 95% of claims of socially and environmentally responsible business behaviour.

Ninety five percent is a large figure, and obviously represents various extremes of greenwashing – at best, it's an honest blurred interpretation of intent, at its worst it can be very costly in fines and compensation and extremely damaging to a company's brand reputation. Consider, for example, the repercussions of Volkswagen's emissions scandal.

Watch the 'Dieselgate' video here: https://www.sbs.com.au/news/what-is-the-volkswagen-dieselgate-emissions-scandal

The literature in this space recognises seven sins of greenwashing:

1 **The Sin of the Hidden Trade-Off**, by emphasizing one good practice to distract from another, potentially more serious, practice.

2 **The Sin of No Proof**, where no evidence or third-party certification can back up the claims of good practice.

3 **The Sin of Vagueness**, where claims are almost meaningless as they are so vague.

4 **The Sin of Worshiping False Labels**, where an award or other certification-like label is introduced to the packaging, but doesn't reflect any genuine standard of production (wines are often a case in point).

5 **The Sin of Irrelevance,** when the claimed good practice is either already enforced by law or doesn't make sense in the context.

6 **The Sin of Lesser of Two Evils,** when an environmental claim makes consumers feel 'green' about a product category that is itself lacking in environmental benefits. Organic cigarettes are an example of this sin.

7 **The Sin of Fibbing,** when claims are outright false.

To help you identify how these sins work in practice, TerraChoice has created a 'name that sin' game. Try it out here: http://sinsofgreenwashing.com/games-tools/name-that-sin/index.html

Greenhushing

While the term greenwashing has gained traction as a concept, a new term has emerged in this space: greenhushing. This is almost the reverse of greenwashing. It is the deliberate withholding from customers and other stakeholders of the sustainability-related actions practiced by a business. The researchers who have investigated this phenomenon in tourism suggest that businesses use this technique to bridge the gap between what they think a customer wants and their own position with regards to sustainability. Some business will greehush up to 70% of their actual sustainability-related behaviours, only reporting the 30% that they feel will not negatively impact on the tourists' experience (Font et al., 2017).

If you are thinking that this sounds familiar, you would not only be right, but also very astute. Greenhushing is a form of moral muteness, brought about by the dual issues of projection preference and false consensus bias. By a tacit agreement that the hedonic nature of tourism is paramount and cannot be affected by sustainability messaging that may evoke feelings of guilt or, worse still, inhibit purchasing behaviour, sustainable businesses choose to "shelter their customers, from the negative externalities of the tourists' enjoyment" (Font et al., 2017, p.1016). In their study, Font and his colleagues found that businesses would resort to euphemisms in relation to the environment and therefore avoid having to moralise what is a hedonic, responsibility-free experience.

One way that this is expressed is that a hotel business designed on principles of minimal environmental impact and to maximise environmental benefits, e.g. native plants to feed native insects and birds, may avoid the term 'eco' and focus on luxury instead, fearing that 'eco' evokes impressions of lower quality and standards of service.

It's a powerful realisation to know that greenhushing may also be occurring alongside the more cynical greenwashing. Whilst we may be witnessing a broader societal shift towards sustainable tourism, on a person to person level, there may still be a reluctance to openly discuss and promote value-laden issues. Why do businesses chose to remain silent about their sustainability behaviours, how do we overcome this moral muteness so that we can discuss what we value, how to act on those values, and bring morality out of the shadows?

Only greater stakeholder awareness (and tourists themselves constitute a major stakeholder) will lead to systematic change in the transition towards sustainable tourism (Gössling et al., 2012) – and greater awareness will only happen through the valuing and discussion of sustainable practices within the sector.

6.4   Speaking up about ethical issues in tourism

One reason moral muteness exists is that ethics and morality tend to join religion, politics and money as taboo topics at the dinner table.

A study by Caruana et al. (2014) on tourists' accounts of responsible tourism noted a clear lack of consistent discourse amongst tourists on what constitutes responsible (or ethical) tourism. As tourists, we often don't know what to look for or how to ask to questions. Nor do we know what to do if the answer we get is one that we don't like – does it mean we don't travel? Do we criticise our host? Do we change our travel plans? So we come back to the point made in the introduction: we put tourism in a different category – one apart from moral and ethics.

However, to move towards greater sustainability, we need to be able to openly discuss value-laden issues. Business programs will generally touch on the issue of ethics, but to become the basis of decision-making and behaviours, this area is like any other, we needs skills, knowledge, training and practice. Ethics training is necessary, as we can't assume that individuals can master complex ethical issues based on their own values, especially considering the ramifications of poor choices.

Personal values can be in conflict with organisational values, therefore a program that identifies risks, raises codes of ethics, training, reporting and the development of ethical leadership is essential. Furthermore, successful ethics programs require communication that encourages individuals to ask questions, voice concerns, communication and identification of ethical issues (Gonzalez-Padron et al., 2012).

One woman has taken on the challenge of helping people voice their values to ask questions about moral dilemmas in way that allows us to act on our values in an authentic and results-oriented way. Mary Gentile starts from the premise that most of us are good people and want the best for others and the planet – figures backed up by studies on green consumers in general and green tourists as well, that show that up to 75% of us care about the environment in some way – but that we don't necessarily know how to engage with ethics and morals in the public arena. Her training program, *Giving Voice to Values*, allows each of us to empowered and skilful and practiced enough to voice and act on our values effectively. It's worth considering if you feel that this is an area where you would like to be able to ask questions and make change. (https://www.darden.virginia.edu/ibis/initiatives/giving-voice-to-values/)

Review

6

The question of ethics is arguably underdeveloped in tourism – and perhaps deliberately so. The tourist experience, particularly as it relates to leisure travel, is seen as an opportunity to escape responsibilities and be carefree. Although a number of guides on responsible tourism exist in response to what is seen as the rise of the green consumer, studies in this area have repeatedly shown a lack of understanding among tourists as to what responsible tourism actually is, and an undeniable gap between what tourists say that they value and want, and what they actually do – the so-called knowledge-attitude-behaviour gap.

Part of the issues stems from the fact that as soon as we decide to travel, we are committing to a carbon footprint, and one that some argue exceeds all the carbon emission savings that we can achieve from everyday behavioural changes. So like the proverbial ostrich, we bury our travelling heads in the sand.

Yet ethics is fundamentally about our relationships with others, and relationships with others is an underlying theme of sustainability – what we do to enhance our relationships with others (including nature) is more than likely to move towards greater sustainability, and conversely, what we do that damages relationships with others is more than likely to move us away from greater sustainability.

So it is important that we find ways to overcome our moral muteness and green-hushing. We need to find ways to bring moral decisions out of the shadows. To do this, it is helpful to have a grasp of the slippery concepts of right and wrong, and understand the various types of reasoning that lead each of us to determine rights vs wrong: for some of us the end justify the means, whereas for others the process of doing has as much ethical bearing on right or wrong as the outcome. We also need to understand the influence of our social groups and culture, and how they might shape right and wrong for us, and others who do not share our socio-cultural norms.

This is where we need to learn to flex our moral muscles by developing our ability to voice our values. Through practice, we develop the highly valuable concept of *phronesis,* practical wisdom through implementing values – what is right, not what is easiest, or even what is sensible. To achieve this, we have a number of barriers to overcome: first and foremost, we must learn to recognise moral dilemmas in tourism.

I have given you four examples of moral issues in tourism to get you started, but there are many others, and it is by having a fundamental grasp of human rights, and the rights of nature (c.f. Chapter 4); keeping your eyes and ears open (one of my most memorable lessons on this topic was on a bus in Dominica, listening to local farmers discuss their involvement with FairTrade); and familiarising yourself with the work of NGOs and others in the area of fair and ethical tourism. Once we have identified moral dilemmas, we need to develop an intent to behave in an ethical manner and carry that intent through into actual behaviour.

These can be tricky – we don't want to upset people, cause confrontation or appear to judge others for their decisions. This is where the GVV program can be useful, as Prof. Gentile points out that the chances are that we are not the only ones wanting to do the right thing, and if we have the moral courage to raise the issue, we may find others are relieved and delighted to follow our lead. We may also not want to trade value for money or luxury or convenience for ethical decisions. That is something that you must decide for yourself. But hopefully in reading this book, you may find opportunities to start moving in that direction – perhaps even become one of those five plane passengers who bought a fight carbon offset – if you aren't already on that path.

Questions and exercises

1 How often do you base your travel decisions around sustainability issues? If you don't, why not?

2 How would you feel about querying the sustainability practices of a tourism business? How would you phrase a question about sustainability practices?

3 In addition to the four examples of ethical issues in tourism given above, can you find any others and describe them.

Multiple choice questions

1 Ethical concerns have been at the forefront of arguments for greater sustainability in tourism: True or false?

2 The view that what is right or wrong depends on the context, and whether the outcome produces the greatest good for the greatest number of people represents which school of ethical thought?

   a) Relativism

   b) Deontology

   c) Utilitarianism

3 Moral dilemmas need careful consideration as there is no wrong or right answer. Moral judgements and moral intent therefore influence the chosen course of action: True or false?

4 The idea that we don't need to discuss moral issues with strangers because they are likely to have the same outlook as us is a case of?

   a) False consensus bias

   b) Projection bias

   c) Both a) and b)

5 The code of ethics in tourism is legally binding: True or false?

References

Brenner, L. & Bilgrin, B. (2011). Preferences, projection and packing: support theory models of judgments of others' preferences. *Organizational Behavior and Human Decision Processes*, **115**, 121-132.

Carroll, A. B. (2015). Corporate social responsibility. *Organizational dynamics*, **44**(2), 87-96.

Caruana, R., Glozer, S., Crane, A. & McCabe, S. (2014). Tourists' accounts of responsible tourism. *Annals of Tourism Research*, **46**, 115-129.

Dahlsrud, A. (2008). How corporate social responsibility is defined: an analysis of 37 definitions. *Corporate Social Responsibility and Environmental Management*, **15**(1), 1-13.

Donyadide, A. (2010). Ethics in tourism. *European Journal of Social Sciences*, **17**(3), 433-426.

Fennell, D. A. (2006). *Tourism Ethics*. Channel View Publications.

Font, X., Elgammal, I. & Lamond, I. (2017). Greenhushing: the deliberate under communicating of sustainability practices by tourism businesses. *Journal of Sustainable Tourism*, **25**(7), 1007-1023.

Garay, L. & Font, X. (2012). Doing good to do well? Corporate social responsibility reasons, practices and impacts in small and medium accommodation enterprises. *International Journal of Hospitality Management*, **31**(2), 329-337.

6

Gössling, S., Hall, C.M., Ekstrom, F., Engeset, A.B. & Aall, C. (2012). Transition management: A tool for implementing sustainable tourism scenarios? *Journal of Sustainable Tourism*, **20**(6), 899-916.

Gonzalez-Padron, T., Ferrell, O., Ferrell, L., & Smith, I. (2012). A critique of giving voice to values approach to business ethics education. *Journal of Academic Ethics*, **10**(4), 251-269.

Groves, K. Vance, C. & Paik, Y. (2007). Linking linear/nonlinear thinking style balance and managerial ethical decision-making. *Journal of Business Ethics*, **80**, 305-325.

Hall, D. R. & Brown, F. (2006). *Tourism and Welfare: Ethics, responsibility and sustained well-being*. CABI

Holjevac, I. A. (2008). Business ethics in tourism–as a dimension of TQM. *Total Quality Management & Business Excellence*, **19**(10), 1029-1041.

Hultsman, J. (1995). Just tourism: An ethical framework. *Annals of Tourism Research*, **22**(3), 553-567.

Jones, T.M. (1991). Ethical decision-making by individuals in organisations: an issues-contingent model. *Academy of Management Review*, **16**(2), 366-395.

MacBeth, J. (2005). Towards an ethics platform for tourism. *Annals of Tourism Research*, **32**(4), 962-984

Malone, S., McCabe, S. & Smith, A. (2014). The role of hedonism in ethical tourism. *Annals of Tourism Research*, **44**, 241-254.

Mossaz, A. & Coghlan, A. (2017). The role of travel agents' ethical concerns when brokering information in the marketing and sale of sustainable tourism, *Journal of Sustainable Tourism*, **25**(7), 989-1006.

Nordlund, A. & Garvill, J. (2003). Effects of values, problem awareness, and personal norm on willingness to reduce personal car use. *Journal of Environmental Psychology*, **23**, 339-347.

Peltonen, A. (2016). Ethics of sex tourism in Thailand: Tourists' stance to prostitution and human trafficking, Thesis, Saimaa University of Applied Sciences.

Rest, J.R. (1986). *Moral Development: Advances in research and theory*. New York: Praeger.

Smith, M. & Duffy, R. (2003). *The Ethics of Tourism Development*. Routledge, London.

Street, M. Douglas, S., Geiger, S. & Martinko, M. (1997). The impact of cognitive expenditure on the ethical decision-making process: the cognitive elaboration model. *Organizational Behavior and Human Decision Processes*, **86**(2), 256-277.

Tzschentke, N. A., Kirk, D. & Lynch, P. A. (2008). Going green: Decisional factors in small hospitality operations. *International Journal of Hospitality Management*, **27**(1), 126-133.

UNWTO. (1999). *Global Code of Ethics for Tourism*. Retrieved from http://cf.cdn.unwto.org/sites/all/files/docpdf/gcetbrochureglobalcodeen.pdf

van der Werff, E., Steg, L., Keizer, K. (2013). It is a moral issue: the relationship between environmental self-identity, obligation-based intrinsic motivation and pro-environmental behaviour. *Global Environmental Change*, **23**, 1258-1265.

Weeden, C. (2002). Ethical tourism: An opportunity for competitive advantage? *Journal of Vacation Marketing*, **8**, 141-153.

Wiltermuth, S., Bennett, V. & Pierce, L (2013). Doing as they would do: how the perceived ethical preferences of third-party beneficiaries impact ethical decision-making. *Organizational Behavior and Human Decision Processes*, **122**, 280-290.

Yaman, H. & Gurel, E. (2006). Ethical ideologies of tourism marketers. *Annals of Tourism Research*, **33**, 470-489.

6

7 Measures and Tools

Introduction

The old adage says that "you can only manage what you can measure". Yet, it is also perhaps true that in the tourism space, where the public and private domains collide, perhaps a little more imagination is required, and sustainable tourism management tools may be required to cover the intangible aspects of tourism as well as the more tangible aspects.

This is because the public domain, as highlighted in Chapter 2, holds places and spaces in the public trust – the places and spaces that we share with family and friends, that recharge and rejuvenate, that hold aesthetic, recreational, functional and emotional values for us, as residents of those spaces and places. Meanwhile, the private sector sees those same places and spaces as opportunities to generate a return on investment, often transforming them into economically productive areas through processes of urban regeneration or concessions on public land.

It is in this chapter on sustainable tourism management tools that the previous chapters on systems, impacts, governance and collaboration, as well as ethics and values, come together to deliver the ways in which we can track how well we are managing tourism for a Triple Bottom Line approach to sustainability, minimising the negative outcomes while maximising the positive outcomes of tourism, for multiple stakeholders and across multiple scales.

It is also in this chapter that we practice our various juggling techniques, and once we have learned how to keep the three balls up in the air, we will take a step back and look at how elegant this process can be when applied to the practice of tourism in Chapter 8.

For now, however, we want to focus on the number of tools available to us to track our progress towards sustainable tourism. These tools come in a range of formats – from measurement instruments to regulatory frameworks and voluntary tools. They can be directed at tourists, tourism businesses, tourism employees, and/or destinations and destination management or marketing organisations. This chapter will introduce you to the range of tools available to you, how they work and what they do, so that you can best select which ones will work in any given context. Briefly, they can be grouped according to their main purpose, i.e.

1 **To measure levels of impact**, and changes (or potential changes) in impacts.

2 **Command and control**, whereby governments can exert strict control over development.

3 **Economic incentives**, that will influence behaviour and send signals through the market.

4 **Voluntary practices**, that showcase best practice to be adopted by stakeholders.

5 **Supporting mechanisms**, which will influence the development of sustainable tourism in other ways.

The remainder of this chapter will cover each of these areas separately, examining the general principles of each type of tool, what they look like in practice and how well they have served the needs of sustainability in tourism. It is important to note as well that they will often be used in ways that are, or at least should be, mutually reinforcing and complementary.

Key words and concepts

- Visitor management tools
- Environmental Impact Assessment
- Limits of Acceptable Change
- Indicators
- Tipping points

- The green economy
- Demarketing
- Eco-certification
- Interpretation
- Soft management techniques

7.1 Visitor impact measurement tools

7

While the notion of sustainable tourism covers the three pillars of sustainability, social, economic and environmental, its origins are very strongly embedded in concerns about the environmental impacts of the sector. This is still true today, with many of the arguments surrounding tourism's lack of sustainability focussing on its carbon footprint and GHG emissions associated with travel to destinations.

There is a significant number of visitor management tools that have been proposed in different areas of the world, for example:

☐ Visitor Impact Management (VIM)

☐ Visitor Experience and Resource Protection (VERP)

☐ Visitor Activity Management Process (VAMP)

☐ Recreation Opportunity Spectrum (ROS)

☐ Tourism Optimisation Management Model (TOMM)

This section will cover two main impact measurement tools and models that are relevant for tourism, Environmental Impact Assessments and Limits of Acceptable Change. Both of these systems rely on identifying and monitoring sustainability indicators and managing to those indicators in an adaptive manner, and often in conjunction with some sort of zoning plan.

Environmental Impact Assessments (EIAs)

EIAs are a key way of understanding the impacts of any future development on the environment, by exploring the relationship between specific human activities and the social, economic and environmental contexts in which they take place. An EIA provides a systematic way of evaluating the positive and negative impacts of any proposed development, with the aim of directing decision-making towards sustainability (Hughes & Morrison-Saunders, 2015).

EIAs are relevant to sustainable tourism management in three ways:

1 They specifically value economic, social and environmental contexts equally, and seek to maximise benefits at the same time as minimise negative impacts;

2 They expand the scope of consideration beyond the immediate development proposal, to take into account the interconnected, systems nature of any development;

3 They adopt a governance approach that includes a broader community of interest, including governments.

Most important is the holistic, systems approach adopted by EIAs: they focus on the complexities and interconnectedness of socio-ecological systems, moving from a single site to include the broader community and geographic region. Transferred to a sustainable tourism context, the EIA process would encourage sustainable tourism managers to move beyond the analysis of any one activity, attraction or destination to consider all parts of the tourism system. For example, the carbon footprint of flying *to* a destination would be captured when accounting for the environmental impacts of tourism *in* that destination.

Furthermore, managers must also focus on maximising the social, environmental and economic benefits of tourism, as well as minimising negative impacts. Again, this is best achieved through a systems approach that moves away from a traditional notion of achieving balance within the system and instead embraces the dynamic nature of tourism systems (e.g. the conditions at tourist-generating regions, changes in transport modes, efficiencies, etc., and conditions at the destination, to name only parts of the system). This also ties in with the concept of resilience, that is, the ability to recover quickly from challenges or crises, by considering the state of a system as a whole and the varied dynamics within that system. Thus, resilience refers to an iterative management process where continuous monitoring and learning are used to improve long-term management outcomes.

One example of this approach is the Ningaloo Coast Regional Strategy, which sets out a tourism development plan within the broader social, environmental and economic context of the Ningaloo Coast Region of Western Australia. The intent of this strategy was to balance tourism development against other concerns, values and development opportunities put forward by a highly motivated and engaged local community, keen to maintain this highly valued, ecologically unique coastal region.

Question

The Ningaloo Coast Regional Strategy is available at https://www.planning. wa.gov.au/dop_pub_pdf/Part_1_Section_1.4.pdf. Review it in light of the material covered so far – what are some of key points that you note?

Limits of Acceptable Change (LAC)

Test yourself

The LAC model has been applied across a number of tourist settings, often through the influence of US Parks and Recreation, who have slowly been transitioning all of their recreation management plans across to this system. For many practitioners and academics, LAC replaces the more widely known **carrying capacity** approach. While the latter advocates a fixed limit on the number of tourists, or tourism providers and activities, basically asking the question "how many people is too many?", the former looks at how much change to an area is acceptable, irrespective of absolute numbers.

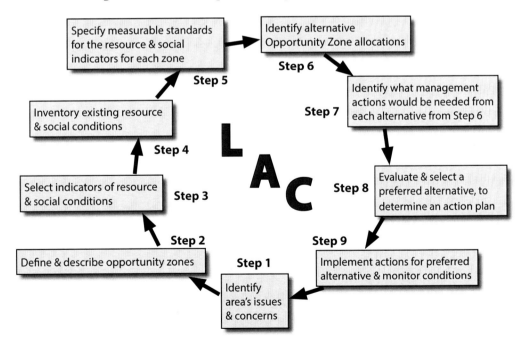

Figure 7.1: The nine steps of Limits of Acceptable Change

It follows an iterative nine step process outlined in Figure. 7.1 that specifically acknowledges that change (it's in the title!) is inevitable and must be embraced by managers. It also explicitly recognises that users of an area will have several goals, some of which will be in conflict and compromises will have to be found. It makes these compromises explicit and considers which goal will constrain the other, at which point and to what extent. Most often the two goals in conflict are preservation of the ecological integrity of an area, versus unrestricted recreational access. Both goals will be compromised to some extent, while one (maintaining ecological integrity) may constrain the other (unrestricted access) when its upper limits of acceptable change are reached. At that point access will be restricted until ecological integrity is back to within the acceptable range.

One significant advantage of the LAC process is the steps, when completed through a governance, i.e. shared decision-making, approach (c.f. Chapter 5), provide a management mechanism that is transparent, explicit and defensible. Step 1 invites stakeholders to explicitly state what value they associate with a site – e.g. wilderness, aesthetic, recreational, social, and so forth, and brings out any concerns associated with those values. Step 2 looks for ways to accommodate diverse, perhaps conflicting values, through a zoning process, while Step 3 explicitly asks users to identify how those values should be measured, i.e. what indicators should be used, and Steps 4 and 5 identify what the acceptable range on those indicators might be. Steps 7 and 8 verify that the best of use the area is being made, by checking alternatives, and only at Step 9 are management actions implemented with an associated monitoring process.

There are several very useful guides and case studies that explore LAC within a tourism context, and numerous studies (mainly out of North America) of its application. Examples include many parks in North America as well as the Balearic Islands (Spain), management of recreational boating (Diedrich et al., 2011), beach management in West Java Indonesia (Komsary et al., 2018), and the Okovango Delta (Mbaiwa et al., 2008).

The role of tourism indicators is vital in these approaches, and deserves attention here. An indicator must be selected to tell us something about the important value of a place, it must be measurable and must vary in line with changes in usage of a place and the impacts of tourism. The UNEP/UNWTO (2005) sustainable tourism guide for policy makers offers five criteria to be used in the selection of indicators:

1 Their relevance to the issue under consideration
2 Their feasibility in terms of data collection and analysis
3 The credibility of the information that they provide
4 Their ease of understanding among stakeholders
5 Their comparability across time and space.

Some of the important questions that must be considered when selecting an indicator include:

☐ What is the question that we want to answer using an indicator, and will the indicator answer that question?

☐ Does the selected indicator demonstrate a direct relationship with the natural, social, or economic status of tourism?

☐ Can the indicator be measured easily and relatively inexpensively, i.e. will it be worth collecting?

And importantly,

☐ Will the indicator trigger action before the conditions have deteriorated to an unacceptable level?

The final point relates to the issue of **tipping points**, where a system can change very quickly from one (acceptable) condition to another (unacceptable) condition very quickly, with no opportunity to revert back to its original condition when a threshold is crossed. An incident such as Fukoshima's nuclear reactor meltdown and the impact on the region for visitors is one example.

Another consideration for indicators is whether they can be measured without negatively affecting the visitor experience. Survey fatigue is a common problem in tourism, so detailed questions to a visitor on her or his experience may be tricky, for example.

The UNWTO has helpfully provided a handbook of tourism indicators that can be used a destination, community or business level. The indicators can be used to measure impacts on the social, environmental and economic aspects of a place, they should also be used to give a baseline assessment of existing conditions, serve to set targets for policies and actions, and assess and revise those actions and policies. Table 7.1. gives some examples of the UNWTO's suggested indicators.

One example where this approach has been used at a destination level is Rottnest Island, a weekend getaway off the west coast of Australia. A Balance Scorecard approach has been implemented on the island as a whole, through a set of performance indicators (e.g. tourist satisfaction) that lends equal weight to business/economic variables, environmental variables and social variables (Mau & Tedesco, 2015). An Environmental Management System monitors the environmental performance of the island's businesses, implemented through an Environmental Performance Framework, again using baseline assessments and monitoring of selected environmental performance indicators.

7

Table 7.1: Suggested indicators to monitor tourism's sustainability

Baseline issue	Suggested indicators
Local satisfaction with tourism	Local satisfaction level with tourism (questionnaire)
Effects of tourism on communities	Ratio of tourists to locals (average and peak period) Percentage of people who believe that tourism has helped bring new services and infrastructure (questionnaire) Number and capacity of social services available to the community (percentage of which are attributable to tourism)
Sustaining tourism satisfaction	Level of satisfaction by visitors (questionnaire) Perception of value for money (questionnaire) Percentage of return visitors
Economic benefits of tourism	Number of local people (ratio of men to women) employed in tourism (also ratio of tourism employment to local employment) Revenues generate by tourism as a percentage of total revenues generated in the community
Energy management	Per capita consumption of energy from all sources (overall and by tourist sector – per person day) Percentage of businesses participating in energy conservation programs or applying energy saving policy and techniques Percentage of energy consumption from renewable resources (at destinations, establishments)
Development control	Existence of a land use or development planning process, including tourism Percentage of area subject to control (density, design, etc)
Controlling use intensity	Total number of tourists arrivals (mean, monthly, peak periods) Number of tourists per square metre of the site (e.g. at beaches, attractions) per square kilometre of the destination (mean numbers/peak period average).

7.2   Regulatory instruments

Many of the policies and regulations that influence tourism development were covered in Chapter 4. These are vital when it comes to protecting vulnerable communities or environments. The UNEP/UNWTO sustainable tourism guide for policy makers recommends that command and control instruments be used to manage the following nine areas (2005, p.78):

1   The location and nature of any tourism development

2   Rights and conditions of the tourism workforce

Test yourself

3   Issues relevant to visitor health and safety, such as food hygiene, fire hazard management

4   Trading practices

5   Management of serious environment damage (e.g. sewage discharge, etc.)

6 Issues that could be a nuisance to local residents, e.g. noise pollution

7 Use of scarce resources, e.g. water

8 Rights of access to services, land and so forth

9 Managing the risk of crime or exploitation between visitors and locals.

At more fine-grained level, local government land use planning and regulations is a key mechanism for managing the development of tourism. Building size, design, density and appearance will all affect the sense of place conveyed to visitors and locals. Councils have the ability to protect existing buildings for their heritage value. Organisations such as the National Trust in the UK contribute to tourism by promoting bundled tours of their heritage locations.

Find out more: https://www.nationaltrust.org.uk/tours-and-overseas

Similarly the design and accessibility of public spaces will have an impact on the provision of tourism and the types of activities that occur. Local governments may also invest specifically in tourism related buildings, for example convention centres, which are typically not build as profit-making ventures, but instead drive growth, investment and employment in surrounding areas. Other tourism-specific investments can include sports venues and entertainment complexes. Some cities have become quite successful sport event destinations through their local government's investment in sports venues.

As well as land-use and building regulations, local government can also influence licensing procedures and permits that will influence the attractions and other support services for tourism. The latter include tourist coaches and taxis, bars and restaurants. These powers can limit the number of visitors (and residents) to a place. Government agencies can also use mechanisms such as concessions to grant private use to a public area, with very specific conditions attached to that use. One example of this is the establishment of private lodges inside national parks such as in South Africa's Kruger National Park.

The balance of power between regulation and access is why the emergence of the shared economy, with businesses such as Airbnb and Uber, have been disruptive to the tourism sector. Early studies of Airbnb show how tourism became much more dispersed through a city, with next to no control over the number of beds available within a destination. Local councils scrambled to catch up with this alternative and informal provision of tourism services that fell outside of normal regulatory and licencing frameworks.

European cities have perhaps been the most pro-active at regulating the shared economy to respond both to concerns over impacts on more traditional accommodation and transport providers as well as to general issues of over-tourism. Amsterdam is reportedly one of the most popular Airbnb cities, and has imposed heavy regulations and taxes on Airbnb as a platform as well as on the hosts themselves, with limits on the number on the number of nights available to hosts, an agreement to collect the city's 5% tourist tax, and a high marginal tax rate (42%) on short-term accommodation rentals.

Test
yourself

7

The provision of infrastructure is another area where governments (local, regional or national) can exert significant powers over the sustainable development of tourism. The decision to open a new airport for example, or to choose to invest in roads versus public transport, or allow schemes such as the Gold Coast's bike share business showcased in Chapter 3, will all influence how tourism develops. This also extends to the provision of utility services such as water, power, telecommunications as well as social services, such as health care, schooling and so forth for the tourism workforce.

One regulatory mechanism that is used in a number of tourism settings, particularly around cultural and natural heritage settings is zoning. Zoning specifically sets out different uses at different densities in different areas of a tourism attraction or destination. If you remember the LAC process, zoning forms an integral part, creating opportunities for different uses, e.g. hikers, cyclists/skiers/horse riders and motorised vehicles within a protected area. It can also be used within marine parks, with extractive activities such as spear-fishing allowed in some areas, while other areas are set aside as no-take zones.

One key point to note in this section is that in order to manage tourism sustainably, a regulatory body must have a mandate for tourism. This is particularly applicable to protect areas, where the general focus is on conservation. Without an explicit framework for tourism, tourism activities cannot be managed sustainably. This becomes known as 'enabling legislation' which allows tourism to be promoted and managed in a sustainable manner. It may also include land tenure provisions, particularly for traditional societies where land rights are not always clearly defined.

7.3 Economic incentives

Economic incentives are another way that governments can influence the development of sustainable tourism. They can work at many levels, where and how to invest as a tourism developer, and how to manage your supply chain, as well as directly influencing consumer (tourist) behaviours. They are arguably more flexible than regulatory mechanisms, and can be adjusted to changing conditions more rapidly, but they are also an indirect influence – whereas regulatory mechanisms are "thou shalt not", economic incentives are more of a "you'd be better off if you don't".

At the most basic level, the pricing set by governments and their agencies on fees to enter attractions such as national parks and museums and for the use of facilities such as car parks. In this sense they are a direct revenue raising mechanism for governments who can then use that revenue to implement sustainable practices.

These types of revenue raising techniques can be managed directly by a government agency (e.g. national park service) or can be managed indirectly, such as when the private sector collect taxes as part of their fees, e.g. bed taxes in hotels and the so-called 'reef tax' collected by marine park tourism operators visiting the Great Barrier Reef. These are often more appealing to business as they are directed at the consumer, rather than the business, and can be relatively easy to collect.

Entry fees will also have a direct impact on the number of visitors to a site, and economic incentives are therefore a good way to change the pattern of demand – an issue sometimes covered in '**demarketing**'.

The process of demarketing can raise prices at a destination or attraction to discourage people from visiting. The term demarketing was coined by Kotler and Levy in 1971 to draw attention to the type of marketing techniques that "deals with discouraging customers in general or a certain class of customers in particular on a temporary or permanent basis" (p.78). In the case of tourism, it can dramatically reduce the number of visitors to a destination.

Two true forms of demarketing exist:

1   **General demarketing**, to reduce total demand;

2   **Selective demarketing**, to reduce demand from specific market segments

A third form, which is not of interest to us here, is **ostensible demarketing**, where the appearance of scarcity can be used to stimulate demand. This can sometimes be used in so-called Last Chance Tourism, where destinations or attractions are promoted as 'disappearing soon' or 'see them before they go'. Examples include the sinking city of Venice, or the extinction-bound polar bears of Churchill, Manitoba. However, virtually by definition, Last Chance Tourism is the very antithesis of sustainable tourism and therefore not covered here.

One interesting case of selective demarketing be could to deter long-haul flying by certain market segments (Gossling et al., 2015). Using four well known tourism destinations – namely Seychelles, USA, Turkey and the Bahamas – the researchers work out the destination's main markets, their size and the distances that they have to travel between origin and destination. This gives a GHG emission value for each market.

In the case of Turkey, for example, the primary market in 2009 (the figures provided in the study) was Germany (1) followed by Russia (2), the UK (3) and the USA (10). In sheer volume and distance travelled, these countries have a cumulative GHG emission total of over 8,200,000 t CO_2. This is nearly three and half times the contribution of the other 6 top ten tourism markets travelling to Turkey – Bulgaria, Iran, Netherlands, Georgia and France.

Based on these figures, Gossling et al., (2015) suggest that one way to manage the GHG emissions from tourism is to encourage lower emissions markets, while demarketing the higher emissions markets. This could be achieved through a combination of active international marketing campaigns that take into account emission-intensities alongside economic value, and regulatory mechanisms, e.g. carbon taxes or emissions trading schemes.

Test yourself

7

Governments will also commonly use economic incentives by creating specific investment conditions. Governments can encourage sustainable tourism through grants, loans, tax concessions, awards and prizes, and so forth. Most often these will have the greatest impact on the tourism firm's own financial performance, representing the economic pillar of sustainability, but they can also be used to encourage businesses to invest in green energy through low interest loans on solar panels for example.

In some cases this can go spectacularly wrong, as in the case of the 'backpacker tax'; the Australian federal government changed backpacker income tax rates with apparently little stakeholder consultation. The primary stakeholders in this case were farmers who rely on backpackers to fill the seasonal jobs, and their surrounding communities who also benefit economically from the presence of backpackers. The scheme is already fraught with issues, but the additional changes left everyone unhappy.

ABC.NET.AU
Survey signals 'backpacker tax' will be a tourist turn-off

Figure 7.2: The backpacker tax. https://www.abc.net.au/news/rural/2016-08-24/backpacker-tax-review-strawberry-employment-jobs/7779286

Taxes may also be commonly used to change behaviour, e.g. directing the revenue raised towards community projects, conservation projects, or to manage resource use and pollution. Carbon taxes are perhaps the best known, and some regions have enforced carbon taxes on their regional flights – the European Union being the best example. They can also be used to minimise packaging and therefore plastic waste, encourage frugal consumption of water, and so forth.

Some regions are investing in whole new 'economies'. The 'green economy' is an increasingly appealing concept for many destinations. It is defined by the International Chamber of Commerce (ICC) as "an economy in which economic growth and environmental responsibility work together in a mutually reinforcing fashion while supporting progress on social development". In 2012, UNEP published its *Green Economy Roadmap* to highlight how business can bring about solutions to common global issues. Tourism was, not surprisingly, one sector that has been frequently highlighted by UNEP (amongst others) as playing an important role in the transition to a green economy.

Read more about the green economy: https://www.cbd.int/financial/doc/ tourism-greeneconomy.pdf
http://www.greengrowthknowledge.org/resource/green-economy- driving-green-economy-through-public-finance-and-fiscal-policy-reform

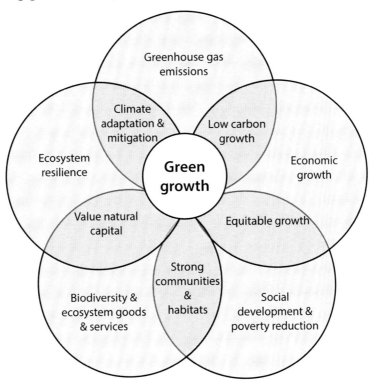

Figure7.3: Principles and outcomes of a green growth strategy.

Related to the green economy is the circular economy – a concept being pioneered by Europe. Instead of our dominant developed nation paradigm of 'make, use, dispose', the circular economy aims to keep resources in circulation for as long as possible, recovering and regenerating them at the end of each lifespan. It focuses on long-lasting design, maintenance, repair, reuse, remanufacturing, refurbishing, recycling, and upcycling (all very familiar practices in economies that have not yet peaked in their consumption paradigm!). These obviously have strong implications for sustainable supply chains, as the waste output of one service delivery provider becomes the raw material input of another.

The circular economy has its most obvious applications in manufacturing, where raw materials can be recycled and upcycled into new products. There have been more recent attempts, however, to apply it to service sectors such as tourism, focusing on waste as a resource (e.g. food waste as a source of compost material), the collaborative economy as a sustainable form of resource sharing and eco-design for buildings such as hotels. The European Union has funded a handbook geared towards introducing circular economy principles into tourism in the South Baltic region; and a recent UN session on tourism and construction and the circular economy was also published on the web, to highlight the types of discussions taking place around how to base sustainable tourism delivery on a circular economy model.

Download the EU's handbook: https://crt.dk/media/90318/Cirtoinno-handbook_CRT_05102017-002-.pdf

Watch the UN session on the circular economy: http://webtv.un.org/watch/tourism-and-construction-circular-economy-solutions-for-sdg12/5810884916001/

7.4 Voluntary mechanisms

When discussing practical tools for developing greater environmental sustainability it is not uncommon for the topic of ecolabels and green certifications, codes of conduct and carbon calculators, and associated offsets, to arise.

Ecolabels operate on the supply side of sustainable tourism and are understood to be a form of establishing compliance with external standards of positive environmental performance. In some definitions, this focus on compliance is key, particularly when associated with some form of third party auditing of standards and performance. In other definitions, the focus is more on ecolabels as a demand-side tool, whereby tourists can inform themselves about the activities and standards of any business. In either case, signing up to an ecolabelling program is voluntary, fee-based, and requiring the business to adhere to a set of best practice principles, which can be audited.

Ecolabels are usually administered through an accredited agency, and monitored by an independent third-party organisation. They are therefore seen to serve three general purposes:

1 Standardise desirable environmental performance levels across the sector,

2 Ensure certified businesses understand and meet those performance levels

3 Serve as competitive point of difference for a market looking for green products.

Ecolabels have been around for over 30 years, and the number of certification programs keeps growing, of which Australia's Earthcheck and the international Green Globe are perhaps the most widely recognised. However, the tourism sector has not readily embraced the concept of ecolabels; at the last count (2005) it was estimated that only 1% of the world's tourism businesses had adopted an environmental certification scheme.

This low uptake begs the question of how useful ecolabels actually are. The general arguments in favour of ecolabels is that they have:

☐ Low implementation costs, when compared to government regulations.

☐ Cost savings from operating more efficiently.

☐ Marketing advantages for the environmentally-conscious tourism market

☐ Credibility through the third party auditing system (although this one is debated within the sector).

Deng-Westphal et al. (2015) attempt to explain the low uptake through a review of the existing literature in this area, and suggest that there are five barriers to their adoption by tourism operators. These include:

☐ The cost of implementation, as businesses sign up to the certification program and must complete the paperwork associated with the environmental performance (and change their practices in some cases).

☐ The low level of consumer awareness of labels, reducing any marketing advantage.

☐ The variability in quality and issue of credibility between programs

☐ The lack of a measure of the effectiveness of ecolabels

☐ The issue of inequality in developing countries.

Another way of looking at the issue of low adoption is from a theoretical perspective, using Roger's (2003) Diffusion of Innovations Theory. Rogers argues that the successful diffusion of any innovation can be explained in large part by specific attributes of the innovation itself, related to its *relative advantage, compliance, complexity, trialability and observability*. For an innovation to succeed, it must be high in most of these, but low on complexity.

Question

Review Rogers' model of innovation diffusion (**http://www.conceptlab.com/notes/illustrationdetail/rogers-2003-p170.png**), and evaluate whether ecolabels represent a case of an innovation in its early stages with low awareness, or an example of rejection at the decision making stage.

7

Another tool that has been covered already is the use of codes of ethics. Perhaps the best known of these is the UNWTO's Global Code of Ethics for Tourism (UNWTO, 1999), covered in Chapter 6. The provides a set of 10 key principles, based on the declaration of Human Rights, that cover the economic, social, cultural and environmental components of travel and tourism, and are addressed to governments, the travel industry, communities and tourists. (See Table 6.1, p 145.)

Codes of practice have been successful in professions where there is a strong sense of professional identity, often accompanied by a commitment to service such as the Hippocratic Oath for doctors or the Nightingale Pledge for nurses. However, codes of ethics in tourism have been criticised as being at best a public relations exercise with little capacity for enforcement (they are a voluntary practice) and little awareness among industry and tourists themselves. At worst, they are seen as a means of avoiding more stringent government regulations of the type presented in Section 7.2.

Nonetheless, there are some sectors where codes of ethics, or codes of practice, have been effective in tourism. Whale watching is one area that has received a lot of attention, and resulted in clear, unambiguous guidelines for many operators, presented in an easy way for vessel skippers to quickly understand and refer to (Figure 7.4).

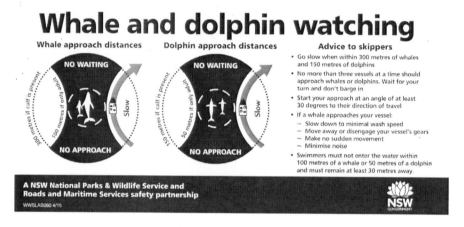

Figure 7.4: New South Wales (Australia) guidelines for boat-based whale watching

Visitors to Antarctica are presented with a strict code of conduct, developed in 2011 as part of the Antarctic Treaty. Visitors are told to protect Antarctic wildlife, be safe, respect protected areas, respect scientific research and keep Antarctica pristine (Figure 7.5). The guidelines are circulated through tour operators under the International Association of Antarctica Tour Operators (IAATO).

Carbon calculators

Another voluntary mechanism that we have already covered in Chapter 3 is the use of carbon calculators and carbon emission offset schemes. As with ecolabels, these schemes have had limited uptake, for a number of reasons. Perhaps first and foremost, most tourists are not yet ready to consider the carbon footprint of their travel behaviour. As mentioned in Chapter 2, Gössling and Buckley (2016) found that up to 15% of respondents from a sample of "green" tourists in Germany would not refer to carbon labelling in their travel behaviour decisions as "such a label would rather scare me off to book my holiday with this tour operator, because I think they try to make me feel guilty about travelling" (p.365).

TEXT OF RECOMMENDATION XXVIII-1 GUIDANCE FOR VISITORS TO THE ANTARCTIC

Protect Antarctic Wildlife

Taking or harmful interference with Antarctic wildlife is prohibited except in accordance with a permit issued by a national authority.

- Do not use aircraft, vessels, small boats, or other means of transport in ways that disturb wildlife, either at sea or on land.
- Do not feed, touch, or handle birds or seals, or approach or photograph them in ways that cause them to alter their behaviour. Special care is needed when animals are breeding or moulting.
- Do not damage plants, for example by walking, driving, or landing on extensive moss beds or lichen-covered scree slopes.
- Do not use guns or explosives. Keep noise to the minimum to avoid frightening wildlife.
- Do not bring non-native plants or animals into the Antarctic such as live poultry, pet dogs and cats or house plants.

Respect Protected Areas

A variety of areas in the Antarctic have been afforded special protection because of their particular ecological, scientific, historic or other values. Entry into certain areas may be prohibited except in accordance with a permit issued by an appropriate national authority. Activities in and near designated Historic Sites and Monuments and certain other areas may be subject to special restrictions.

- Know the locations of areas that have been afforded special protection and any restrictions regarding entry and activities that can be carried out in and near them.
- Observe applicable restrictions.
- Do not damage, remove, or destroy Historic Sites or Monuments or any artifacts associated with them.

Respect Scientific Research

Do not interfere with scientific research, facilities or equipment.

- Obtain permission before visiting Antarctic science and support facilities; reconfirm arrangements 24–72 hours before arrival; and comply with the rules regarding such visits.
- Do not interfere with, or remove, scientific equipment or marker posts, and do not disturb experimental study sites, field camps or supplies.

Be Safe

Be prepared for severe and changeable weather and ensure that your equipment and clothing meet Antarctic standards. Remember that the Antarctic environment is inhospitable, unpredictable, and potentially dangerous.

- Know your capabilities, the dangers posed by the Antarctic environment, and act accordingly. Plan activities with safety in mind at all times.
- Keep a safe distance from all wildlife, both on land and at sea.
- Take note of, and act on, the advice and instructions from your leaders; do not stray from your group.
- Do not walk onto glaciers or large snow fields without the proper equipment and experience; there is a real danger of falling into hidden crevasses.
- Do not expect a rescue service. Self-sufficiency is increased and risks reduced by sound planning, quality equipment, and trained personnel.
- Do not enter emergency refuges (except in emergencies). If you use equipment or food from a refuge, inform the nearest research station or national authority once the emergency is over.
- Respect any smoking restrictions, particularly around buildings, and take great care to safeguard against the danger of fire. This is a real hazard in the dry environment of Antarctica.

Keep Antarctica Pristine

Antarctica remains relatively pristine, the largest wilderness area on Earth. It has not yet been subjected to large scale human perturbations. Please keep it that way.

- Do not dispose of litter or garbage on land. Open burning is prohibited.
- Do not disturb or pollute lakes or streams. Any materials discarded at sea must be disposed of properly.
- Do not paint or engrave names or graffiti on rocks or buildings.
- Do not collect or take away biological or geological specimens or man-made artifacts as a souvenir, including rocks, bones, eggs, fossils, and parts or contents of buildings.
- Do not deface or vandalize buildings, whether occupied, abandoned, or unoccupied, or emergency refuges.

Figure 7.5: Code of conduct for visitors to Antarctica. **https://iaato.org/documents/10157/13325/Visitor_Guidelines-1.pdf**

Second, carbon calculators are not easy to understand or use. Studies of European air travellers found that when faced with a choice of carbon calculators aimed at reducing carbon footprints and recommending carbon offsets, many travellers refused to engage with them, finding them confusing (Juvan & Dolnicar, 2014; Gössling & Buckley, 2016). At their simplest level, they will calculate emissions from immediate sources/direct operations (e.g. the fuel consumption of a plane from point A to point B) – these are labelled Scope 1 and Scope 2 in the Greenhouse Gas Protocol. Some calculators will take a lifecycle approach, i.e. the fuel used on the flight + emissions associated with building the plane and the airport + emissions from disposing of decommissioned planes, and so forth. This approach, Scope 3, requires significantly more knowledge of the tourism system and a great deal more data from each service or products lifecycle, and therefore becomes quite difficult to use accurately.

Even for those that do want to use them, they are not always easy to find. A common problem for airlines is that bookings made through travel agents rarely include the option of carbon offsetting. This could be linked to the false consensus bias that tourists want a hedonic, responsibility-free trip and are therefore not interested in offsetting their carbon emissions. By way of example, a google search for "hertz carbon offsetting" does turn up results

7

(see below). However, a thorough search of Hertz's website does not. Even if you did manage to find their carbon offset scheme, it's still not quite clear how to access it!

Read about Hertz's scheme: https://images.hertz.com/pdfs/09_2016_PDF_Carbon_Offsets_Support.pdf

Question

Pick a travel company that you are familiar with, perhaps an airline, car rental agency or all-inclusive package tour provider. Search for their carbon offset programs. How easy are they to find and use?

7.5 Supporting mechanisms

As well as the varied tools and techniques listed above, there are also a number of soft management techniques that are often used in tourism to promote sustainability. Soft management techniques are persuasive in nature – they encourage tourists to undertake a particular behaviour without the use of regulations. Three common ones include interpretation, social marketing or sustainability marketing techniques

Interpretation is perhaps the best known soft management tool for greater sustainability in tourism. Interpretation serves to connect tourists to their environment by providing information that is relevant, accessible, and meaningful to the tourist. It represents a type of informal learning which is often used to raise awareness of the environmental or social issues of a place.

Managers can use well-designed interpretation to draw attention to the types of tourist behaviours that they want to minimise, or alternatively maximise, at a site (Ballantyne et al., 2011; Ham & Weiler, 2002). Used in this way, interpretation can help manage site-specific environmental behaviours. It is a soft management tool that can be useful to, e.g. ask visitors to maintain a minimum distance during wildlife interactions, or to behave respectfully in cross-cultural interactions.

Interpretation has shown more limited usefulness in managing deliberately harmful actions, e.g. collecting souvenirs in a no-take zone, or in encouraging longer-term pro-environmental behaviour, once the visitor leaves the site (Roggenbuck, 1992). We have already explored Mann's et al. (2017) experiments with asking tourists to pledge to engage in more pro-environmental behaviours once they leave a site. This initiative is one of the few that appear to have worked well in creating a spill-over effect between the tourist experience and pro-environmental behaviour in general. Another example is Howard's (2000) study of tourists at a turtle watching tour, who continued to engage in turtle-related pro-environmental behaviours up to six months after the tour.

What we do know about interpretation, however, is that done well, it can significantly add to the quality of the tourist experience, and therefore tourist satisfaction – although the actual relationship between high-quality interpretive experiences, visitor satisfaction, and changes in pro-environmental behaviours and attitudes has not been proven. Whether or not interpretation does work to change environmental behaviours and attitudes appears to depend on visitor characteristics, and situational factors, especially the type of pro-environmental behaviour being considered (Ballantyne et al., 2009; Weaver, 2013).

Interpretation is primarily for the benefit of tourists (although some residents may enjoy it too!). When similar principles are applied to other tourism stakeholders, e.g. host communities, tourism NGOs or management agencies and businesses themselves, this is usually referred to as *capacity building*. It's a term that surfaced when we were talking about governance and partnerships (c.f. Chapter 5), as it refers directly to developing people's potential to make and implement good decisions, by increasing their understanding, knowledge and skills in sustainable tourism.

Governments and industry peak bodies have an important role to play in capacity building. For example, the UNWTO has developed a Hotel Energy Savings Toolkit, which you can try out. The toolkit allows small to medium sized enterprises to calculate, record and track their energy usage, through an online tool. The toolkit itself contains much more than just the carbon calculators, as it also gives advice on how to save energy, how to make good return on investment decisions, and how to communicate the hotel's energy initiatives. As more businesses start to use the toolkit and plug their data into the online system, it will be able to provide comparative data, regionally and for similar business type and size.

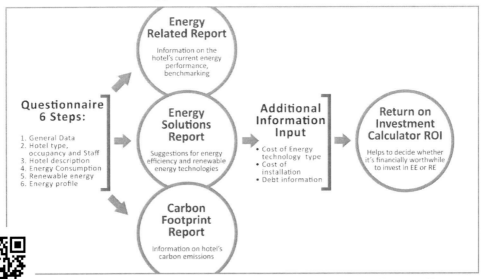

Figure 7.6: The process of the WTO's Hotel Energy Savings toolkit initiative. http://www.hes-unwto.org/hes_root_asp/index.asp?LangID=1

The Hotel Energy Savings toolkit therefore combines many of the themes that we have discussed to date: a business case for sustainability, knowledge partnerships, indicators and benchmarks and marketing activities to communicate sustainability efforts to green consumers.

My Green Butler

One final tool that I would like to cover is much closer to home, as it evolved out of the thesis of one of my postgraduate students. We'll also cover it in Chapter 8, on how to operationalise sustainable tourism, but for this chapter, we'll look at how Christopher Warren took what he learned from making his own business more sustainable and developed My Green Butler, a package that can be applied to any business. At the heart of the package are two things: a smart metering system and a persuasive communication host/guest interaction model, where guests are invited to co-create their sustainable tourism experience. For an overview of the program, see the video below:

https://youtu.be/XLk4M0lp9sU

My Green Butler requires the business to do several things:

1   Provide the systems and infrastructure that enable guests to act sustainably during their stay (e.g. providing recycling bins).

2   Install metering systems that track resource use (water, electricity, gas, food waste, etc.) at a fine grained level, and collate that data in a format that can be presented to guests daily.

3   Interact with the guests in a way that invites them to be greener, by introducing them to sustainability-oriented facilities and activities, report back their performance and, wherever possible, pledge the business' savings from guests' reduced consumption to some on-going sustainability project.

Any business can sign up to the My Green Butler program, where they will be invited to audit their current resource use and opportunities for guest savings, be given advice on the smart metering systems, and trained in persuasive communication to invite guests to co-create their sustainability-oriented experiences. In the next chapter, we'll have a look at how he put these into practice in his own business and what the sustainability outcomes were.

Review

At the core of sustainable tourism is understanding the impacts of tourism, setting a vision for sustainability that minimises the negative impacts and maximises the positive ones, being able to track one's path on that vision, and having the means to alter one's practices in response to one's progress on that path. Indicators, combined with an adaptive management mindset, provide the best mechanism to do so, whether these are targeted at the business, community or tourist.

We have reviewed a number of these under the visitor management plans, which combine formalised ways of identifying values, selecting appropriate indicators from, for example, those provided by the UNWTO, and adaptive management mechanisms that allow the performance of a business or destination to be reviewed in light of those indicators.

In many cases, the application of indicators can be reinforced through soft management measures, e.g. interpretive signs, or hard management measures, through regulators mechanisms at an international, national, regional or local level. Ultimately, the latter are doing the same as indicators, tracking business performance against a set of desirable criteria. The former, soft management measures, support regulation by communicating what the harder measures aim to achieve and how.

The importance of communicating sustainability efforts was highlighted in our previous discussions of ethics and norms – when we become accustomed to sustainability as part of our everyday activities, then it will be the absence of sustainable practices that will shock us, not their presence (just think of the community reactions to the phasing out of plastic bags, if you live in a place that has been progressive enough to ban them).

Because of the inseperabilty of tourism, i.e. it is produced and consumed at the same time, and the consumption of tourism almost inevitably involves host communities, tools to manage sustainable tourism will often be most successful if they communicate their efforts to stakeholders, e.g. through certification programs, and invite them to co-create the sustainability of tourism, a theme that we will return to in the next chapter. This can be done through training of staff as well as a clever design of the tourism experience that create inherently enjoyable

7

Questions and exercises

1 Consider the value of ecolabels. How often have you used the presence of an ecolabel on a tourism product to decide between two tourism offerings? If you answered "not very", ask yourself why not.

2 In your view, why does pro-environmental interp retation work best on-site, with little spill over into people's every day behaviours? Can you support this view from the readings presented below?

3 Explain in your own words what the Green Butler is all about. How does it differ from other programs? What makes it unique?

Multiple choice questions

1 The Limits of Acceptable Change model relies on first defining the maximum number of visitors that a tourism site can cope with (carrying capacity): True or false?

2 Some of the key characteristics of a useful indicator include?

a) Their relevance, feasibility to collect, credibility, their ability to be compared across space and time.

b) Their relevance, acceptability to stakeholders, usefulness, and measurability.

c) Their relevance, credibility, comparability and usefulness.

3 All tourism indicators suggested by the WTO need to be objective and measured by a third party to be useful: True or false?

4 The UNEP/UNTWO suggests using regulatory instruments for how many distinct areas of tourism management?

a) 7

b) 8

c) 9

5 Demarketing represents which kind of sustainable tourism management tool:

a) Economic

b) Voluntary

c) Regulatory

Further reading

Simpson, M. C., Gössling, S., Scott, D., Hall, C. M. & Gladin, E. (2008). Climate change adaptation and mitigation in the tourism sector: frameworks, tools and practices. UNEP/UNTWO.

Michailidou, A. V., Vlachokostas, C., Achillas, C., Maleka, D., Moussiopoulos, N., & Feleki, E. (2016). Green tourism supply chain management based on life cycle impact assessment. *European Journal of Environmental Sciences*, **6**(1).

Miller, G. & Twining-Ward, L. (2006). Monitoring as an approach to sustainable tourism. In D.Buhalis & C. Costa, *Tourism Management Dynamics: Trends, management, and tools*, Heinemann, 51-57.

References

Ballantyne, R., Packer, J., and Hughes, K. (2009). Tourists' support for conservation messages and sustainable management practices in wildlife tourism experiences. *Tourism Management, 30*, 658-664.

Ballantyne, R., Packer, J., and Falk, J. (2011). Visitors' learning from environmental sustainability: Testing short- and long-term impacts of wildlife tourism experiences using structural equation modelling. *Tourism Management, 32*, 1243-1252.

Deng-Westphal, M., Beeton, S. & Anderson, A. (2015). The paradox of adopting tourism ecolabels: what is the problem? In Hughes, M., Weaver, D. & Pforr, C., *The Practice of Sustainable Tourism: Resolving the paradox*, Oxford: Routledge, 228-246.

Diedrich, A, Balaguer Huguet, P. & Tintoré Subirana, J. (2011). Methodology for applying the Limits of Acceptable Change process to the management of recreational boating in the Balearic Islands, Spain (Western Mediterranean). *Ocean & Coastal Management* **54** (2011) 341-351.

Gössling, S. & Buckley, R. (2016). Carbon labels in tourism: persuasive communication? *Journal of Cleaner Production, 111*, 358-369.

Gössling, S., Scott, D. & Hall, C.M. (2015). Inter-market variability in CO_2 emissions-intensities in tourism: Implications for destination marketing and carbon management. *Tourism Management, 46*, 203-212.

Ham, S. H. & Weiler, B. (2002). Interpretation as the centrepiece of sustainable wildlife tourism. In R. Harris, T. Griffin, and P. Williams (Ed.) *Sustainable Tourism: A Global Perspective*, (pp 35-44). Oxford, UK: Butterworth-Heinneman.

Howard, J. (2000). Research in progress: Does environmental interpretation influence behaviour through knowledge or affect? *Australian Journal of Environmental Education, 15/16*, 153-6.

Hughes, M. & Morrison-Saunders, A. (2015). Promoting interdisciplinary sustainable tourism. In Hughes, M., Weaver, D. & Pforr, C., *The Practice of Sustainable Tourism: Resolving the paradox*, Oxford: Routledge, 38-51.

Juvan, E. & Dolnicar, S. (2014). Can tourists easily choose a low carbon footprint vacation? *Journal of Sustainable Tourism, 22*(2), 175-194.

Komsary, K.C. Tarigan, H. & Wiyana, G. (2018). Limits of acceptable change as tool for tourism development sustainability in Pangandaran West Java. *IOP Conference Series: Earth and Environmental Science, 126*, 1

Kotler, P., & Levy, S. J. (1971). Demarketing, yes, demarketing. *Harvard Business Review, 79*, 74-80.

7

Mann, J.B., Ballantyne, R., & Packer, J. (2017). Penguin Promises: encouraging aquarium visitors to take conservation action. *Environmental Education Research,* **24**(6), 859-874.

Mau, R. & Tedesco, J. (2015). Sustainable tourism–the Rottnest Island experience. In Hughes, M., Weaver, D. & Pforr, C., *The Practice of Sustainable Tourism,* Oxford: Routledge, 285-300.

Mbaiwa, J.E., Bernard, E.E. and Orford, C.E. (2008). Limits of Acceptable Change for Tourism in the Oka vango Delta *Botswana Notes & Records,* **39**, 98-112

Rogers, E.M. (2003). *Diffusion of Innovations.* 5th ed., New York: Free Press.

Roggenbuck, J.W. (1992). Use of persuasion to reduce resource impacts and visitor conflicts. In M.J. Manfredo (Ed) *Influencing Human Behaviour: Theory and Applications in Recreation Tourism, and Natural Resources,* Campaign, Illinois, 149-208.

UNEP & UNWTO (2005). *Making Tourism More Sustainable: a guide for policy makers.* UNEP/UNWTO.

UNWTO. (1999). Global Code of Ethics for Tourism. Retrieved from http://cf.cdn. unwto.org/sites/all/files/docpdf/gcetbrochureglobalcodeen.pdf

Weaver, D. (2013). Protected Area Visitor Willingness to Participate in Site Enhancement Activities. *Journal of Travel Research,* 52, 377-391.

8 Operationalising Sustainable Tourism

Introduction

As well as simply (!) learning to keep the three sustainability balls in the air, it's important to know how to juggle these balls in a coherent and pleasing manner – after all tourism is part of the experience economy and we want to deliver something that is engaging and attractive to its end users, tourists.

This chapter therefore discusses how to operationalise sustainability in tourism. Some have tried to do this at the level of a destination, creating the 'Green Destinations' brand (Figure 8.1). It's a laudable effort and one which hopefully will lead to greater sustainability for the sector as a whole in the long run. Given what we know about the complexity of the tourism system, creating a green destination is, however, perhaps outside the scope of this book, and of most of us as practitioners or tourism business managers.

Figure 8.1: Green Destinations. http://greendestinations.org/

Instead, we will aim for a more achievable target – in the words of Norman Peale (author of *The Power of Positive Thinking*):

Shoot for the moon. Even if you miss, you'll land among the stars.

This chapter will combine what we have learned to date in Chapters 1-7 and integrate them, using a case study approach of a tourism business that strives to make sustainability a core part of its ethics, business practice and tourism experience. We'll review how it engages with other stakeholders and other partners, how it strives to maximise its positive impacts and minimise its negative ones, as well as its use of indicators and the outcomes of its efforts.

We'll also introduce some new concepts in this chapter. First, we'll review some important considerations of sustainability in tourism, not least of which are tourism as an experiential economy and the characteristics of the 'green market', then we'll look the importance of business models that support sustainability as part of a value creation approach. We'll look at the concept of co-creation and smart systems that support sustainability. The latter will serve as our segue into Chapter 9 on innovation, our final 'content' chapter.

Key words and concepts

- Experience and transformation economy
- Service Dominant Logic
- Green market
- Business models

- Value creation
- Circular economy
- Co-creation
- Demarketing

8.1 The experience economy – integrating sustainability into the tourist experience

The previous chapters have provided a fair amount of knowledge about what should be done to make tourism more sustainable. The World Travel and Tourism Council (2002) reminds us of the 10 priority areas for sustainable tourism as:

1 Waste minisation, reuse and recycling.
2 Energy efficiency, conservation and management
3 Management of freshwater resources
4 Transport
5 Involving staff, customers and communities in envronmental issues
6 Design for sustainability
7 Partnerships for sustainability.
8 Wastewater treatment
9 Land use planning and management
10 Hazardous substances

Test yourself

Of those ten, the first five explicitly require the participation of tourists themselves: tourists need to play an active role in creating a sustainable tourism experience. This leads us directly to the issues of understanding the characeristics of the experience economy and the process of co-creation, and to introduce the concept of Service Dominant Logic.

Tourism has long been positioned a key part of the experience economy; a progression from the agrarian economy (farming, etc.), the industrial economy (manufacturing, etc.), and the service economy (education, IT services, etc.), to the experience economy (entertainment, etc.), where memories themselves become the sales 'product' (Pine & Gilmour, 1999). The next stage, known as the 'transformation economy', may arguably be more relevant to sustainability than the experience economy, and will also be discussed here.

In the experience economy (our current position), customers pay to enjoy a series of memorable events that engage them in a personal way and create feelings of pleasure and arousal. It's not hard to see the relevance for leisure travel, and this sets the tone for how to design tourism for successful sustainability outcomes. It reminds us not to neglect consumer expectations and desires as a key factor in designing successful sustainable tourism experiences. We'll cover this by considering who 'green tourists' are and what they are looking for in their tourism experience, as part of understanding the co-created experience.

Pine and Gilmour (1999, p.206) argue that "experiences are not the utmost in economic offerings", but that the next stage is the 'transformation economy'. Here, success lies in understanding the aspirations of individual consumers, designing an experience that guides them to fully realise those aspirations and transform them. To achieve this, the experience stager must create a bond with the buyer, who must be engaged in personal purposes. As part of this relationship, the 'transformation elicitor' stages a series of experiences to help the buyer persevere towards a common goal. This is the approach adopted by the business owner in the case study that we will be using in this chapter, and we'll unpack how and why it is a useful approach in this context.

Adopting this approach requires a good understanding of how tourists might engage with a sustainability-focussed experience. We'll divide this into three parts; (i) what do we know about green tourists, (ii) why co-creation is so important in tourism experiences and (iii) how the concept of Service Dominant Logic is important to furthering sustainable tourism experiences.

First, lets recap what we know about green tourists (c.f. Chapter 6). Studies consistent show that up to 75% of us care about the environment in some way, but that the majority don't necessarily know how to engage with sustainability in a consumption setting. The proportion of us willing to put our money where our mouth is in buying green products and services is still comparatively small.

Instead, some authors talk about an *emerging* green tourism market, as yet unaware of the benefits of green travel products and services and unfamiliar with the environmental language, but who may be sensitised to green tourism under the correct circumstances (Bergin-Seers & Mair, 2009). An emerging market approach shifts the focus from niche markets such as ecotourism towards mainstream markets.

8

Importantly, research has found evidence that mainstream tourism markets are also concerned with energy efficiency, renewable energy and carbon offsets, recycling, using local produce, waste management and other green initiatives (Andereck, 2009; Dolnicar & Leisch, 2008). So we can assume that there is a benefit to focussing on the future wants and latent needs of this emerging market, as way of introducing them to sustainability and its operationalisation in tourism.

8.2   Co-created experiences and Service Dominant Logic

Enter the term co-creation, and its relative, Service Dominant Logic. The co-creation of value through experiences depends upon the presence of three dimensions: personalisation (meeting individual preferences or needs); engagement (a sense of involvement or identification with the offering); and finally, co-production, whereby the customer is actively involved in forming the product (Minkiewicz et al., 2014). The process of personalisation that allows individuals to co-create their experiences fosters maximum meaning and satisfaction for tourists (Binkhorst & Dekker, 2009).

Such co-created activities can contribute positively to sustainability by involving guest participation, which stimulates positive experiences (Warren & Coghlan, 2016). However, such approaches are not common in mainstream tourism which has been slow to design their experiences around value propositions that embrace sustainability (c.f. the greenhushing in Section 6.3).

Service-dominant logic embraces concepts of the value-in-use and co-creation of value rather than the value-in-exchange and embedded-value (Lusch & Vargo, 2006; Vargo, 2008). The latter is characteristic of a Goods-Dominant Approach, which is arguably still the dominant paradigm in tourism value creation. Table 8.1 shows the transition from a Goods (or products) Dominant Logic to a Service Dominant Logic.

Table 8.1: Underlying conceptual transitions from a Goods Dominant Logic to a S-D Logic, taken from Lusch & Vargo (2006).

Goods Dominant Logic Concepts	Transitional Concepts	S-D Logic Concepts
Goods	Services	Service
Product	Offerings	Experiences
Feature/attribute	Benefit	Solution
Value-added	Co-production	Co-creation of value
Value-in-exchange	Value-in-use	Value-in-context
Profit maximization	Financial engineering	Financial feedback/learning
Price	Value delivery	Value proposition
Equilibrium systems	Dynamic systems	Complex adaptive systems

Test yourself

The key is that we transition from features and attributes (e.g. a pool at your hotel) to a benefit (relaxing and fun environment) to a solution (help you de-stress and make the most of your holiday). The first is value added (here it is for you to enjoy), the second provides the means for guests to actively participate, while the latter is curious about what the guest might enjoy and personalises its recommendations to suit the guest's needs and wants.

To help us think about how to transition to a S-D logic, Lusch and Vargo (2006) have represented by 10 fundamental premises, presented in Table 8.2.

Table 8.2: The 10 Foundational premises for a S-D Logic (taken from Lusch & Vargo, 2006).

FP1	The application of specialised skills and knowledge is the fundamental unit of exchange.
FP2	Indirect exchange masks the fundamental basis of exchange.
FP3	Goods are a distribution mechanism for service provision.
FP4	Operant resources are the fundamental source of competitive advantage
FP5	All economies are service economies.
FP6	The customer is always a co-creator of value.
FP7	The enterprise cannot deliver value, only offer value propositions.
FP8	A service-centered view is inherently customer oriented and relational.
FP9	All social and economic actors are resource integrators.
FP10	Value is always uniquely and phenomenologically determined by the beneficiary.

Some of these are easier to intuitively grasp than others – the sixth, seventh, eight and tenth foundational premises should require little explanation; the tourism provider sets the scene for value to be created, and the tourist determines the actual value that arises from the experience at the tourism location.

The other premises are perhaps not quite so obvious and may need a little more explanation.

The first premise originated from the idea that it is the application of specialised skills and knowledge that is the fundamental unit of exchange in services. My ability to show you around, connect you to the place through stories and interpretation, navigate the local geography as well as culture, keep you safe and look after your basic needs, form the basis of exchange in tourism's SD-Logic.

The second premise "indirect exchange masks the fundamental basis of exchange" speaks to the nature of the tourism supply chain or value chain. The end 'product' of tourism is delivered through a complex combination of goods, money, institutions and so forth, so that its service nature might not always be apparent.

An example of this premise combined with the third premise "goods are a distribution mechanism for service provision" is apparent in volunteer tourism. It always strikes me as interesting that volunteer tourists who pay

8

a third party provider to organise their trip, later question why they paid so much, when they could have paid the actual host volunteering organisation so much less and organised the trip themselves. This relates to these two premises – they are paying for a curated and verified list of projects, branded and packaged, with the reassurance of a known contact point and a registered organisation that can be held to account if anything goes wrong. They are not simply being upsold a bed and meals at a host volunteering organisation! The goods are being used in a complex web of providers to create the end experience.

The fourth premise, "operant resources are the fundamental source of competitive advantage" is a little more complex. As with the first foundational principle, it arose out of the idea that knowledge is the fundamental source of competitive advantage – an *operant* resource that acts on other resources (while an *operand* resource is the resource on which an act or operation is performed). It is therefore the skills and knowledge of employees, the tourism firm's resources, that act upon other types of resources (e.g. the culture of a place, its natural features) to create a competitive advantage.

The fifth premise, "all economies are service economies", refers to the idea that essentially everything boils down to a service, now increasingly apparent through specialisation and outsourcing.

The ninth premise, "all social and economic actors are resource integrators" also refers to the value/supply chain, or networks, required to deliver a tourism experience.

The trick here is to use the SD-Logic model to build sustainability into the value created through SD-Logic within the experience itself. Using traditional model approaches that look at how value is created and captured within a business can therefore be useful to understand where and how sustainability-related activities can be integrated into the tourism experience rather than bolted on, as an awkward, semi-visible addition to the tourism experience, e.g. "hang your towels up and we won't wash them" and yet we'll provide you with new single-use water bottles daily, won't allow you to open your windows to cool your room and so forth.

Green Tourism-Scotland strives to make tourism business incorporate a green philosophy at the core of their members' businesses: "sustainability and the environment are at the heart of what we do" (Figure 8.2). It combines the areas where tourism businesses can take practical steps, e.g. energy and water savings, new habitats for biodiversity, fairly traded and/or local products, waste recovery, creating awareness of environmental issues in customers and so forth. The figure also lists the value of this approach captured for the business (savings, reduced costs, marketing advantage) as well as value created for customers (better customer experience and better understanding of green issues).

Figure 8.2: The value creation cycle proposed by Green Tourism-Scotland. Read the full report: https://www.green-tourism.com/wp-content/themes/gtbs/data/Green%20Tourism-Scottish%20Impacts%20Report%202018.pdf

8.3   Business models for sustainability

Business models are primiarily concerned with value creation and value capturing for businesses and their clients. And this is where we want to include sustainabilty considerations so that they become a core part of the value creation process. Business models can be viewed from two distinct, but interrelated angles: as an *object*, the business model focusses on a firm's attributes that can be directly measured and/or observed (e.g. its activities and products, its processes and profit formulas); as a *cognitive schema*, it captures that way that businesses think and talk about their value. In contrast to the business model as an object, the business model as a schema allows us to think of it as something that is malleable and which can either guide or impede action and decision making. The latter approach is encouraged where the goal is to allow for much more flexible approaches to value creation that can lead to innovation in tourism.

One key aspect of any successful business model is to focus on the integration of activities that create and capture value. An integrated approach captures all the complex interactions between all stakeholders, both producers and consumers, that play a part in co-creating the final business unit. It deliberately considers both the value that a customer derives from the business offering and the value that the supply chain is able to capture, and is able to take into consideration a wider range of players, some of whom may disrupt traditional ways of producing value (Reinhold et al., 2017).

In an applied context, we talk of business models as a tool, such as the well-known Business Model Canvas (Osterwalder & Pigneur, 2009). This is a visual chart with elements describing a firm's or product's value proposition, infrastructure, customers, and finances. The gaol of a good business model is to keep the focus on the value proposition, the relationships that will enable that value proposition to manifest and the business structure that will support its sustainability.

Table 8.3 describes the business model canvas of a social enterprise in Fiji that aims to empower local village women by giving them employment as stand up paddle tour guides. The value proposition is to offer an active and cultural activity to resort guests, through a benefit sharing mechanism.

Table 8.3: The business model canvas for a new tourism business, Ocean's Daughter in Fiji.

Key partners	Key activities	Value propositions	Customer relationships	Customer segments
Resorts Villages Blue Planet SUP board suppliers Banks Insurers Hotel Association	Board sales to resorts SUP tours led by village ladies Finding Nemo & friends family SUP tours Retreats for women	Doing something fun, active and healthy, that gives an insight into local culture and supports local communities/ empowers women using a recognised brand for its products/ activities	Face to face encounters during tours, with post-tour hospitality, and supported by social media engagement (e.g. FaceBook page)	Active women Honeymooners Couples Families with young children New SUPers Experienced SUPers
	Key resources Fijian Women in Business mentoring group Blue Planet Boards & equipment Training & guides Certification agencies Banks Storage facilities		**Channels** Social media Reviews Inbound tour agents Direct marketing Hotel industry associations	

Cost structure	Revenue streams
Equipment and merchandise Certifications Insurance Commissions and taxes Marine operator licences	Selling boards to resorts SUP tours Retreats Merchandise

Test yourself

Question

Taking into consideration what you've learned in Section 8.1 and 8.2, which of the boxes in the Business Model Canvas should be the focal point of your planning, from which the content of all the other boxes will be derived?

8.4 Case study: integrating sustainability into the business model

Crystal Creek Meadows in an interesting case of integrating sustainability into the business model for several reasons: first, it is one that I am very familiar with as I supervised the PhD study that led to a co-created sustainability tourist experience, and the evaluative research that logged the initiatives impacts. Second, the owner and driver of this transformation will readily admit that sustainability was not part of his agenda when he first started the business with his wife, as part of a lifestyle change. Fortunately, he has both tracked his progress towards a holistic and co-created sustainability experience for his luxury tourists (c.f. Warren et al., 2018).

Crystal Creek Meadows is a hospitality business offering rural tourism in Kangaroo Valley, near Sydney in New South Wales in Australia. The business can accommodate up to 14 persons/night, spread across 4 self-catered cottages on the 16 acre property. The cottages are rated 4.5-star; the business is not currently marketed as an eco-business, instead customers are mainly attracted by the rural setting, interior comforts, children's activities, day spa services and self-catering facilities.

The cottages and other buildings are between 10 to 30 years old using timber frames and boards, energy mix is electricity, LPG and firewood, rainwater is harvested in each cottage using a 22,000 litre tank. More and more sustainability-oriented features have been added over the last decade, e.g. the addition of a solar panel system and switch to green energy, a carbon offset program by planting local trees, as well as operational plans to minimise their carbon emissions as well as those of their suppliers, and finally certifications in ecotourism and Climate Action (Table 8.4).

Similar to other forward-thinking properties, the owners established a baseline of resource use (electricity, gas, fuel, water, gas, waste) that allowed them to track their use in relation to the sustainability initiatives that they were implementing. However, the owners' on-going monitoring of resource use on the property as a whole indicated that their sustainability-oriented actions had a reached a 'green ceiling' (i.e. a type of glass ceiling in pro-environmental behaviours) in terms of resource savings.

8

Dr Warren decided to do something that most tourism properties would consider *radical* – he wanted to involve the guests in creating a more sustainability business. Now remember that these are not eco-tourists, they have no strong attachment to the environment, and relatively little knowledge about how to behave in a pro-environmental manner. In addition, they have paid a substantial nightly rate to relax and be free of responsibility for 2 or 3 nights. And yet, Dr Warren felt strongly enough to trial inviting guests to become part of his effort to break through that green ceiling.

Table 8.4: The progressive addition of sustainability features into the business (adapted from Warren et al., 2018).

Sustainability-oriented features of the business	Date	Sustainability focus
Eco-efficiency: house and cottage floor, roof and veranda insulation	2005/14	Environment
Policy: 12 years on the Kangaroo Valley Tourist Association board	2004-12	Social
Construction: Grey water irrigation and citrus orchard	2005	Environment
Guest engagement: complimentary bikes with baskets to promote fresh local produce picnics	2006	Environment
Guest engagement: Counter bins for food scraps to feed chickens, recycle bins	2006	Environment
Guest engagement: designed range of ecotourism activities within the local area	2006	Environment
Knowledge: commenced state and national tourism awards	2006-12	Economic
Knowledge: gained Ecotourism Certification and Climate Action certification	2006–17	Environment
Eco-efficiency: switched to accredited firewood supplier	2007	Environment
Community: Green Kangaroo carbon calculator involving 24 local businesses	2007	Environment
Eco-efficiency: 1 kWh solar system benefiting from grant	2008	Environment
Eco-efficiency: offset carbon balance by planting 55 trees (later including guests in tree planting activities) and firewood plantation for cottage fireplaces (replacing electric heating)	2008	Environment
Eco-efficiency: purchase 100% Green Power	2008	Environment
Guest engagement: card requests separating jars for reuse	2008	Environment
Guest engagement: offer free rail and coach transfers	2008	Environment
Guest engagement: guest wildlife donation option when booking	2008	Economic
Guest engagement: smart electricity meter in Rose Cottage and house	2008	Social
Eco-efficiency: pelmets across all rooms and thermal back curtains throughout	2008–14	Environment
Plan: office and home green practices, and builder, tradesmen emissions reduction practices contract	2009	Environment
Plan: Climate change risk mitigation & adaptation	2009	Economic
Knowledge: share business case history at over 20 conferences, seminars, onsite tours	2009	Social
Construction: Three in one 5 kWh solar, wood store, water harvesting facility	2009	Economic
Plan: Food Miles & Green Suppliers Report	2011	Environment
Plan: EMS including electricity audit	2011	Environment
Knowledge: sponsored UNSW PhD student climate change prize	2011	Social
Guest engagement: Aboriginal interpretative guide book linked to local operators	2012	Social
Guest engagement: Establish vegetable garden, scissors, gloves, basket	2012	Social
Renovation: replacing cottage spa bath with 130 litre claw foot bath	2013/4	Environment
Eco-efficiency: replaced top loading washing machine for efficient front loader	2013	Environment
Guest engagement: join TripAdvisor Green Leaders	2014	Economic
Guest engagement: counter top compost bins	2017	Environment

The starting point for his approach was anecdotal observations by the owner of the business that some guests are more willing than others to participate in his green initiatives, e.g. segregating food scraps to feed the chickens or add to composting. His gut feel was that guests who are more positive are more responsive to pro-environmental messages, and are more willing to test out new pro-environmental behaviours if invited to do so. This led to a search for wellbeing measures that could test this hunch, as well as ways to boost wellbeing through sustainability-related activities during guests' stay at Crystal Creek Meadows. This is another way of saying how do we include sustainability in the value created through the tourist experience.

Wellbeing is a growing areas of research with a number of established measurement scales, e.g. Life Satisfaction scale, Hope scale. After trialling these with friends and colleagues, it was felt that they could not easily be applied to guests visiting Crystal Creek Meadows in a way that did not interfere with their holiday experience. Instead the authors turned to a less formalised clinical approach called 'strengths spotting'. This identifies which of the 24 character strengths that make up a person's personality, e.g. hope, gratitude, kindness, perseverance and passion or zest for life, are being used in any given situation. We particularly want to spot signature strengths, character strengths that we are both very good at, but more importantly make us happy when we act on them.

Why spot guests' signature strengths in relation to the sustainability of a tourism business? Encouraging people to identify, and enact their signature strengths is a type of positive psychology intervention that is proven to boost wellbeing. Asking people to consciously use their signature strengths has been found to encourage positive behaviours in a range of contexts, e.g. education, health and veteran programs. Could they also work in tourism to encourage pro-environmental behaviours? Could this perhaps represent the type of new approach needed to deliver intrinsically rewarding engagement in pro-environmental behaviours.

THECONVERSATION.COM
A green and happy holiday? You can have it all

Figure 8.3: A green and happy holiday? Read more about Crystal Creek Meadows here:
https://theconversation.com/a-green-and-happy-holiday-you-can-have-it-all-65038

Table 8.5 lists the 24 signature strengths that are recognised in the literature and specifically how we might think of them in a pro-environmental context.

Table 8.5: Park et al.'s (2004) definition of values in action – inventory of character strengths, adapted for pro-environmental behaviour (Warren & Coghlan, 2016).

Character strength	Applied to pro-environmental behaviour
WISDOM & KNOWLEDGE	
Creativity [originality, ingenuity]:	Coming up with/putting into practice novel, different ways of living/consuming to minimize impacts on the environment
Curiosity [interest, novelty–seeking, openness to experience]:	Taking an interest in all of an ongoing environmental experience; exploring and discovering about one's impact on the environment; interested in new ways of living which minimize negative environmental impacts and might be positive impacts.
Judgment [open–mindedness, critical thinking]:	Thinking environmental things through and examining them from all sides; not jumping to conclusions; judging environmental claims, defining environmental problems; changing one's mind in light of information; weighing all evidence (environmental, societal, social norms) fairly.
Love of learning:	Mastering new pro-environmental skills, topics and bodies of knowledge, whether on one's own or formally; beyond curiosity to describe the tendency to add systematically to what one knows.
Perspective [wisdom]:	Looking at the bigger picture, placing pro-environmental behaviours within a larger context.
COURAGE	
Bravery [valour]:	Not shrinking from a natural environmental threat, difficulty, or pain, speaking up for what is right for the environment even if there is opposition; acting on convictions even if unpopular and/or costly includes physical bravery but not limited to it.
Persistence [perseverance, industriousness]:	Finishing what one starts; persisting in pro-environmental action in spite of obstacles (internal and external); "getting it out the door"; taking pleasure in completing pro-environmental tasks.
Integrity [authenticity, honesty]:	Speaking the truth about ones pro-environmental behaviour and practices, presenting oneself in a genuine way; being without pretence; taking responsibility for one's feelings and actions towards nature and the environment.
Zest [vitality, enthusiasm, vigour, energy]:	Describing a passion for the environment that translates into pro-environmental behaviours; not doing pro-environmental practices or behaviour halfway or half-heartedly; feeling alive and activated to enjoy the environment.
HUMANITY	
Love:	Valuing a close relationship with nature (animals and planets); being close to animals and plants; valuing 'mother earth'.

Kindness [generosity, nurturance, care, compassion, altruistic love, "niceness"]:	*Undertaking an action because we feel a sense of care for nature.* Doing favours and good environmental deeds for nature and natural resources; positively improving nature.
Social intelligence [emotional intelligence, personal intelligence]:	Being aware of the motives and feelings of other people and oneself and how they conflict with the desire for pro-environmental behaviour; knowing what to do to be more pro-environmental; knowing one's own limitations.

JUSTICE

Fairness:	Treating the environment according to notions of fairness and justice; not letting personal feelings bias decisions about nature; moderating behaviour to give nature a chance
Leadership:	Encouraging a group of which one is an member to get things done such as; encouraging pro-environmental change in a public-sphere; trying to see pro-environmental actions happen
Citizenship [social responsibility, loyalty, teamwork]:	Working well as a member of a group which cares for the environment; recognising that everyone has a role to play in protecting the environment, wanting to do one's bit, being loyal to the group; doing one's share; signing a petition, making a donation; belonging to an environmental group

TEMPERANCE

Forgiveness and mercy:	Being understanding of how we as a species impact the environment, and wanting to do better. Forgiving those (including oneself) who have done harm to the environment; giving people a second chance; not being vengeful
Modesty and humility:	Letting one's pro-environmental accomplishments speak for themselves: not seeking the spotlight for one's actions; not regarding oneself as more special than one is
Prudence:	Being careful about one's choices; not taking undue risks; not saying or doing things that might later be regretted for the environment. Weighing up alternatives and taking the one that is the least damaging.
Self–regulation [self–control]:	Formally regulating one's consumption to not waste natural resources, pollute nor harm habitats; to choose alternatives even when they do not offer financial benefits

TRANSCENDENCE

Appreciation of beauty & excellence [awe, wonder]	Noticing and appreciating the beauty of the natural world and its symmetry
Gratitude:	Expressing an appreciation of nature. Being aware of and thankful for the good environmental things that happen in society by a company, community, institutions or individual; taking time to express thanks
Hope [optimism, future–mindedness, future orientation]:	Expecting the best from society for environmental care in the future; believing that a good future for nature and the environment is something that can be brought about by themselves, and others

8

A first step in this approach was to identify whether guests who were more receptive to pro-environmental messages and behaviours displayed certain signature strengths through a strengths spotting exercise. And sure enough, tourists who displayed character strengths were more likely to report engaging in pro-environmental behaviours or hold pro-environmental attitudes (Warren & Coghlan, 2016).

They expect more information about the environmental impacts of their stay, are more willing to make small behavioural changes during their stay to help the environment. For example, they search for opportunities to be involved in conservation whilst on holiday, access to local fresh produce, donating to wildlife conservation, viewing carbon footprint, having the room cleaned with eco-friendly products and having electricity used in the room powered by solar panels. They are also more likely to rate the responsibility for dealing with environmental impacts of a holiday as resting with the individual, rather than external agents.

Even more interestingly, this approach uncovered findings that were not known to us prior to the study: Chapter 6 introduced us to the issue of the Knowledge – Attitude – Behaviour gap, an issue that we still try to overcome by filling the gap with more knowledge through information. And it's true that, among the signature strengths are curiosity and judgement. Equally important through are social intelligence, self-regulation, hope and citizenship, which were more prevalent in the strengths spotting analysis.

We concluded that tourism experiences designed to appeal to specific character strengths can encourage tourists to adopt pro-environmental behaviours. Guests' character strengths simply need to be built into the experience in a way that focusses on sustainability. Warren and Coghlan (2016) look at how the character strengths model can be overlayed on to Pine and Gilmour's experience model discussed in Section 8.1. In cases where we are looking for tourists to be both immersed and active (key characteristics of co-created experiences) we are actually looking to target strengths such as zest, bravery, citizenship, kindness and integrity

Next the results needed to be implemented as a system that could be applied across the business to integrate the character strengths into the experience, to link wellbeing with sustainability in a way that the tourists could co-create. The system consists of a technological (smart meters for resource use and computer-based guest information system) and a sociological component, applying persuasive communication and politeness theory. Basically complementing old fashioned welcoming and engaging hospitality with technology.

Applying politeness theory to hosted visitor accommodation allowed hosts to engage guests by providing them with information on the sustainable infrastructure and equipment of the rooms and facilities, and persuading them to 'use less'. The host, in this case, Dr Warren, gives the guest a tour of the cottage and explains how to use various everyday items such as kettles, curtains and fans in a way that promotes sustainability within the context of his climatic micro-climatic environment and knowing how tourists like to enjoy his property.

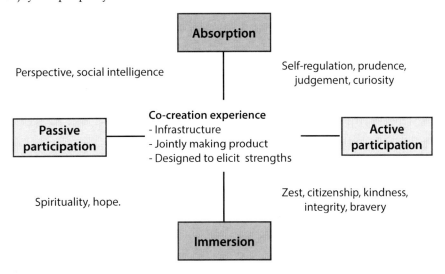

Figure 8.4: Realms of experiences which can appeal and nurture guest character strengths to co-create (taken from Warren & Coghlan, 2016))

The smart system monitors guest resource used, for each cottage and captured each minute. Daily advice on the previous day's resource consumption, in combination with suggestions on how to stay comfortable depending on the weather, are provided to guests in the form of a daily report card.

The combination of a guided tour on how to behave sustainability, the invitation to do so by the host (and his pledge to donate all fiscal savings made to a local wildlife group), monitoring and direct feedback, benchmarked against other guests, as well as ongoing advice on how to minimise resource use, were found to result in reduced resource consumption, but also maintain or enhance levels of guest satisfaction (Warren et al., 2017). Table 8.6 summarises the approach that integrates the personal touch with the pledge with the guided tour and the smart metering and feedback.

This approach could also be considered a form of pro-environmental gamification of tourist pro-environmental behaviours in hospitality. Games are often used to encourage pro-social and pro-environmental behaviours, commonly by gamifying those behaviours. Gamifying refers to "the process of using game thinking and game mechanics to solve problems and engage users" (Deterding et al., 2011, p.10), Gamification techniques in tourism create more memorable experiences, by enhancing the social, emotional and immersive aspects of the tourist experience, creating more engaging, interactive and entertaining experiences during travel, and driving loyalty, experience sharing and memories post-experiences (Xu et al., 2017).

Test yourself

8

Table 8.6: Overview of the approach to integrate sustainability considerations into the guest experience (adapted from Warren et al., 2018)

At Check-in, the guest is invited to participate in sustainability initiatives	*Breaking the ice:* Hand shake, light joke, meet the chickens, connect with the children	
	Pre-giving: Explain local attractions, highlight free property facilities, give free wifi pass	
	Exchange norm Offer to make restaurant booking, carry luggage from car	
	Appeal:	
	(Test 1) Showcase self-benefits of cottage followed by direct appeal to conserve resources	(Test 2) Showcase technical eco-friendly nature of cottage, personally specific recommendations, make appeal to converse resources
	Conclusion: Inform them of daily eco feedback and Invite them to sign pledge	
Daily guest experience	*Strengths-based sustainability-oriented activities:* Invite guests to feed the chickens as a form of kindness, use the shower timer as a form of self-regulation, check the feedback sheet to engage curiosity & perspective	
	Feedback: Smart system monitoring of guests' daily resource use, and daily eco feedback sheet provided to guests on their usage.	
Occasional intervention by the host	*Assistance:* Advice, recommendations as requested	

A review of the literature on gamification shows that encouraging sustainable consumption is a focal area for gamification, alongside education, health and exercise, commerce and innovation/ideation (Hamari et al., 2014). It has been applied for example in reducing domestic energy consumption (Johnson et al., 2017) and tourist accommodation (Warren, Becken & Coghlan, 2018). Negruşa et al., (2015) found games can be used to develop economic, social and environmental sustainability in tourism, although this represents a relatively new areas of research within the gamification literature.

The new approach therefore combined aspects of positive psychology and gamification into a pro-environmental intervention that aimed to be an intrinsically rewarding, co-created positive tourism experience, and used persuasive communication and politeness theory to "sell" the intervention to guests upon arrival. The gamification of the intervention allowed guests to track their progress against benchmarks of pro-environmental performance.

It's an approach that had never been used before, and came about through what is known as action research, where a problem that needs solving is identified – in this case, how to break the green ceiling of resource savings in hospitality. Action research allows the researcher to implement, test, and review their approach based on the test results, achieving practical improvements through reflection and critical analysis.

In terms of co-creation, the guests partnered with the host in a power-sharing relationship where the host was able to provide advice and information and guests were able to collaborate with other members of their party and collectively solve the problems to use resources most efficiently. As part of the progressive involvement of guests, guests had 'scaffolded' learning opportunities, and at the end of their stay the host was able to discuss guests' reflections on the experience. Under the ethics approval conditions approved by the authors' institution, guests were not aware of the research aspect of the interaction until the end of their stay.

So what did they actually do in their co-created experience?

As shown in Table 8.6, the owners of Crystal Creek Meadows invited guests to take part in the sustainability practices of the business in a way that encouraged the use of the types of character strengths described in Table 8.5. Zest (vitality, enthusiasm) was encouraged through the use of bicycles with baskets and fresh produce for picnics offsite.

Kindness (nurturance, care and generosity) could be expressed by saving food scraps in a separate bin to use to feed the chickens. Curiosity was encouraged through the Aboriginal interpretive guide book linked to local operators and the guide to local ecotourism activities. Self-regulation and prudence were encouraged through a range of smart metering of resource use (i.e. water, electricity and gas meters for each cottage) and daily feedback sheets. Citizenship was encouraged by giving guests the opportunity to donate to a local wildlife protection organisation as well as by joining the tree planting activities to offset their travel-related carbon footprint.

Meanwhile ingenuity (or creativity) was showcased by encouraging guests to visit the grey water irrigation system in the citrus orchard and pick fruit, as well as the three-in-one 5 kWh solar, wood store, water harvesting facility, while appreciation of beauty was facilitated through the availability of gardening implements to cut the local flowers, the locally produced aromatherapy products and the five senses walk of plants used in the aromatherapy products.

What was the outcome?

Because this was part of an action research project, it is possible to evaluate the outcomes of this way of integrating sustainability into the value proposition of the business. Consumption data were collected for each guest stay and two questions were asked as part of a broader departure survey administered to all guests, to determine how receptive guests were to this approach. The quantitative part of the study provides objective measurement of research use, whereas the qualitative components reveals guests' own perceptions of their consumption. The owner also kept reflective memos which helped to

8

identify influencing factors in guests' responses, and enabled progression to discussion points with other guests.

Table 8.7 indicates the resource savings made by providing the right infrastructure in the cottages (e.g. the improved insulation, smaller bath and so forth) and by inviting guests to incorporate sustainability practices into their experience in a way that is known to boost wellbeing and value adds to their time at Crystal Creek Meadows.

Overall, the study showed the guests who received the welcome by the hosts, the tour of the cottages and their sustainability features, and the daily monitoring feedback (based on the smart metering) as well as advice on how to be more sustainable used significantly less electricity (27.4%), gas (22.3%), water (21.6%) and firewood (10%). These are significant savings and demonstrate just how sustainability efforts can be incorporated into the tourist experience, so tourists might become actively involved and play their part in greater sustainability, when the conditions are provided for them to do so.

For the business as a whole (remember as this was an experimental study, some guests carried on as normal) electricity usage was reduced by nearly 1/3 from a mean of 28,386kWh in the 2007 baseline recording, to a mean of 17,574kWh, as the business incorporated more and more sustainability initiatives. Gas measures also showed a decline, although not as substantial as electricity, and finally firewood use decreased by nearly a quarter. The business savings are also reported for those readers who prefer the Green is Gold approach (c.f. Chapter 2).

Table 8.7: Resource savings for the business as a whole, in relation to its sustainability efforts.

Electricity	Gas LPG	Firewood
Baseline (2007) kWh 28386	Baseline (2007) 900 kg	2009-15 mean tonne 16.070
2008-16 mean kWh17574	2016 585 kg	2016 tonne 12.000
Mean saving kWh 10812	Mean saving 147	Saving tonne 4.070
@0.27 cents per kWh = $2,919 pa	Current rate $107 per 45 kg	Current rate $ 300 per tonne
Seven year saving $20,434	Seven year saving $3,668	Single year saving $400

It is particularly important to point out here, that this approach added to the guest experience, rather than detracting from it, as many business owners fear that it might. Remember, also, that these are mainstream tourists – the business is not marketed as 'eco' and the guests report typical travel motivations (rest and relaxation, spending time with family and friends) in their pre-arrival surveys, and are no more or less green than you or I.

Test yourself

The guests that did receive the full experimental treatment reported engaging in twice as many resource-saving actions than the control group. Guests' reported level of satisfaction of their experience at Crystal Creek Meadows was no different between the two groups.

Indeed some of the guests reported that the experience enhanced their stay because they were learning new techniques to keep comfortable in different temperature using natural ventilation, or because they knew that the fiscal savings were going to a good cause (local wildlife NGOs) or because they appreciated the advice to help them have an more enjoyable stay, e.g. recommending local attractions which were also applying more responsible business practices. Those guests who were acting as the control sample in the experience were less enthusiastic about the idea of receiving eco-feedback on their consumption (34%) compared to the guests who had been approached with the intervention who felt knowledge of resource use would add or strongly add to their stay experience (70%).

As part of this case study, Dr Warren reflected on the lessons learned from trying to make sustainability a core part of his value proposition. His experiences reinforced his point of departure: that conserving resources represents a low cost method to achieve savings compared to buying eco-efficient technologies. Since energy and water can account for a high proposition of SMEs expenditure, guest conservation behaviours represent a prudent positive strategy

By inviting guests to be a part of the scheme, he discovered that what prevents conservation progress is perhaps more to do with the values and attitudes of the hospitality managers than to do with guests' attitudes. Reiterating what we have covered in Chapter 2, he argues that if managers have a low comprehension of resource use then they will not be able to appreciate opportunities for conserving, and will certainly not be able to invite guests to help them in this endeavour.

He believes that for tourism business to be more sustainable, tourism management stakeholders need to move away from the classic 'measure, monitor and manage' mantra. Instead, we need to build radically new ways of consuming sustainably at accommodation and boldly confront our current ways of life in the built environment, giving tourists a direct and active role to play in their consumption in a way that enhances their wellbeing and places sustainability at the core of a tourism experience. Chapter 9 will continue to develop these ideas by talking about innovation and sustainable tourism.

8

Review

One of the key issues of sustainable tourism is how to operationalise sustainability – a tricky issue for many reasons – not least that sustainability in tourism represent a form of wicked problem, the systemic issues that affect sustainability in tourism, and its fragmented, networked nature. Where do we even apply sustainability? At the level of the tourist? The business? The destination? The supply chain? At a policy level?

All of these apply – we need policy to create the right ecosystem to support sustainability, and we want all our tourists to have green inclinations. In this chapter, however, we've explored an approach based on combining character strengths/values (c.f. Chapter 6) and building these into the co-created experiences available at a tourism business, to create a value proposition based on integrating sustainability considerations in the core of the business operations.

This chapter has introduced you to how to create value in service sectors, combining business management concepts (e.g. Service-Dominant Logic), with practical tools (e.g. the Business Canvas Model, and the 24 character strengths in an environmental framework) and illustrated these in the context of a specific case study, with the accompanying video. Hopefully, this has given you a clear perspective on all the ways that a business can include sustainability considerations in its operations and invite tourists to be part of the solution in a fun, engaging and satisfying way.

If you look closely, you'll also see many of the other elements covered in the previous chapters integrated into this chapter!

Questions and exercises

1   Review the case study material in light of what you have learned in Chapters 1-7. Which concepts can you see in practice here (think of ethics, supply chains, knowledge hubs, impacts, carbon calculators, circular economies, partnerships, policy and so forth)? Use the tables, particularly Table 8.5 to guide you.

2   Based on your answer to the previous activity, which concepts could be further build into this approach to reinforce the operationalisation of sustainability.

Multiple choice questions

1   Which of the 10 priority areas for sustainable tourism, as per WTTC, require the participation of tourists themselves?

a) Management of fresh water, transport options and waste minimisation

b) Management of fresh water, partnerships for sustainability, wastewater treatment

c) Waste minimisation, transport options and partnerships for sustainability

2   The concept of 'value-in-exchange' is a feature of the type of service-dominant logic that want to see in tourism? True or false?

3   The value proposition should always be at the centre of a business model as it dictates the rest of the decisions for the business: True or false?

4   Which character strengths were particularly useful in designing a co-created sustainable tourism experience at Crystal Creek Meadows?

   a) Strengths associated with knowledge and temperance (curiosity, love of learning, self-regulation).

   b) Strengths associated with courage and justice (integrity, citizenship, zest).

   c) Strengths associated with transcendence and humanity (kindness, social intelligence, hope).

5   The greatest resource savings recorded by Chris were in guests' use of?

   a) Water

   b) Gas

   c) Electricity.

Further reading

Fesenmaier, D. & Xiang, Z. (Eds) (2017*). Design Science in Tourism: Foundations of Destination Management.* Cham: Springer.

Shove, E., Pantzar, M. & Watson, M., (2012). *The Dynamics of Social Practice: Everyday Life and How it Changes.* Sage: London.

References

Andereck, K.L. (2009). Tourists' perceptions of environmentally responsible innovations at tourism businesses. *Journal of Sustainable Tourism,* **17**(4), 489-499.

Bergin-Seers, S. and Mair, J. (2009). Emerging green tourists in Australia: their behaviours and attitudes. *Tourism and Hospitality Research* ,**9**(2), 109-119.

Binkhorst, E. & Dekker, T. D. (2009). Agenda for co-creation tourism experience research. *Journal of Hospitality Marketing & Management, 18*(2-3), 311-327.

Deterding, S., Dixon, D., Khaled, R. & Nacke, L. (2011). From game design elements to gamefulness: defining gamification. In *Proceedings of the 15th international academic MindTrek conference: Envisioning future media environments.* pp.9-15, ACM.

Dolnicar, S. & Leisch, R. (2008). An investigation of tourists' patterns of obligation to protect the environment. *Journal of Travel Research, 46,* 381-391.

Hamari, J., Koivisto, J. & Sarsa, H. (2014, January). Does gamification work?– a literature review of empirical studies on gamification. In *2014 47th Hawaii international conference on system sciences (HICSS)* (pp. 3025-3034). IEEE.

8

Johnson, D., Horton, E., Mulcahy, R., and Foth, M. (2017). Gamification and serious games within the domain of domestic energy consumption: A systematic review. *Renewable and Sustainable Energy Reviews*, **73**, 249-264.

Lusch, R. F. & Vargo, S. L. (2006). *The Service-Dominant Logic of Marketing: Dialog, debate, and directions*. Armonk, N.Y: M.E. Sharpe.

Minkiewicz, J., Evans, J. & Bridson, K. (2014). How do consumers co-create their experiences? An exploration in the heritage sector. *Journal of Marketing Management*, **30**(1-2), 30-59.

Negruşa, A. L., Toader, V., Sofică, A., Tutunea, M. F. & Rus, R. V. (2015). Exploring gamification techniques and applications for sustainable tourism. *Sustainability*, **7**(8), 11160-11189.

Osterwalder, A. & Pigneur, Y. (2009), *Business Model Generation - A handbook for visionaires, game changers, and challengers*, Osterwalder & Pigneur, Amsterdam.

Park, N., Peterson, C. & Seligman, M. (2004). Strengths of character and wellbeing. *Journal of Social and Clinical Psychology*, **23**(5), 603–619.

Pine, J. & Gilmore, J. (1999). *The Experience Economy*. Boston, Harvard Business School Press.

Reinhold, S., Zach, F.J. & Krizaj, D. (2017). Business models in tourism: a review and research agenda. *Tourism Review*, **72**(4), https://doi.org/10.1108/TR-05-2017-0094

Vargo, S. L. (2008). Customer Integration and Value Creation: Paradigmatic Traps and Perspectives. *Journal of Service Research*, **11**(2), 211-215. doi:10.1177/1094670508324260

Warren, C. & Coghlan, A. (2016). Using character strength-based activities to design pro-environmental behaviours into the tourist experience. *Anatolia*, **27**(4), 480-492.

Warren, C., Becken, S. & Coghlan, A. (2017). Using persuasive communication to co-create behavioural change: Engaging with guests to save resources at tourist accommodation facilities. *Journal of Sustainable Tourism*, **25**(7), 935–954.

Warren, C., Becken, S. & Coghlan, A. (2018). Sustainability-oriented Service Innovation: fourteen-year longitudinal case study of a tourist accommodation provider. *Journal of Sustainable Tourism*, 1-20. DOI: 10.1080/09669582.2018.1511721

Xu, F., Buhalis, D. & Weber, J. (2017). Serious games and the gamification of tourism. *Tourism Management*, **60**, 244-256.

Section 3:
The Future of
Sustainable
Tourism

9 Change and Innovation

Introduction

By its very definition sustainable tourism is a both a current- and a future-oriented activity; it's tourism "that takes full account of its current and *future* economic, social and environmental impacts, addressing the needs of visitors, the industry, the environment and host communities" according to the UNWTO. Understanding sustainable tourism and managing therefore has a very strong future-oriented component, which is the focus of this chapter.

Often, when we want to understand the future, one of the first things that we need to do is look to the past to identify the trends that have got us to where we are now, and that, in all likelihood, will continue to be trends into the future. The context for tourism's future is a history of spectacular and sustained growth, measured in terms of volume, geographic spread, economic benefits, as well as environmental and social impacts. Going back 40 years to the 1970s, tourism has grown from under 70 million international tourist arrivals, to over 1 billion international tourist arrivals in 2012, according to UNWTO estimates.

This chapter focusses on the future-oriented considerations. We look at what changes are coming, how to understand those changes, ride the wave of change where it is our interest, and weather the storm of change when it isn't. We cover innovation and structural changes, those tipping point type of changes that once they have occurred are unlike to ever revert back to their original state (unlike temporal change such as seasonality through peak, shoulder and low seasons).

Innovation, in particular, is a buzzword in tourism – we speak of digital disruptions, smart tourism, shared economy/peer-to-peer platforms and so forth. These are all exciting terms, which in many cases can directly impact on sustainable tourism by reducing waste and/or consumption, or creating a more equitable playing field for smaller tourism providers in more remote areas.

It's important not to conflate change with progress, however. As we'll see in talking about innovation, the very first characteristic that an innovation must possess to be successful is a relative advantage over what already exists. If it doesn't offer a relative advantage, it's important to ask yourself – why do it? Have you fallen into the trap of "pro-innovation bias" – that innovations are inherently superior and should diffuse more rapidly through a system than existing products of services.

In this chapter will consider both the changes, and challenges, that the tourism sector is facing going into the future, we'll discuss what innovation actually is, how we can classify innovations to better understand what they are, and how they either get adopted or rejected. This chapter will also look at an example of an innovation from my own work, to illustrate these concepts in practice and give a personal perspective on what it takes to get a new product or idea from the state of an invention (where it exists in your head or your lab only) to an innovation (where it is available on the market).

Key words and concepts

- Temporal and structural change
- Black swans, wildcards, X factors, disruptors
- Forecasting
- Environmental scanning
- STEEP

- Scenario-based planning
- Delphi analysis
- Business as usual
- Green economy
- Innovation

9.1 Understanding change

Change can come in several forms – seasonality is one well-known example in tourism, and is a form of changing demand patterns, where holiday peak periods are followed by shoulder and low seasons, and these repeat yearly. This type of change can usually be predicted and managed through planning based on prior experience. We know that last year's summer season visitor numbers were 20,000, and winter season were about 7,000, so we can expect more or less the same this year.

If you have been paying attention, you'll notice how the previous chapters in this textbook will serve you well in understanding change. In Chapters 5 to 8 you've learned to carefully research your particular situation, speak to stakeholders, decide on a desirable end state for your business, attraction, host community and/or destination, engaged in planning, selected appropriate indicators to track change and then monitored what those indicators have told you about the state of the system and adjusted your management accordingly. That is almost (although not quite, in practice) the easy stuff.

It is the unpredictable change – the wildcards, disruptors or black swans that come out of nowhere and severely disrupt your system – that you also need to understand and manage. It is the structural change, changes to the system as a whole, occurring incrementally until you reach a tipping point of no return that will affect how you run your day to day operations. It is the changes in the broader system that you need to be aware of and be able to respond to. And finally, it is the radical innovations that you need to keep up to date with.

Whatever the type of change, you will need to learn to recognise it, understand its implications and know how to respond to it. Often it is the incremental change occurring outside the immediate sphere of influence of tourism that are the hardest to spot and so this is where we will start our discussion of change.

Types of change

One common way of scanning for relevant change is to adopt what is known as a STEEP approach. Here you consider different aspects of our interconnected systems focussing on Social, Technological, Economic, Environmental and Political dimensions of that system. Understanding current and past changes can then be used to forecast future tourism development, as well as inform contingency analysis of a range of future forecasts (we'll talk about both forecasting, environmental scanning and scenario-based planning in the next section).

Social factors

Scott and Gossling (2015) have identified several significant trends that have affected the growth of tourism in the past and will continue to affect growth into the future.

Starting with social factors, we want to consider how changing demographics, ethnic diversity, religion and cultural factors might influence tourism. Perhaps one of the demographic changes that has received the most attention is this notion of an ageing population; many people (in developed countries in particular) are living longer, the average life expectancy has gone up approximately 10 years over the last couple of generations, meanwhile families are getting smaller with parents having fewer children. These two trends combined means fewer youths, and more elderly people.

Test yourself

An ageing population has varied impacts on tourism. Retirees have more leisure time, and often, enough disposal income to be able to travel (whether that is a luxury cruise, or a caravan-based road trip). Some tourism sub-sectors are well positioned to capitalise on an ageing population – the travel section of the British newspaper the Telegraph recently ran with a story about what happens if you die on a cruise ship (Figure 9.1).

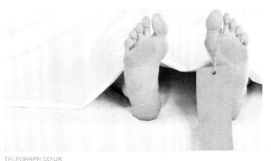

TELEGRAPH.CO.UK
What happens when someone dies on a cruise?

Figure 9.1: What happens when someone dies on a cruise? https://www.telegraph.co.uk/travel/cruises/articles/What-happens-when-someone-dies-on-a-cruise/#

Older tourists might also have different health concerns – at the very least mobility factors should be taken into consideration with older markets, so that there are opportunities for seating, easy access using ramps, and so forth. Some have also suggested that larger print might be beneficial in signage and promotional material, and greater emphasis on comfort and safety. Accessible travel is likely to become a strong trend in the future of tourism, applying the seven principles of universal design (e.g. equitable use, flexible use, low physical effort) to make tourism experiences and infrastructure accessible to more people.

Along with these changes, several studies are looking at generational differences in needs and expectations. The so-called Millennials, individuals born in the 1980s and 1990s, are clearly digital natives, with a greater propensity to use Web 2.0 as a primary source of information, and a strong desire for greater work life-balance than their predecessors. They have also been described as the ME generation, with the implication that the "what's in it for me" message is clearly communicated, as well as the importance of customised and flexible experiences that speak to the individual's values and needs and how they add to a person's sense of (perceived/portrayed) identity.

Millennials have also been described as more socially conscious, although this can sometimes be related to slacktivism (low investment social activism, e.g. online petitions, social media shares or likes towards a social cause). The importance of visuals in marketing can also be attributed to this younger generation, both in terms of imagery, but more generally in the way that information is provided. Consider for instance, Airbnb's at-a-glance integration of available accommodation with photos alongside a visual representation of where these listings are situated (Figure 9.2).

9

Figure 9.2: The importance of visuals in tourism – not just marketing imagery but also quick visual guides of the location of listings.

Another socio-demographic trend that is growing ever more prominent is the emergence of multicultural markets, resulting from combined trends of globalisation (many of us now have parents of different nationalities), a growing diaspora of migrants around the world and the rise of new markets from BRICS nations (Brazil, Russia, India, China and South Africa). This leads to an increasing appreciation of cultural diversity, with various impacts on business practices and hospitality provision (think, for example, of the varying diets across religions and regions).

Technological factors

The importance of trends in technology cannot be overstated. As someone born in the 1970s, I still remember the days of travellers' checks. These were used before it was possible to withdraw cash from cash machines anywhere in the world and certainly before internet banking and online transactions, smartphones, apps and contactless payment systems.

Technological changes cover both ICT and all its associated applications in communication channels, database management, information systems, artificial intelligence and smart systems, but also advancing technology in transport (think of the new non-stop flights between Australian and London launched in March 2018, made possible through advances in fuel efficiency and aircraft design) as well as more efficient building designs, green energy and so forth.

Improved transport-related infrastructure (e.g. the expansion of highways and airports) and advanced technology have enabled people to travel more easily and comfortably. The decreasing cost and increasing speed of travel (e.g. high-speed rail and aviation) have combined to create a time-space compression that allow more travellers to travel greater distances in shorter times.

Arguably the most obvious technological change has been development of information and communication technology (ICT) systems. The internet in

Test
yourself

particular has been instrumental in changing the way tourists connect with businesses in travel planning and booking phases, as well allowing direct communication between customers and businesses and tourism destinations. Moreover, social media applications have increased transparency in travel service quality and provided peer-to-peer platforms for travellers to share information, shifting the balance of power between customers and tourism providers.

The rise of mixed realities (augmented and virtual reality) will be covered in Section 9.2 on innovation and in the case study. Guttentag (2010) was one of the first tourism scholars to clearly mark the potential of VR to contribute to the tourism sector, particularly in planning and management, marketing, entertainment, education, accessibility and heritage preservation – a prediction that has proven largely correct.

Whether Virtual Reality will replace travel entirely, creating Virtual Tourism, as some commentators are predicting, remains to be seen. It has the obvious benefit of eliminating much of tourism's carbon footprint, and managing issues such as overtourism, but the economic impacts of Virtual Tourism on tourism businesses and host communities have yet to be quantified.

Economic factors

When it comes to economic factors, the first E in STEEP, we know that economic growth in key markets has been a major driver of tourism development. Traditionally this focussed on OECD countries, but now increasingly the emerging economies of the BRICS nations are responsible for the continued and accelerating growth of tourism. The UNWTO estimated that Chinese tourists are responsible for up to 21% of the worlds international tourism spending and is the world's fastest growing source market (UNWTO, 2018).

The growing prosperity of prospective tourists, as well as the introduction and expansion of paid holidays have been important economic and social drivers of tourism growth. Tourism's contribution (direct and indirect) to gross domestic product (GDP) has increased from an estimated $5.5 trillion in 2003 to $6.9 trillion in 2013 (representing 9.55% of global GDP). Similarly tourism's (direct and indirect) contribution to global employment has increased from 7% in 1980s to 8.1% (or 214 million jobs) in 2004 to 8.9% (or 265 million jobs) in 2013. There have been downturns in international tourism arrivals, particularly with the Global Financial Crisis of 2007-2008, but the general trend has been for growth in tourism.

9

The environment

Test yourself

The second E in STEEP is the environment. Chapter 3 covered the impacts of tourism on the environment. Many of these trends are unlikely to be halted and/or reversed in the near future. The future of tourism will undeniably be shaped by climate change, as it affects the attractiveness of destinations, will impact on transport and destinations through the increase of extreme weather events and potentially through carbon taxes to reduce carbon emissions.

The rapid rise of the consumption of natural resources (including freshwater), changes in land cover, habitat loss and species extinction, changes in biogeochemical processes, the release of pesticides and herbicides, as well increasing air pollution, landfill and plastics in the ocean are all environmental trends that will affect tourism within destinations. Frightening statistics exist around the volume of plastics now polluting our waterways and oceans – the most comprehensive study of ocean plastic pollution dates back to 2010, with results suggesting that 8 million tonnes of plastics end up in our oceans in one year alone. And that figure is expected to double every 11 years, i.e. by 2021.

As a diver and marine biologist, this is an issue close to my heart. Even if you are not like me, but you have commented on the pollution at beach holiday destinations, then you will know what why this is an issue. This report from the popular destination of Bali is just one example of the problem:

TELEGRAPH.CO.UK
Bali declares rubbish emergency as rising tide of plastic buries beaches

Figure 9.3: Plastic waste on a beach in Bali. Read more here: https://www.telegraph.co.uk/news/2017/12/28/bali-declares-rubbish-emergency-rising-tide-plastic-buries-beaches/

Political factors

Political changes (the P in STEEP) have also played a role in the growth of tourism, particularly through changes in border regulations as well as the liberalisation of travel markets. Europe's Schengen Agreement has made travel within Europe much easier, whilst the dissolution of the USSR has removed the barriers for travel between Eastern and Western Europe. It is estimated that approximately 136 million travellers now come out of ex-USSR countries. China has also seen major changes in its outbound tourism policy, with packaged tours to 146 destination countries permitted as of 2013.

On the other hand, after the terror attacks of September 11, political upheaval during the Arab Spring, various disease outbreaks (e.g. SARS) and natural disasters such as Iceland's volcanic eruption in 2010, and the major tsunamis in South East Asia in 2004 and Japan in 2011.

9.2 Forecasting

Adopting a business as usual (BAU) philosophy, we can argue that these trends are likely to continue shaping tourism development into the future, and forecasting can therefore build on these trends and their growth data to predict future tourism development. Scott and Gössling describe how a wide range of forecasting techniques are available to "assess well-established trends, or influencing factors for which there is a reasonable understanding of" in order to plan several years ahead.

Many national tourism organisations, as well as government departments and international institutions such as the UNWTO and World Travel and Tourism Council (WTTC), make tourism forecasts available at regional, national and international scales. They include expected economic growth to US$10.9 trillion contribution to global GDP by 2023 (WTTC, 2014), global employment increase to 345 million by 2023. The UNWTO anticipates an increase in international tourist arrivals to 1.8 billion by 2030, and a doubling of the commercial aircraft fleet and RPK. In short, they forecast a sustained economic growth for tourism, as well as a continued shift towards Asia, the Pacific and the Middle East.

Scenario-based forecasting

An alternative way of planning for the future is to use scenario-based forecasting. Scenario techniques allow planners to explore greater complexity and uncertainty of more distant futures. They are different to forecasts or predictions, in that they present alternative and plausible futures. Instead of extrapolating predictions based on current trends, scenario-based planning is used to constructively challenge the BAU approach, or at the very least complement it so that we can open up our eyes to alternative futures.

Scenario-based planning is not commonly used in tourism, but we can learn a lot from scenario-based planning used in other sectors such as energy, demography, economic development, biodiversity and ecosystem change, transportation and mobility, agriculture and food production and water security.

Tourism will have to respond to the changes already described throughout this book and in this chapter. Most of these are described by Scott and Gosling as slower evolving trends, such as:

Test yourself

☐ Regional demographic change (ageing, population growth, increased urbanism).

☐ Climate change and the requisite transition to a low carbon economy.

☐ Technological change (social media, mobile computing, the Internet of Things, automation).

These are all relevant for the future of sustainable tourism and have been explored by the UN Environment Programme-led Green Economy Initiative

9

as part of building scenarios of what sustainable tourism might look like in the future if we actively plan and manage for it.

The report provides a comprehensive coverage of the types of tourism growth trends and impacts covered in this textbook, and couples these with advances in environmental and social sustainability made in other economic sectors (e.g. renewable energies). It then posits what would happen to tourism if these advances became part of mainstream tourism planning, development and management. It is therefore a blend of scenario-based planning and forecasting.

The initiative compares tourism development under a Business-as-usual (BAU) situation with two green investment scenarios. The latter scenarios still led to increased international tourism arrivals by 2050, but these were 30% lower than in the BAU predictions. Meanwhile, tourism's contribution to global GDP was estimated at US$ 9.3-10.2 trillion, and direct employment estimated at US$531-580 million. Under the same scenarios, water consumption was reduced by 18-23% and CO_2 emissions reduced by 31-52%, suggesting that tourism growth was still compatible with improved social and environmental outcomes.

 Download UNEP's Tourism in the Green Economy report here: http:// www.greengrowthknowledge.org/sites/default/files/downloads/resource/ Tourism_in_the_GE_%20UNWTO-UNEP.pdf

Scenario-based planning has another noteworthy advantage; it helps overcome what is known as the 'optimism bias' where businesses focus on familiar patterns, leaving them "vulnerable to being blindsided by unexpected, disruptive events" (Scott & Gössling, 2015, p. 278).

It explores the interactions between major known drivers of change (such as those presented above), as well as encouraging planners to consider the strategic implications of game changers, also known as 'black swans' or X-factors, that can result in high-impact, non-linear changes. Examples of black swans or X-factors that could severely disrupt the tourism system are pandemics (global diseases whose spread would be facilitated through international travel), a supervolcanic eruption (e.g. Yellowstone), global terrorist attacks, including cyber-attacks and so forth.

Question

Taking each of the STEEP elements, try to think of at least one black swan or X-factor event that has occurred in global tourism in the last decade.

Tip: The 9/11 attacks, Hurricane Katrina or the volcanic eruption are some examples. Try to think of others.

Scenario-based planning may be useful to understand the future of tourism development under the type of deep decarbonisation of our economic activities required to reach the 70% GHG emissions reductions needed to prevent severe climate change. Deep decarbonisation aims to provide ways to limit global warming to an increase of less than 2^0 Celsius, while still allowing for economic prosperity in a decarbonised world. Due to its large carbon footprint tourism will eventually become an area of focus for deep decarbonisation.

Foreseeing this, the Queensland Government commissioned an interesting report on tourism's Climate Change Response Plan (Becken et al., 2018). The table on page 50 of the report provides ways in which tourism can lead the way to carbon neutrality in that Australian state.

Read the report: https://www.qld.gov.au/__data/assets/pdf_ file/0036/68697/building-resilient-tourism-industry-qld-ccr-plan.pdf

Meanwhile a country that we have already discussed a few times for its progressive thinking reports being the world's only carbon *negative* country:

Watch Tshering Tobgay at TED: https://www.ted.com/talks/tshering_ tobgay_this_country_isn_t_just_carbon_neutral_it_s_carbon_negative

YOUTUBE.COM

This country isn't just carbon neutral — it's carbon negative | Tshering Tobgay

Deep in the Himalayas, on the border between China and India, lies the Kingdom of Bhutan, which has pledged to…

Figure 9.4: Bhutan, a carbon negative country

Other black swan-type scenarios that might seriously disrupt the growth of tourism include a serious pandemic, where travel becomes personally risky and is highly regulated to prevent further spread of the biohazard; a regional conflict in the Middle East that disrupts oil supplies; another prolonged volcanic eruption that interrupts aviation routes; or abrupt climate change that leads to stricter GHG emissions regulations. These events would all have serious impacts on the future economic sustainability of tourism.

Ask the expert

A third way of thinking about the future of sustainable tourism is to ask experts for their opinion. This can be done informally or in a more systematic way. The advantage of the latter approach, e.g. using a Delphi analysis, is that it elicits both a range of views and some level of consensus on those views. A Delphi analysis is a structured communication technique that allows for systematic, interactive forecasting through the use a panel of experts. The experts answer questionnaires in two or more rounds, with results of each round presented back to the panel for further comment to develop a list of key ideas or concerns with some level of consensus by experts.

9

A number of Delphi analyses have looked at the future of sustainable tourism. For example, Scott and Gössling (2015) present a comparison of issues considered important by the tourism sector based on a Delphi analysis and compares it with a list of the global risks deemed to be of highest concern for 2014-2024 according to the World Economic Forum's global panel, 2014. Table 9.1 presents the two lists. The difference between the two lists raise concern about tourism's state of preparedness for an apparently uncertain future – and one which presents significant sustainability-related challenges across sectors and countries.

Table 9.1: A comparison of the most important challenges of the next 10-20 years (taken from Scott and Gössling, 2015)

Rank	Most prominent challenges facing tourism in the next 20 years (von Bergner and Lohmann, 2014)	Global risks of highest concern for 2014-2024 (World Economic Forum, 2014)
1	The preservation of nature in destinations despite pressure from tourism to use it	Fiscal crises in key economies
2	To maintain sustainability, meet the rising impact on the environment as well as increasing demand from new markets and stay attractive at the same time.	Structurally high unemployment/ underemployment
3	Quick reaction on unforeseeable events (volcanic eruptions, terrorist attacks, natural disasters, etc.) in the form of more prepared contingency plans	Water crises
4	Tourism facilities and destinations need to take green development into consideration	Severe income disparity
5	The uncertainty of climate change effect, especially at local level	Failure of climate change mitigation and adaption
6	Further development of sustainable tourism management strategies in a globalised travel world	Greater incidence of extreme weather events (e.g. floods, storms, fires)
7	Growing need for investments in qualified human resources despite high cost pressure on employers in tourism	Global governance failure
8	The implementation of tools to promote sustainable tourism development in order to create rising awareness and better understanding of sustainable tourism and its effects for a local and global community and to support its development	Food crises
9	To handle the increasing cost pressure (rising costs for transportation, increasing global competition etc) in tourism	Failure of a major financial mechanism/ institution
10	Tourism needs to adapt to the different (and fast changing) communication tools and information platforms	Profound political and social instability

Scott and Gössling (2015) drive home this point with specific reference to carbon emissions. In order to phase out CO_2 emissions, tourism will have to plan for and implement a future powered by 100% renewable energy within the next 40 years – a plan that is not yet apparent at any level of governance or within any part of the tourism sector.

One common response that we have to these changes is to call for innovation, and in particular innovation that can tackle the big questions of sustainability and a greener economy in tourism.

9.3 Innovation in tourism

Innovation is one of those buzzwords that seems to be sticking around. Many people view innovation as the 'lifeblood' of business – businesses need to innovate to stay alive; they need to predict and stay ahead of changing consumer demands and other STEEP trends to remain competitive. Another argument in favour of innovation is that if we are to successfully meet the challenges of the future, whether it be climate change, global governance or development opportunities, we need new ways of doing things.

Much of what we know about innovation come from the manufacturing sector (e.g. innovations in smartphones, green energy sources, food production processes), with less focus on the services sector, and even less on governance. As covered in Chapter 8, services have this unique aspect of co-creation which also affects the type and nature of successful innovations. Surprisingly, tourism is an area which does quite poorly in the innovation space (Hjalager, 2010).

I have my personal views as to why this is so, and it comes down to the discretionary and experiential nature of tourism. Because we treasure our holiday time as something so important to our identity, relationships and physical and mental health, I feel it is difficult to test inventions (pre-market innovations) with tourists in-situ, or in real live tourism contexts.

Businesses don't want to risk a bad customer experience, and the ensuing bad customer review, by asking tourists to trial a new product, service or way of doing things during their holiday. You could do what many manufacturing companies do, ask a panel of people to trial an innovation in a more controlled way or environment – but does that practice have 'ecological validity', i.e. do the tests provide results that mimic tourists' views and attitudes during a travel experience?

Another, systems-based, explanation for the paucity of innovation in tourism is presented by Hall and Williams (2008). They visually represent all the different elements required for innovation in tourism, from an openness to international research and development, to local government policies that support innovation through funding and regulatory acts, sectorial connectedness and individual firms' human capital. These are represented in Figure 9.5 and it is a both a complex picture and perhaps somewhat of a demoralising one, given what we have covered in previous chapters.

9

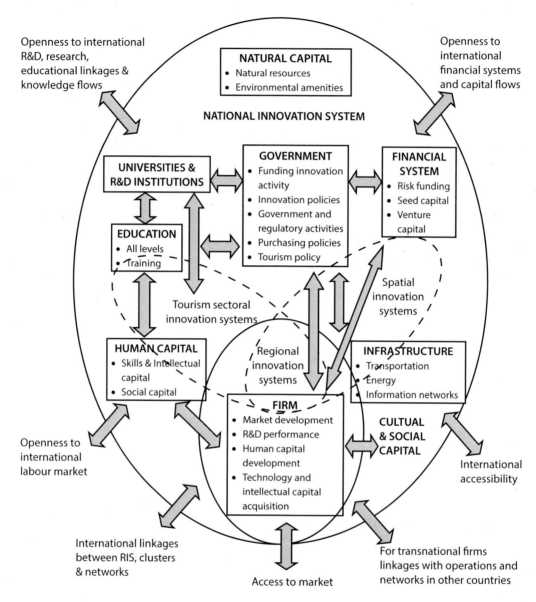

Figure 9.5: Elements of national innovation system (from Hall & Williams, 2008, p.113)

Innovation in tourism therefore tends to be relatively rare and often quite conservative – with a general approach of "if it ain't broke, don't fix it". In the language covered in the next section, most tourism innovations fall into the 'newness' category of imitative innovations or incremental innovations.

Defining innovation

Innovation refers to "an idea, practice, or object that is perceived as new by an individual or other unit of adoption" (Rogers, 2003, p. 12). It is defined as the implementation of organisational learning, new ideas, new processes and products within an organisation (Calantone et al., 2002). Taking the perspective of marketing, innovation refers to a product or service which is perceived new by consumers (Ram, 1987).

There are three widely used approaches to categorise innovations:

1 Newness,

2 Area of focus and

3 Attributes.

The degree of **newness** of an innovation evolves from 'imitative', 'incremental' and 'discontinuous' to 'really new' and 'radically innovative', and combines one or both of new technologies and new markets for a product or service.

Imitation innovations are new to a firm but similar to existing market products or services whereas *incremental* innovations occur through on-going product development (Garcia & Calantone, 2002). The *discontinuous* innovations stage comprises line extensions or new product lines that do not replace existing infrastructures. The *really new* innovations stage replaces either technology or market (but not both) externally of the firm and internally (either or both). The most advanced stage, *radical* innovations, holds both new technologies and penetrates (or generates) new markets.

The second approach to innovation categorisation looks at the **area of focus** of an innovation: does it involve a new product, or process, or marketing focus (Adams et al., 2011). Being able to categorise an innovation by area of focus allows a business to achieve two things: first, to be very precise about what the goal of the innovation is, and second, to reflect on whether its innovation focus is too narrow and whether it could focus on other areas as well.

The third type of categorisation considers innovation **attributes**. These are more descriptive properties, features or intangible qualities that reflect people's perceptions of an innovation. In terms of innovation research, innovation attributes have been perhaps one of the most applied areas of research.

Rogers (2003) identifies five attributes required for successful market diffusion for innovation:

Test yourself

1 Relative advantage,

2 Observability

3 Compatibility,

4 Complexity (too complex is a negative) and

5 Trialability.

9

Innovations that are strong in these areas are more likely to successfully diffuse through a market, as people become aware of the innovation, are persuaded that the innovation offers them benefits. They will then decide to use it, or not, and their attitudes towards the innovation will be confirmed or disconfirmed. Rogers (2003) presents a model of innovation diffusion (Figure 9.6) with these stages and attributes, and a range of other variables that contribute to the successful diffusion of innovations into a market place. If you have an innovation that you want to launch into the market place, this model is an excellent starting point to evaluate whether your innovation has what it takes to be successful.

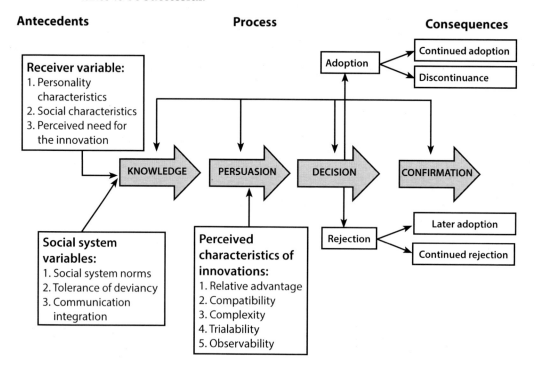

Figure 9.6: Rogers' Diffusion of Innovations Model, integrating the attributes of an innovation, the stages of innovation adoption (or rejection) and the other variables necessary for an innovation to successfully diffuse through a market.

Of course the flip side of this, are those innovations that fail. A lot less is known about the failures, partly due to this innovation bias that we discussed earlier, and partly because unsuccessful innovations don't survive to tell the tale. There is some literature in this area, although not much (Bagozzi & Lee, 1999; Heidenreich & Spieth, 2013).

Innovations can fail as a result of issues in three very different domains:

1 The characteristics of the innovation

2 The characteristics of (non)adopter

3 Behavioural constraints.

Innovation characteristics that will impede diffusion are not surprisingly the inverse of the attributes that lead to successful diffusion. The literature suggests that where there is no perceived added value to be derived from the innovation, or where it is (perceived to be) difficult to use, or where it has a poor image or its adoption might reflect badly on the image of the user, and/or there are significant risks (image, financial or other) associated with its adoption, innovations are more likely to fail, regardless of the market for them.

The market itself may be resistant to innovation, either through consumer inertia, or individual resistance to change. Personality characteristics associated with general trust/agreeableness, openness to new experiences as well as extraversion tend to be more associated with the adoption of innovations, and conversely those who scores lower on these traits tend to be more resistant to innovations.

Finally, there may simply be behavioural constraints that impede the diffusion of innovations. People may have already invested in an alternative product or service, and perceive the switching costs to be too high, or feel that there are sunk costs too great to allow for new alternatives. There may be a lack of awareness of an innovation, and finally habits can be very difficult to break! Adopting an innovation may simply go against the grain.

Sustainability-oriented innovations

Not all innovations focus on competitiveness alone. More recently researchers have started to describe innovations that focus on sustainability as their main driver. These are often pitched under the 'green is gold' banner that we covered in Chapter 2, and wherever possible are described as adding value to the tourist experience. Although relatively new to the literature, these are becoming known under the banner of sustainability-oriented innovation (SOI).

SOI is the deliberate action of becoming more sustainable by purposefully improving all functions, products and services, changing the firm's role within society, and linking sustainable goals and technical methods (physical and social) to achieve a competitive advantage (Adams et al., 2016; Klewitz & Hansen, 2014).

Research into SOIs often have one or a combination of three distinct aspects:

1 **Resource-driver**: when resources are scarce or unaffordable for small businesses or communities

2 **Social-mindedness**: when there are equity concerns in small businesses or communities

3 **Environmentally-driven**: where there are concerns about the impact of business or lifestyles on the local natural environment.

Figure 9.7 breaks these drivers down into further sub-drivers, and also provides examples of some of the ways these types of innovations might be

9

described by the people who champion them. Understanding how people describe their SOI allows you to better identify and discuss what outcomes they are seeking from the SOI, as well as what other outcomes they haven't yet considered but may be possible from it.

The model is built on research in developing countries, but applies equally well to sustainability innovations in more developed nations, particularly where these have been developed by SMEs, who represent the largest number of business in the tourism sector.

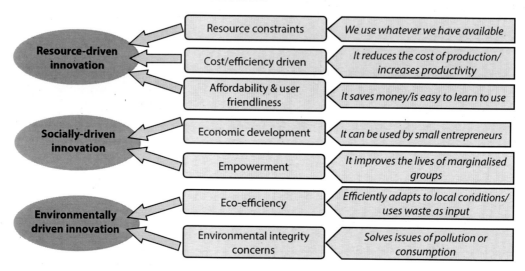

Figure 9.7: The drivers of sustainability-oriented innovations, adapted from Sarkar & Pansera, 2017

The concept of sustainability-oriented innovation (SOI) provides a sharper focus to firms seeking to progress towards sustainability (Adams et al., 2016). In tourism, SOIs tend to centre on resource use and waste, often through renewable energies, smart systems (including smart meters), ICT and the shared economy. The latter has received a lot of attention as a 'disruptor' in tourism (c.f. Section 9.1), and in this sense could classed as both resource and socially-driven sustainability innovation, in the sense that it opens up SME to the market place through digital innovations.

Christopher Warren, who we encountered in Chapter 8 is a man who is passionate about sustainability-oriented innovations. Using his own experiences as well as those of his business acquaintances and friends, and combining those experiences with the literature, Chris proposed his own model of SOI adoption and/or rejection in tourism SMEs. He describes it as a much messier progression than typical models, with fuzzy boundaries between types of innovation and leaps and starts and lags and gaps in the various skills and knowledge and implementation of SOIs. His conceptualisation of SOIs in tourism is presented in Figure 9.8.

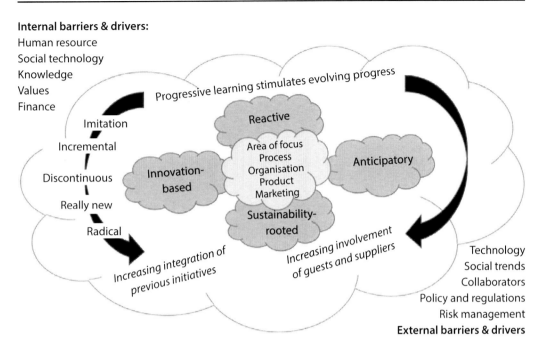

Figure 9.8: Fuzzy boundaries of sustainability oriented service innovations (adapted from Warren, Becken & Coghlan, 2018)

The peer-to-peer accommodation and experience provider, Airbnb, is often provided as a case study in tourism innovations (Dolnicar, 2017; Volgger et al., 2018). Although the model is continuously evolving, the original accommodation providers of Airbnb were hosts with spare beds, rooms or entire apartments/houses, providing cheaper alternatives for travellers, offering authentic connections between hosts and travellers and allowing private home-owners access to the market (Guttentag, 2015). Other similar peer-to-peer offerings have followed suit, and in many cases, are offering alternative forms of mobility for travellers and more efficient use of resources.

Many smaller businesses can benefit from some more quirky innovations. The following videos highlight some of my favourites when it comes to resource consumption. I plan to use the SmartFlower solar power generator in my own holiday home, and currently do use Luminaid when I am camping and LifeStraw when I am travelling to avoid buying bottle water. Many of the ecotourism businesses that I work with in developing countries are also investing in similar products to reduce their consumption through changing guest behaviour, e.g. promoting filtered water over bottled water (c.f. Chapter 8 on the importance of a co-created sustainable tourist experience).

9

https://www.youtube.com/watch?v=btdX8Qdb
yRQ&feature=youtu.be

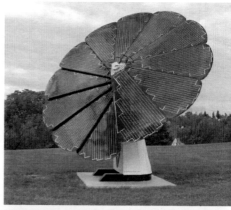

Figure 9.9a: SmartFlower solar power generator

https://www.youtube.com/
watch?v=8HQNnUNwFms

Figure 9.9b: Luminaid solar rechargeable light

https://www.youtube.com/
watch?v=i82YD7uvi2s

Figure 9.9c: LifeStraw water purifier.

The type of smart metering system described in Chapter 8's case study is another example of feedback mechanisms that allow tourists to modify their consumption behaviour in response to real-time consumption data, and a colleague of mine is following up that line of research with smart meters, artificial intelligence and digital message board in hotel showers that encourage guests to use less water.

Other areas that could potentially be transformative for the sustainability of the tourism industry are Virtual Reality (discussed in more detail in the following section) and low carbon transport such as the proposed hyperloop. The article below describes what the hyperloop is and its potential social and environmental impacts.

GLOBALRAILWAYREVIEW.COM
How will hyperloop systems affect society and transport?

Figure 9.10: Hyperloop systems. https://www.intelligenttransport.com/transport-articles/74281/hyperloop-systems-society-transport/

9.3   Innovation case study: Virtual Reality

Virtual Reality (VR) has quickly established itself as a buzz word in tourism, generally referring to the types of immersive computer-generated audio-visual experiences, sometimes with tactile input (Krueger, 1991), or more commonly to 360^0 photo or video experiences (e.g. Fabola et al., 2015).

While there are calls for VR to enhance the co-created tourist experience, it is not clear how best to achieve this using VR, particularly during the tourism experience. Indeed, the tourism-related VR experience is often limited to creating destination awareness at the pre-purchase stage, as an alternative to travel or to preserve artefacts that may not be displayed to the general public.

This case study looks at a new way of using virtual reality to assist in connecting tourists to nature-based tourism assets to better protect them. My IT colleague Lewis Carter and I believe that new ways of linking tourism and the protection of its nature-based assets can be delivered through technology. To make this link fun, informative and interactive, we have been developing a Virtual Reality coral reef game that helps reef tourists get a better sense of what they have witnessed during their tourism experience at Australia's Great Barrier Reef and unpack the complexity of a World Heritage Listed protected area that is both fragile and unique.

The Great Barrier Reef is as an underwater, offshore natural attraction that presents unique interpretation challenges for operators. Our game was designed in response to a very specific tourism need – underwater attractions can create interpretation issues as communication (you have a snorkel in your mouth!) and access can be problematic.

We went with a VR game, as games are an excellent educational tool and have been researched in tourism to create memorable experiences by enhancing the social, emotional and immersive aspects of the tourist experience (Xu et al., 2017). They identify the benefits of games as increasing brand awareness and interest, as well as increased sales conversions in the pre-travel stage, creating more engaging, interactive and entertaining experiences during travel, and driving loyalty, experience sharing and memories post-experiences.

To date, tourism games focussing on natural environments have mainly used location-based approaches such as those reported in Nunes & Mayer's (2014) study. These allow tourists to check in at certain locations, collect rewards to be used at a nearby tourism businesses, and discover information about the site. We wanted our game to be more interactive, dynamic and responsive than that, with a strong educational and emotional component to it, that would achieve three aims:

1   Be fun!

2   Create a deeper sense of connection and understanding of the reef environment

3   Lead to direct conservation outcomes.

Our Virtual Reality game allows players to build their own reef ecosystem, and develop an understanding of what constitutes a healthy reef ecosystem through playful trial and error. Players start with an empty seascape, and place coral to increase the biotic coverage of their system, encouraging other wildlife to move in as the game progresses. The player must manage the system, dealing with bleaching events and coral aggression to continue expanding their reef, and eventually create an ecosystem that is healthy enough to support apex predators such as a shark.

The game is strongly based on a realistic simulation of a reef, and teaches an understanding of ecosystem complexity and resilience. The VR aspect of the technology creates an immersive, 360°, 3D underwater seascape, replicating what tourists have just seen and allowing the chance to explore in more detail the marine life and ecosystem processes on the reef.

Our case represents the first case (to the author's knowledge) to apply games to a nature-based tourism attraction and UNESCO-listed heritage site which does use not use a location-based approach or 360° degree imagery, but instead seeks to 'unpack' the functioning of the ecosystem itself, and lead directly to conservation outcomes for the nature-based tourism attraction that it represents.

To achieve our desired outcomes, the work required an interdisciplinary approach, i.e. that "…analyses, synthesizes and harmonizes links between disciplines into a coordinated and coherent whole", drawing on ICT and game development, business and tourism, marine biology and conservation science, to make the VR game fun, engaging, educational and accurate. It is also a good example of the type of sustainability-oriented innovation that can happen when colleagues from different disciplines get together to create positive change.

Review

Change in sustainable tourism is both inevitable and desirable. Inevitable because tourism responds to the STEEP structural changes that are going on around it, and desirable because sustainability is effectively a change in itself from our current production and consumption patterns, both at an individual and structural level.

This chapter highlights the various types of change, both temporal and structural, and how the tourism sector must respond to these if it is to be sustainable. While the latter can be planned and managed with a fair degree of certainty, the latter requires different techniques. Environmental scanning is one such technique, looking for changes in the areas of social, technological, environmental, economic and political trends, that might impact on tourism.

Each of the STEEP areas are important, but it is perhaps in the environmental area that tourism has the greatest responsibility to change its own practices, notably its carbon footprint. Equally, it is the technology area that holds the most promise for this sector to become more sustainable as well as undergo the most significant forms of change.

Technological advancements allow us to innovate, be it imitative, incremental, really new or radical innovations, that can have a positive impact on our natural and social environment. Smart systems, artificial intelligence, augmented and virtual realities will all continue to disrupt the tourism sector, hopefully in ways that reduce our consumption and build our connections to the places and communities that we visit.

We must also be aware of the innovation bias that exists and remember to consider the relative advantages of various innovations as well as the possible reasons why people may not accept an innovation even if it does offer a relative advantage (and has the four other attributes that allow an innovation to successfully diffuse through a market).

The old adage "if it ain't broke don't fix it" is, of course, true. Yet we know that sustainability in tourism is a dynamic process, that requires constant adjustment, practice and skill. There is at least one area where it is broke, and that is its carbon footprint, and many other areas, covered in Chapter 3, which warrant at least some level of change in order to really drive tourism towards greater sustainability.

The final chapter of this book will bring together the areas where tourism still needs to change in order to be become more sustainable.

9

Questions and exercises

1 There a number of annual tourism innovation awards, e.g. *Tourism for Tomorrow* lists the sustainable tourism award winners and finalists. Have a look for some of these in your area or internationally and describe the innovations using the concepts and terms we have covered in this chapter.

2 In what ways is the peer-to-peer economy promoting sustainability (or not). Think about their structure, their products, the types of suppliers and the market as you give your answer.

3 Search for two of your own innovations that you think can make a contribution to the sustainability of tourism. Feel free to share them with the author too!

Multiple choice questions

1 Environmental scanning based on STEEP is a good method for detecting disruptive change, or wildcards: True or false?

2 The changing consumer preferences of related to the use of visual information represents a changing trend in which STEEP area?

   a) Technology

   b) Social

   c) Economic

3 It is the BRICS nations that will be driving the future trends in tourism: True or false?

4 Scenario-based planning relies on what type of information?

   a) Current trends and hard data

   b) Expert opinions on what might happen

   c) Both a) and b)

5 Which represents the sequence of types of innovation based on their degree of newness from the existing state?

   a) Imitation → incremental → discontinuous → really new → radical

   b) Imitation → incremental → really new → discontinuous → radical

   c) Imitation → incremental → really new → radical → discontinuous

Further reading

Cooper, C. and Fayos-Solà, E. (2019), *The Future of Tourism: Innovation and sustainability*. Cham, Switzerland, Springer International Publishing, 337 pp..

Gössling, S., Hall, C. M., & Weaver, D. B. (2009). *Sustainable Tourism Futures: Perspectives on systems, restructuring and innovations*. New York: Routledge.

Moscardo, G. (2008). Sustainable tourism innovation: Challenging basic assumptions. *Tourism and Hospitality Research*, **8**(1), 4-13.

OECD (2013), *Green Innovation in Tourism Services*, OECD Tourism Papers, 2013/01, OECD Publishing, Paris. http://dx.doi.org/10.1787/5k4bxkt1cjd2-en

References

Adams, R., Heanreaud, S., Bessant, J., Denyer, D. & Overy, P. (2016). Sustainability-oriented innovation: A systematic review. *International Journal of Management Reviews*, **18**(2), 180–205.

Adams, R., Tranfield, D. & Denyer, D. (2011). A taxonomy of innovation: Configurations of attributes in healthcare innovation. *International Journal of Innovation Management*, **15**(2), 359–392.

Bagozzi, R. P. & Lee, K. H. (1999). Consumer resistance to, and acceptance of, innovations. *Advances in Consumer Research*, **26**, 218-225.

Becken, S., Montesalvo, N. & Whittlesea, E. (2018). Building a resilient tourism industry: Queensland Tourism Climate Change Response Plan. Brisbane, Australia. Available at www.qtic.com.au

Calantone, R., Cavusgil, T. & Yushan, Z. (2002). Learning orientation, firm innovation capability and firm performance. *Industrial Marketing Management*, **31**, 515–524.

Dolnicar, S. (2017). Unique features of peer-to-peer accommodation networks In S. Dolnicar (Ed.), *Peer-to-Peer Accommodation Networks: Pushing the boundaries* (pp. 1–14): Oxford: Goodfellow Publishers.

Fabola, A., Miller, A. & Fawcett, R. (2015). Exploring the past with Google Cardboard. In *Digital Heritage* (pp. 277–284). Granada: IEEE Press. doi:10.1109/DigitalHeritage.2015.7413882

Garcia, R. & Calantone, R. (2002). A critical look at technological innovation typology. *The Journal of Product Innovation Management*, **19**, 110–132.

Guttentag, D. A. (2010). Virtual reality: Applications and implications for tourism. *Tourism Management*, **31**(5), 637-651

Guttentag, D. (2015). Airbnb: disruptive innovation and the rise of an informal tourism accommodation sector. *Current Issues in Tourism*, **18**(12), 1192-1217. doi:10.1080/13683500.2013.827159

Hall, C. M. & Williams, A. (2008). *Tourism and Innovation*. Routledge.

Heidenreich, S. & Spieth, P. (2013). Why innovations fail—the case of passive and active innovation resistance. *International Journal of Innovation Management*, **17**(5), 1–42. doi:10.1142/s1363919613500217

Hjalager, A. (2010). A review of innovation research in tourism. *Tourism Management*, **31**, 1–12.

Klewitz, J., & Hansen, E. (2014). Sustainability-oriented innovation of SMEs: A systematic review. *Journal of Cleaner Production*, **65**, 57–75.

Krueger, M. W. (1991). *Artificial Reality II*. Addison-Wesley.

9

Nunes, M., & Mayer, V. (2014). Mobile technology, games and nature areas: The tourist perspective. *Tourism & Management Studies*, **10**(1), 53–58

Ram, S. (1987). A model of innovation resistance. *Advances in consumer research*, **14**(1), 208-212.

Rogers, E. (2003). *Diffusion of Innovations* (5th ed.). New York: The Free Press.

Sarkar, S & Pansera, M. (2017). Sustainability-driven innovation at the bottom: Insights from grassroots ecopreneurs. *Technological Forecasting & Social Change*, **114**, 327–338.

Scott, D. & Gössling, S. (2015). What could the next 40 years hold for global tourism? *Tourism Recreation Research*, **40**(3), 269-285

UNWTO (2018). *Penetrating the Chinese Outbound Tourism Market: successful practices and solutions.* http://cf.cdn.unwto.org/sites/all/files/pdf/exe_summary_chinese_outbound.pdf

Volgger, M., Pforr, C., Stawinoga, A. E., Taplin, R. & Matthews, S. (2018). Who adopts the Airbnb innovation? An analysis of international visitors to Western Australia. *Tourism Recreation Research*, 1-16. doi:10.1080/02508281.2018.1443052

Warren, C., Becken, S. & Coghlan, A. (2016). Using persuasive communication to co-create behavioural change – engaging with guests to save resources at tourist accommodation facilities. *Journal of Sustainable Tourism*, **25**(7), 935-954.

Xu, F., Buhalis, D., and Weber, J. (2017). Serious games and the gamification of tourism. *Tourism Management*, **60**, 244-256.

10 Concluding Remarks

I hope that by now you can see that 'sustainability', a deceptively simple word, is a journey itself. The guiding principles of sustainability are to strategically plan using a holistic and adaptive approach; preserve essential ecological processes as well as protect human heritage and biodiversity; develop in a way that sustains productivity over the long-term for all generations; and achieve a better balance of fairness and opportunity between nations. No small task and one that defies our current business-as-usual approach.

According to the UNWTO, the end goal for sustainable tourism as a sector is to "take full account of its current and future economic, social and environmental impacts, addressing the needs of visitors, the industry, the environment and host communities". It's a constant process of measuring your impacts, adjusting your practices, working with stakeholders and supply chains, keeping abreast of sustainability-oriented innovations, and scanning your social, technological, environmental, economic and political environments to be able to manage the changes that are inevitably coming your way. In this way, we move from linear thinking to a more systems-based approach that sees tourism as part of a wider, complex whole.

Sustainable tourism is also a structural issue. Our focus on economic growth through consumption has led to what Pope Francis has called our 'throwaway culture'. It affects production mechanisms as much as it does the service sector and experiences themselves. When was the last time you stopped to really savour a travel experience once you returned home? Or did you immediately start looking for the next experience? Do you revisit those photos posted on social media or have they drowned in a tidal wave of the newest best thing?

Many tourism academics will argue that sustainable tourism is not achievable, that the rhetoric never matches reality (e.g. Buckley, 2012), and that the challenges are too big. And to some extent this is true; Chapter 2 presented seven challenges that impede the execution of sustainable tourism. Several of these require the support of government and other stakeholders to shift tourism to a more sustainable state, e.g. the private/public sector nature of tourism, integrating sustainable practices across the various scales at which tourism operates, as well as the need for local, context-based, yet multi-disciplinary knowledge.

Solving these requires the type of planning, governance partnerships and knowledge networks covered in Chapters 4 and 5. It is essential for each destination, attraction and business to have its own sustainability plan. The WTO/UNEP (2005) published a guide to making tourism more sustainable based on three guiding principles:

1   Understanding tourism as part of a wider system and engaging with the relevant stakeholders in that system,

2   Adopting a lifecycle approach for all tourism products and services and wherever possible start to engage with circular economies, and

3   Continuing to monitor your efforts within a broader STEEP context.

These are all ideas that have echoed throughout the book.

Fortunately a number of umbrella organisations exist that offer resources for us to build our networks and our knowledge of sustainable tourism. We are definitely not being asked to reinvent the wheel on our own.

☐ The UNWTO One Planet Program (http://sdt.unwto.org/members-one-planet-stp) provides a number of good resources for better understanding best practice in sustainable tourism.

☐ The World Travel and Tourism Council (https://www.wttc.org/priorities/sustainable-growth/) also has a page dedicated to sustainable growth.

☐ UNEP has also offered a report and other useful material on making tourism part of the Green Economy (http://www.greengrowthknowledge.org/sites/default/files/downloads/resource/Tourism_in_the_GE_%20 UNWTO-UNEP.pdf).

☐ UNESCO also offers a set of resources targeted at tourism attractions which hold World Heritage Listed status for their outstanding universal cultural and natural heritage values. (https://whc.unesco.org/en/tourism/)

It is true, however, that a strong regulatory framework for sustainable tourism development is still lacking. While Chapter 4 presented the many declarations exist, e.g. *Manila Declaration on the Social Impact of Tourism* (1997), *Quebec Declaration on Ecotourism* (2002), the 2007 *Davos Declaration on tourism and climate change*, the *Buenos Aires Declaration on tourism and the illegal Wildlife Trade* (2018), as well as other broader declarations that protect communities and ecosystems and wildlife (e.g. the Human Rights declaration, CITES, RAMSAR).

On balance, it would seem that these declarations rarely hold much sway in the face of the 'Big End of Town', as the on-going legal fight with Australia's state and federal governments over Adani's proposed coal mine in 2018 and ensuing impacts on one of the seven natural wonders of the world, the Great Barrier Reef, would attest to. This is where legal frameworks, such as the ones put forward by the Rights of Nature movement, might soon have the biggest impact on sustainability in sectors such as tourism.

Which leads to perhaps the biggest multi-stakeholder, private/public, regulatory issue of them all, climate change. Described as the elephant in the room in Chapter 2, almost any discussion of sustainable tourism will eventually turn to both its carbon footprint as well as tourism's vulnerability to an unstable climatic future. The most recent calculations of tourism's carbon footprint, using a lifecycle approach, are not pretty (Lenzen et al., 2018). Tourism accounts for 8% of the world's carbon emission. The aviation industry accounts for nearly 2% of all GHG emissions, ranking 12th if it were a country, and approximately 80% of the aviation industry is tourism-related (Gössling et al., 2015).

As we saw in Chapter 3, neither tourism nor aviation are currently covered by the 2015 Paris climate treaty, to keep global warming below a 2^0 increase in temperature rise. The tourism sector has set its own targets for a 50% reduction in GHG emissions by 2035, from a 2005 baseline. But we are all still scratching our heads with regards to how this will come about with no strong emissions reduction regulations in place (Gössling et al., 2013). If you remember, a back of the envelope calculation suggests that one international trip is the equivalent of an entire year's household (i.e. when you stay at home!) emissions, and more tourists are travelling more frequently and further! We urgently need a strong and comprehensive decarbonisation strategy for the tourism sector, if it is to become more sustainable, and with only 1% of international travellers purchasing flight carbon offsets, that is will not be our 'get out of jail' card.

Other tourism sustainability challenges are more focussed and could perhaps be tackled by the tourism sector itself, with support from us travellers. The footloose nature of the tourism sector can result in some tourism businesses moving on to newer, more pristine destinations as tourism areas go through Butler's lifecycle model and potentially start to suffer from overtourism and Doxey's irritation index. Strong corporate social responsibility programmes are one way of confronting that issue, particularly with larger multinational businesses that can have a strong impact on local communities and natural environments.

We also discussed the issue that many tourism businesses are classed as SMEs, and they have limited time, knowledge and resources to invest in strong sustainability practices. Yet we saw in Chapter 8 that some SMEs not only implement sustainability, but can be leaders in that space. Chris Warren's Banksia Award for small business contribution to sustainability attests to that. (http://banksiafdn.com/2018-banksia-small-business-award/)

Chris Warren's award winning green tourism initiative (www.mygreen-butler.com) also shows how another of the seven major challenges facing sustainable tourism can be addressed. In Chapter 2, we discussed this idea of inseperability in tourism where production and consumption are linked in ways that do not occur in most sectors – a tourist can contribute up 40% of tourism's carbon emissions through his or her holiday behaviour, not to

10

Test
yourself

mention tourists' other social and natural impacts covered in Chapter 3. The answer to this issue of inseperability in tourism is to focus on co-created sustainable experiences, inviting the tourist to be part of the solution through his or her travel choices.

As well as the MyGreenButler program, which specifically requires the host to lead the guest to be more sustainable, there is a vast number of sustainable tourism NGOs and small businesses willing and able to engage tourists in greener, more sustainable tourism experiences. Chapter 1 presented some of the tourism NGOs around the world who produce guides for ethical, responsible and green travel. A quick google search will bring up a number of these guides for travellers. And it is the responsibility of each of us to become responsible travellers who travel in ways that:

> *"maintain ecological processes and conserve natural heritage and biodiversity; respect the authenticity, traditional values and cultural heritage of host communities and contribute to cross-cultural understanding; and, ensure viable businesses, and distribute economic benefits to all stakeholders equitably"*
> (the definition of sustainable tourism, UNEP & UNWTO, 2005).

For me personally, this is where the value of an ethics-based approach, discussed in Chapter 6, comes into its own. Garay and Font (2015) describe sustainability as a "value-driven journey, influenced primarily by the development of environmental consciousness and personal, socio-cultural and situational factors of the individual business-owners" (p. 336). And yet of all the reasons to become more sustainable, ethical and moral arguments are often deliberately excluded as being the least considered factor by most tourism businesses (Hall & Brown, 2006). One tourism academic, Donyadide (2010) was blunt in his assessment that "the absence of ethical leadership in the tourism industry has been truly 'astounding'" (p. 429).

Meanwhile, Hall and Brown (2006, p.6) outline at least five reasons why tourism would particularly benefit from the application of ethics:

1 It is an activity focussed on human behaviour.
2 It includes several different actors representing a range of perspectives and objectives.
3 It has an applied context.
4 It has social, cultural, economic, ecological and political dimensions.
5 It can create a range of different combinations of impacts in a wide variety of contexts across the globe.

Our accepted social norms, as well as our own self-identities, are shaped by the stories we tell and share. Discussing our sustainability-oriented values may go against the grain of business, for reasons such as false consensus biases, preference projections and so forth. Yet these conversations are so important if we do want to see the type of paradigm that is required to make tourism more sustainable and avoid the type of moral muteness or green hushing (Font et al., 2017). This is perhaps where the Dalai Lama's statement below comes most into play:

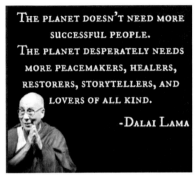

THE PLANET DOESN'T NEED MORE SUCCESSFUL PEOPLE. THE PLANET DESPERATELY NEEDS MORE PEACEMAKERS, HEALERS, RESTORERS, STORYTELLERS, AND LOVERS OF ALL KIND.
-DALAI LAMA

Figure 10.1: Dalai Lama

Over the years I have met many SME tourism business managers and owners that are trying their very best to minimise their negative impacts on the social and natural environments that surround them, while actively trying to improve their local ecosystems by removing weeds, restoring native vegetation, removing light pollution, as well as spreading the economic and social benefits to as many in their communities as they can. I have seen the beneficiaries of these efforts talk with pride about the types of psychological and social empowerment as a result of tourism in their area.

It is because these business owners are explicit about their sustainability-oriented values that others, both locals and guests alike, follow their lead and jump onto the sustainability bandwagon. These people are not necessarily adopting a 'green is gold' business case approach to sustainability, which we covered in Chapter 2 and produces mixed results at best. In fact, many of these sustainable tourism business owners will privately discuss how tiring and costly being sustainable can be at times, with little direct financial recompense.

Some of the most prominent tourism academics warn us not to think of sustainable tourism as a 'wicked problem' because it may seem unachievable and lead to a trap of denial, evasion or trying to maintain the status quo (Weaver et al., 2015). But for me, and maybe others, thinking of sustainable tourism as a wicked problem can sometimes help to reframe why we find it so hard to make tourism more sustainable. This way of looking at it can therefore stop us from looking for easy solutions and silver bullets, and remind us to do the hard work necessary to get there. If you remember, Chapter 4 lists the characteristics of a wicked problem as follows:

☐ There is no definitive formulation of a wicked problem, unlike an ordinary problem.

☐ Wicked problems have no stopping rule, the search for solutions is ongoing, as the problem is never fully resolved.

Test
yourself

10

- ☐ Solutions to wicked problems are not true or false, but are largely a matter of judgment.
- ☐ There is no immediate and no ultimate test of a solution to a wicked problem, there are likely to be unexpected consequences over time, making it difficult to measure solutions' effectiveness.
- ☐ Every solution to a wicked problem is a "one-shot" operation, there is no trial and error, as every implemented solution has consequences that cannot be undone.
- ☐ Wicked problems do not have an exhaustively describable set of potential solutions.
- ☐ Every wicked problem is essentially unique, experience does not help you address it.
- ☐ Every wicked problem can be considered to be a symptom of another, and is entwined with other problems, meaning there is no one root cause.
- ☐ A wicked problem can be explained in numerous ways, and each stakeholders will have different ideas about what the problem really is and what its causes are.
- ☐ The planner has no right to be wrong, problem solvers dealing with a wicked issue are held liable for the consequences of any actions they take, because those will have such a large impact and are hard to justify.

If you look at it this way, it becomes clearer why sustainable tourism is such a large challenge, and the tendency to dismiss sustainability as utopian or unachievable is perhaps lessened. Some academics working in sustainable tourism suggest some essential paradigm shifts that will help transform the sector. For example, Nepal et al. (2015) espouse a grassroots approach of thinking global and acting local, and propose a number of guiding principles that would facilitate the move towards greater sustainability, including a focus on development beyond materialism, a valuing of wellbeing and quality of life, and a socially just understanding of development.

To guide sustainable tourism practices away from a rhetoric that cannot be implemented, Nepal et al. (2015) outline four main premises:

1 Development must be redefined beyond its materialistic interpretations.
2 Non-material systems and ideas, such wellbeing, happiness and quality of life, need to be mainstreamed.
3 The focus of sustainability needs to be scaled down from global sustainability, which they argue is both impractical and impossible, to community sustainability
4 Renewed interests need to be focussed on grassroots development and activism.

They highlight "the contradictory duality of environmental protection coupled with economic progress" (p.62), i.e. that we cannot keep growing and be green. Instead we must focus on socially just forms of tourism that facilitate the empowerment of local communities and allow to tourists to engage in meaningful, ecologically sustainable experiences. We should look beyond measures of economic progress and focus on human development measures such as wellbeing, happiness and quality of life. This is the approach that Bhutan has adopted at a nation-wide level, but also that Chris and others have adopted within their business. It is important not to forget that tourism's supply chain linkages operate at a global scale, so that the cumulative community efforts at moving towards sustainability would come to represent a significant global effort.

There are some of the broad, global challenges facing sustainable tourism. The UNWTO is quick to point out the growing demand for tourism, as a measure of its success and resilience. Tourism's spectacular growth comes (i) from the large emerging markets (the BRICS nations), (ii) as existing markets live and travel longer, and (iii) as tourism continues to represent a highly desirable form of conspicuous consumption in an increasingly materialistic, homogeneous global culture. Travelling to more and more exotic locations becomes a badge of honour, while at the same time we demand a level of comfort while we travel that is simply not possible within the social and natural resource boundaries of many destinations.

Chapters 3 and 9 point out some of these social and natural challenges that tourism faces now and into the future. These include the depletion of natural resources, particularly the hydrocarbons that underpin our current economic systems, an unequal distribution of natural resource use, and the growing challenges of climate change. As if these were not enough in themselves, one of the most cited tourism researchers, Butler (2015) says tourism itself is characterised by an inherent inertia, where there is a significant lock-in effect in the practice of tourism, as well as a demand sector habituated to certain destinations, attractions, and travel routes, and tourists who are reluctant to embrace sustainability unless it is presented as being cheaper and more convenient than traditional options.

Keeping all three of those juggling balls in the air becomes even harder when the balls have a mind of their own and each want to move in different directions. As I said in the introduction, keeping all three in the air at any one time will take skill, practice and focus. To start off with, it is likely that at least one of the three balls will be dropped on at least some occasions; trade-offs must be made to move towards greater sustainability. But with focus, we identify our shared values, articulate a vision, bring together stakeholders, select, measure and communicate appropriate sustainability indicators and respect non-negotiable social, environmental and economic thresholds. In this way incremental steps can be taken towards sustainability, now viewed an ongoing process rather than a final destination.

10

If I were to summarise the key points around sustainable tourism for an academic audience, I would broadly state the following points:

☐ The notion and desire for growth remains one of the guiding doctrines of tourism. Increasing numbers of tourists are generally seen as a positive by destination managers, and mass tourism will continue to be the main form of tourism.

☐ Environmental and social impacts from tourism development are inevitable. It becomes a question of identifying what impacts are considered acceptable and/or manageable through a modelling system of indicators and thresholds.

☐ The stakeholders of tourism are many and varied. A good governance structure must underpin any sustainable tourism plans, and obviously planning must be undertaken.

And finally,

☐ Aiming for incremental progress towards sustainable tourism is more realistic than practicing sustainable tourism per se.

If however, you were to ask me over a coffee how I see sustainable tourism, I would answer that:

☐ **It must be seen as a journey** – progress, not perfection, towards better outcomes for people, planet and profit.

☐ **Practice is everything**, it will improve skills, knowledge and focus

☐ **The structural issues of sustainable tourism must be addressed** – individuals can only go so far without facilitative policies, regulations, infrastructure and social norms around them.

☐ **It is a largely a supply-side issue** - do not expect the market to lead, but don't underestimate their willingness to try to be more sustainable if they are asked to in the right way.

☐ **Remember the rule of thumb**, if what you're doing is building relationships, it is more likely to support sustainability than if it's not building relationships.

Finally, start by making a pledge or two for your own travel behaviours. Some of mine are to think about the whole supply chain, actively manage my carbon footprint, buy locally so that the economic benefits stay in the community and compensate somewhat for my inevitable social and natural impacts, and finally, respect local wishes – if they ask you not to do it, see that as part of building a relationship, and refrain from doing it.

Test yourself

Question

What pledge will you make to support sustainable tourism?

_____

_____

_____

Multiple choice questions

1 The three areas that WTO/UNEP encourage sustainable tourism managers to consider are?

   a) The wider system and its stakeholders, a lifecycle approach, STEEP monitoring

   b) Consumer demand, partnerships, STEEP trends

   c) Strategic planning, investment, black swans

2 The single biggest challenge facing tourism is climate change: True or false?

3 Thinking of tourism as a wicked problem can be helpful because we understand the nature and scale of the problem and stop looking for a silver bullet: True or false?

4 Nepal et al. (2015) suggest that sustainable tourism be built around which two fundamental ideas?

   a) Intangible outcomes such as wellbeing must be given more weight in decision-making, and bottom-up change is the most desirable approach

   b) Development needs to take into account local communities and global systems of governance have a responsibility to do so

   c) Development needs to focus on wellbeing, and community-level sustainability

5 Each of us has a personal responsibility and ability to make tourism more responsible: True or false?

References

Buckley, R. (2012). Sustainable tourism: Research and reality. _Annals of Tourism Research_, **39**(2), 528-546.

Butler, R. (2015). Sustainable tourism – a way forward? _The Practice of Sustainable Tourism: Resolving the paradox_, Oxford: Routledge.

Donyadide, A. (2010). Ethics in tourism. _European Journal of Social Sciences_, **17**(3), 433-426.

Font, X., Elgammal, I. & Lamond, I. (2017). Greenhushing: the deliberate under communicating of sustainability practices by tourism businesses. _Journal of Sustainable Tourism_, **25**(7), 1007-1023.

10

Garay, L. & Font, X. (2012). Doing good to do well? Corporate social responsibility reasons, practices and impacts in small and medium accommodation enterprises. *International Journal of Hospitality Management*, **31**, 329-337.

Gössling, S., Scott, D. & Hall, C.M. (2013). Challenges of tourism in a low carbon economy. *Wiley Interdisciplinary Reviews: Climate Change*, **4**(6), 525-538

Gössling, S., Scott, D. & Hall, C.M. (2015). Inter-market variability in CO_2 emissions-intensities in tourism: Implications for destination marketing and carbon management. *Tourism Management*, **46**, 203-212.

Hall, D. R. & Brown, F. (2006). *Tourism and Welfare: Ethics, responsibility and sustained well-being*. CABI

Lenzen, M., Sun, Y.Y, Faturay, F., Ting, Y.P., Geschke, A. % Malik, A. (2018). The carbon footprint of global tourism. *Nature Climate Change*, **8**, 522–528.

Nepal, S.K., Verkoeyen, S. and Karrow, T., (2015). The end of sustainable tourism? Re-orienting the debate. In R. Butler (ed.) *The Practice of Sustainable Tourism: Resolving the paradox*, Oxford: Routledge.

UNEP & UNWTO (2005). *Making Tourism More Sustainable - A Guide for Policy Makers*, p.p.11-12

Weaver, D., Hughes, M. & Pforr, C. (2015). Paradox as a pervasive characteristic of sustainable tourism: Challenges, opportunities and trade-offs. In R. Butler (ed.) *The Practice of Sustainable Tourism: Resolving the paradox*, Oxford: Routledge. pp. 281-290.

Index